Is God real?

Does He care about me personally?

Can I find Him and know Him?

Will He help me in my life?

What will happen to me after I die?

Find answers
In these true accounts
Glorifying God,
Through Jesus Christ,
In the Power of the Holy Spirit.

Real life stories of God's
Supernatural Power
working in the lives of ordinary people
to change their lives
and eternal destiny forever.

"These things have I written unto you
that believe on the name of the Son of God;
that ye may know that ye have eternal life,
and that ye may believe on the name
of the Son of God." (I John 5:13)

DIVINE APPOINTMENTS

Charlie Deitrick

Love To ~
Kelly & Jerrod,
& family ~
We are hoping
you both enjoy our
book and feel show our
close Jesus is near to us
in any situation ! We Love your
parents and so glad to see you
on Facebook ~ maybe we'll meet someday
if not ~ we'll see you in our Fathers House!!
God Bless you as you
read the wonderful
miracles we've been
Blessed to be a part of
In Christ's Love
Charlie & Doug
2021

BookLocker
Saint Petersburg, Florida

Print ISBN: 978-1-64719-077-4
Epub ISBN: 978-1-64719-078-1
Mobi ISBN: 978-1-64719-079-8

Published by BookLocker.com, Inc., St. Petersburg, Florida.

Printed on acid-free paper.

BookLocker.com, Inc.
2020

First Edition

Cover photo: © Charlie Deitrick

(Some names and identifying details have been changed to protect the privacy of individuals.)

ACKNOWLEDGEMENTS

There are no words to express my gratitude and appreciation to my Lord and Savior Jesus Christ; Who gave Himself on the Cross for me; Who brought me out of the darkness and into His glorious Light; and has allowed me to know Him personally. He is my life; He watches over me; and He alone deserves all the thanks and praise for making this book possible.

I also want to thank my dear husband Doug ~ who has been my constant encourager, helper, and prayer warrior. He has worked tirelessly in the arranging, typing, research, continuity, and editing of this work.

We want to thank our dear friends, Mary and Ed, for their many years of encouragement, and for Mary's professional guidance and help in completing this book.

A special thank you to my best friend, Kath, her husband Ed, and my dear sister Ginny; our faithful prayer partners and encouragers, who have always been there for us!

Thank you to our many dear friends and wonderful supporters all around the world for your faith, encouragement, and your consistent, effectual, and heartfelt prayers.

Lastly, thank you to all those mentioned in this book. We love you and will be forever thankful for you, and for all of God's "Divine Appointments."

DIVINE APPOINTMENTS

Charlie Deitrick

CONTENTS

INTRODUCTION

What is a "Divine Appointment?"

Divine Appointment *n* : An apparently coincidental encounter or event that has actually been arranged by God for some specific purpose. This purpose may be obvious during the encounter, or the purpose may only become apparent some time later.

This book is comprised of true stories that will inspire and encourage followers of Jesus Christ...and also those seeking answers to life's meaning and purpose. I believe these stories will stay with you, as they have with me, and I believe God wants to use them in your life.

From Genesis to Revelation ~ the Bible is filled with "Divine Appointments."

There are appointments with patriarchs, priests, prophets, kings, heroes, and God Himself!

God has "Divine Appointments" for each and every one of us. The only questions are; how do we recognize them? How do we find God's purpose in sending them? And what will we do with them?

Find answers in my personal first-hand accounts of God's leading, guidance, kindness, and power, as witnessed in my own life, just as I experienced them.

These stories prove the reality of God, His Son Jesus Christ, and God's Holy Spirit; and show that His Divine Power is still available to all who believe, obey, and seek to serve Him. They provide hope and inspiration, comfort and faith, and a deeper glimpse into the heart of our loving God.

I came to realize that God never intended for me to keep these wonderful stories to myself; I needed to share them to help others. My ultimate goal in sharing these testimonies is to see precious souls come to the Saving knowledge of our Lord and Savior, Jesus Christ.

After many requests from followers of my on-line ministry, and seeing the hunger in those wanting to know more about God's power and miracles, I have been led to share some of my most memorable "Divine Appointments."

These personal stories include a wide variety of people, in many different circumstances, all confirming the nearness of God in each of our lives. They demonstrate His willingness to help, and Save, anyone who will come to Him in faith and sincerity.

I hope to encourage believers in their faith; promote the preaching of the Gospel, and inspire service to our Faithful, Loving, and most Merciful God. I pray that this book might even turn out to be one of *your* "Divine Appointments!"

This book is intended to glorify God, to demonstrate His constant abiding love, and to confirm His promise that; "I will instruct thee and teach thee in the way which thou shalt go: I will guide thee with mine eye." (Psalm 32:8)

"Dear LORD, please bless this book to all who read it. And Thank You, for Your Divine Appointments in all of our lives." Amen!

Love, Charlie.

"And let us not be weary in well doing: for in due season we shall reap, if we faint not." (Galatians 6:9)

"And, behold, I come quickly; and my reward is with me, to give every man according as his work shall be." (Revelation 22:12)

1. AGAINST ALL ODDS

I. {In the Beginning; and The Night God Stepped In}

I met my only true love ~ in Junior High School. His name was Doug. I knew he was wild, but then, . . . so was I! Doug and I both grew up around 'hood's' ~ black leather jackets, gangs, switch-blades, brass knuckles, gang fights, car clubs, (and a lot of criminal activity.)

Neither of us cared anything about school, except for acting out in class, meeting up with friends, and hanging out after school, smoking, drinking, and causing trouble.

We both really enjoyed skipping classes, which led to trouble with the principal and the vice principal. Their offices became our 'second home.' Doug and I often met up there with other mutual friends, (and partners in crime.)

Doug was very bright ~ he never had to study for tests, and then when test time came ~ he always aced them. I never did understand that about him!

Now myself, I was gifted in other ways ~ (but tests were not my strong point.) Many times, I knew the answers, but suffered from fear at test time. My teachers always said ~ that they knew I could do the work, but 'I wasn't working up to my potential.'

I excelled in art class, and I was a gymnast ~ so I was always great in sports. Our gym teacher even bought a 'balance beam,' and let me teach the other students how to perform routines on the beam.

I was popular, and involved in school activities, (like the school paper,) but I had a lot of problems and worries that eventually led me to act out to the point where I was expelled, and thrown out of high school right before graduation!

I was a 'chronic run-away' ~ I often 'hitchhiked,' and many times didn't care if I lived or died. Doug had already dropped out of school ~ so we ended up at the same parties, and ended up in jail a few times.

We had started dating at age fifteen. We were considered like an 'item,' and people knew we loved each other.

When we were seventeen years old, we lived in a 'commune' with seven other people, (and sometimes occasional drop-ins.)

My relatives used to ask me questions about our communal living. It was actually a lot like "one big family" I told them. My family were all Lutheran and never put us down about it. They just loved us and prayed for us, and were really sweet people.

Doug and I had decided that we didn't need a 'marriage license' to prove our love to each other, (or to anyone else.) We lived by 'our own rules.' We had both attended Sunday school, and church, (when we were kids) and said a few prayers along the way, (when we got in a jam,) but we didn't have a clue what Christianity was all about.

Doug rode a motorcycle, (a Harley Davidson.) It was the 60's and we were definitely hooked into the drug scene, hanging with 'outlaw' bikers, and open to almost every wild idea that came along. Some of our own friends told us that we were living life "way too fast," and that we'd better slow down!

Doug also played guitar and sang in a local 'rock' band. His band had been 'black-balled' by all the legitimate clubs in the entire state, because of their acting out and cussing on stage, and because of the 'banned' psychedelic rock music they played. As a result, they mainly played underground fraternity parties, keggers, and biker parties. (A lot of people knew who Doug was, especially the police!)

One night, the President of the bike club, and some club members, came to our small apartment and told us, (even though we were only seventeen,) that Doug's band was now the 'Official Biker Band,' for their chapter. It was obvious that there was 'no choice!'

The longer we went that way ~ the worse our lives spiraled down!

The old saying ~ that bikers were all 'brothers' and took care of each other; we'd soon find out was a lie from hell.

Many of them were married, some were divorced, but most had 'old ladies' as they called them, (biker groupies.)

This particular day, several club members walked into our friend's house where we were hanging out. They carried in a big bottle of hard liquor, . . and handed it to me. I said, "No thanks," and this six-foot-six bully said, "You too good to drink with 'Big Don'?" I took the bottle, and took a couple of swigs just to get him to back off!

We drank a lot ~ but I didn't like anyone bullying me, and making me drink when I didn't want to! Doug and I had been drinking since we were young kids, so we were used to it all, but neither of us liked being 'told' what to do. There were a lot of things we got involved in ~ but it was always 'our choice.'

The night 'God stepped in' and saved our lives, these 'brothers' asked us to go with them to a run-down bar, known to be a rat hole, in a bad part of town. I told Doug ~ I had a bad feeling about going with these guys when they'd been so pushy with me earlier. He said ~ 'he wanted to go' ~ they would be meeting other 'chapters' there, (bikers we didn't know from other states.)

At that point I decided to bring up my concerns to our friends; (the 'President' of the entire multi-state club, and his 'old lady.')

They both assured us, "You'll be fine going with us."

I still had a very bad feeling; so much so ~ that I was only going along to make sure Doug was okay. I couldn't have rested knowing he was with them by himself, and not knowing what was happening.

Our friends had decided to "drop (take) mescaline" before we left for the bar. They asked us to ride with them.

When we got to the bar, I saw there was an older couple running the place alone. They call them "Mom and Pop Bars." Both Doug and I were brought up to respect our elders, and as wild as we were, this night would be a turning point in our lives.

I was not in a 'party' mood ~ I just wanted to go home with Doug!

I made my way through the crowd over to the jukebox, and this dirty, slobbish, uncouth biker from Kansas City, (who was drunk out of his mind,) came over and grabbed my arm! I jerked my arm away, and he got mad and threw his beer on the older couple behind the bar!

They looked scared to death!

There were at least fifty drunk, rowdy, insane, and 'evil' bikers crowded in there, and the bar was full of pot, and cigarette smoke.

(It was so hot in there . . it was hard to breathe!)

The music was pounding; the voices and laughter raging, and this same slobbish biker, suddenly snorted, and spit on the older couple behind the bar! (He spit right in their faces!!) They were humiliated, and absolutely terrified! (So was I!)

That was it!! I was so mad at this point; I hated what he did!!

They had no air conditioning. The front and side doors were open, but the air was still and muggy! (You could just 'feel' the evil in that bar!) ~ I wanted this all to stop! It was like we were in a nightmare!

Over all the noise, I told Doug I wanted to leave, and his answer was, "Well, we rode with them, and we haven't been here that long." I felt trapped, with my feelings of doom.

~ I had felt something bad was coming before we ever got there. (My 'sixth-sense' had told me not to go!)

I told Doug I could hitchhike home. He said, "No, we're in too bad of an area!" Hah! We were in a living nightmare 'now!'

By this time, the bikers had taken over the whole bar! (They had the older couple tied to chairs, back to back, behind the bar, and were busy handing out "free liquor!") I was so upset about the older couple being abused and humiliated ~ I couldn't stand it!!

Then all of a sudden, this biker with long red hair and a long red beard, came up and grabbed my arm and said, "You're mine!"

Doug grabbed my other arm and said ~ "She's with me!"

He said, ~ "You in the club?"

Doug said, "Just about!"

Doug hollered to our friends, who at this point in time, were just 'coming on' to the drugs they took before we left for the bar!

Doug asked our 'friends,' "Hey, can't you help us out here?" They were just 'snickering' ~ 'high as kites!'

This biker called them out, saying ~ "Well, are they in the club or not?"

Our friend's 'old lady,' then got up and told him, "Well, it isn't 'official' yet, but yeah, they're gonna join."

He said, "Right! They aren't initiated yet ~ so she's mine!"

At that point in time ~ Doug hung on to my arm, and this guy was pulling really hard on my other arm ~ and telling us I was his old lady tonight!

This was one of those jams ~ where you cry out in your head and pray for God to help you! (We both knew, this could get 'real bad' . . . 'real fast'!!) Doug prayed in his head ~ "God, if you get us out of here somehow, and not let Charlie get hurt ~ I'll give these bikers up!" I was praying in my head, "God please help us to get out of here alive!"

Well, right after we both prayed ~ this biker let loose of my arm, walked over to our friends, and started throwing his arms in the air yelling about, "Rules are rules man!" Doug will tell you, (and I felt the exact same thing,) that something 'supernatural' happened at that moment! We actually 'felt' time stop, . . and we had just enough time to get out the side door, before all hell broke loose!

Doug grabbed my arm and whispered, "Come on, let's get outta here!" ~ We hurried out the side door (and miraculously, nobody saw us!)

When we got outside, Doug said, "Let's run!"

As we were running to the car across the street, we heard yelling and loud crashes coming from inside the bar ~ and then guns began to fire off!

About a minute later, our friends came running out the side door! When they got to their car ~ they got 'their gun' out of the dash!! He said, "C'mon, let's go back in!"

I said, "You're crazy!! We just got outta there with our lives ~ we're not goin' back in there! Sorry ~ we'll walk or hitchhike!"

Right then, a "Paddy Wagon," and a swarm of cop cars converged on the parking lot of the bar! The four of us jumped in the car and got outta there!

We had gotten out just in time! God had truly watched over us and kept us safe, and answered both our prayers that night! (And we knew it!)

We heard later, that most of the bar ended up in jail, and many were hurt bad. ~ The bikers had all turned on each other and started breaking the place up!

They had even started beating their 'old ladies,' and even breaking wooden chairs over their heads! ~ A couple of the club members had been shot! So much for 'the brotherhood!'

But God had definitely shown us His 'power and protection,' and 'His will' for us that night, to never be around those people again!

There were evil forces pulling us in every direction.

(We believed there was 'a God,' but we had no way of knowing how to find Him, let alone have a personal relationship with Him!)

After this insane experience, Doug and I decided to just lay low in our apartment for a while.

In our apartment I had a huge Bible my Mom had given me on my sixteenth Birthday, and I threw a fit about it! I had asked her what she paid for it? She said, "Why?"

I asked her again, "How much?!"

She said, "Thirty-two dollars."

I said, "That's thirty-two dollars you wasted, cause I'll never read it! Why didn't you just give me the money?"

She had replied, "So you could spend it all on drugs?"

(I still remember how disappointed I was, getting a 'Bible,' on my sixteenth birthday!)

Well, while we were both still 'laying low,' Doug was 'high' one day and he decided to start looking through my Bible, "just to look at the pictures." He began to read some in it too.

Just a few weeks later, he came down with a really terrible inner-ear infection, which he'd had several times when he was younger. It was so painful that all he could do was hold his head, and roll back and forth in pain! It had always taken him at least 'two weeks' to get over it!

He remembered what he had been reading in my big Bible, about Jesus healing the sick, and the blind, and the deaf. He decided to pray to "Jesus," and ask 'Him' to heal his ear infection.

Immediately after he prayed ~ that terrible pain was gone! He was healed instantly! We were both shocked!

(The Lord was getting Doug's attention!!)

"He that walketh with wise men shall be wise: but a companion of fools shall be destroyed." (Proverbs 13:20)

"Forsake the foolish, and live; go in the way of understanding." (Proverbs 9:6)

II. {From Witches to Wisdom}

We had made a break with the bikers, and hadn't been going out except for necessities. Then, one early evening about a month later, my girlfriend from high school asked us over to her house. (She still lived at home.) We decided to go over and get out for a while.

She and I partied together, and I had known her for years, . . but I was about to find out some things I didn't know, (and didn't want to know!)

They were very wealthy and had a huge home. My girlfriend went out with a good friend of ours, 'John' ~ who her mother hated! He rode a Harley too, and we had 'hung around' with John for years as well. When Doug and I went over to her house, it was just her and her mother, and Doug and I.

After we had talked a while, her mother surprised us, when she asked if we were "familiar with Tarot Cards?"

We knew of them, but we never had anyone read them in front of us before. Her mother was obviously a 'pro.' She grabbed our hands and checked out our palms, and before we knew it, we were feeling very strange being there! We all heard a noise upstairs and she said, "That's just my 'familiar spirit'!" She told us his name, and said that the 'other noise' we heard ~ was her pet rabbit's "spirit," thumping across the attic floor! (We were both getting spooked at this point!)

We knew about the occult, but we had never experienced anything like this before!

Then she asked us to join in around a 'Ouija Board!' We had one at home when we were kids, but it was more of a joke than anything else! So, we both sat down expecting to laugh; instead, the feeling in that room became very eerie and 'scary!'

What we didn't know, was that my girlfriend and her mother had been in a big, heated argument before we got there, (about my friend planning to spend the night at a motel with John.) Her mother strongly disapproved, and sarcastically asked her, what she planned to take along to sleep in? My girlfriend had yelled back at her mom, and said, "Well you don't expect me to wear 'Doctor Denton's' do you?" (Old time, one-piece pajamas.)

It's important that you know ~ we knew 'nothing' about the big argument that had taken place.

We were just sitting there, with our hands on the Ouija Board, and Doug and I started laughing, and messing around with it. Her mother gave us an evil look and said, "Take your hands off, . . Now!" So, we did!

Suddenly, . . the "planchette," (pointer hand piece,) began to move freely, all on its own! We couldn't believe our own eyes! If we hadn't of seen it ourselves, we would have never believed it!

As we both watched, it spelled out a very personal message; ~ 'the board' spelled out, "Watch out for 'Jammican' John," (referring to the 'Doctor Denton' pajamas!) "He will be here in ten minutes."

Just 'exactly' ten minutes later, Doug and I were shocked to hear the doorbell ring, and there stood our friend 'John' at the door! My girlfriend said, she'd be upstairs a minute to get her things.

She bounced right back down with a small bag, and out the door she went, hopping on his Harley, and leaving Doug and I there alone with her mother! We felt completely 'out of place!'

Her mother was angry beyond words! She told us to, "Stay there." ~ She was going upstairs a minute, and would be right back.

When she returned, she had her hand up to her neck, covering a necklace she had put on. She said, "I rarely show this to anyone, but this is an old necklace, that has been passed down to me from my mother, and in turn, her mother to her." She pulled her hand away and the necklace was five-pointed stars and crescent moons, alternating all the way around. It was 'antique gold,' and very 'ornate.' She said, "I don't do this often, but I am going to cast a spell, to show my daughter ~ I mean business! She knows I don't want her with John!"

She put her hand up again to the necklace, closed her eyes, paused a few moments in concentration, and then told us that she was "a white witch!" She told us, she wasn't "evil," but sometimes she had to "make decisions to stop someone from making a mistake." (But we knew it was evil. We could actually 'feel' it!)

Within minutes, her daughter showed up at the door ~ more angry than I can say here! She was cussing, and accusing her mother of interfering by ~ 'using her powers!' Her mother glared at her and said, "No I didn't!"

Her daughter screamed back, "You just don't get two flat tires on a motorcycle ~ at the same time!!" (Both tires went flat at the end of her street before they could even pull out on the main road.) They had pushed it downhill, back to her driveway.

At that point we were both scared, and wanted out of there for two reasons; first, not to be in the middle of a huge argument between my girlfriend and her mother, but second, we were wanting to drive away from all the 'weirdness,' and never go back!

We left right away, and Doug and I talked nervously for a long time, as we traveled back home.

We discussed what we had just witnessed, and 'felt,' and been a part of! I asked him, "Do you feel as weird inside as I do?" He said, "Yeah, and it feels like 'something' is in here with us; following us ~ something evil!"

I said, "I feel it too!"

I told him my girlfriend had given me a beautiful, expensive ring with a polished stone on it; but now, I didn't want anything to do with any connections to their jewelry, or evil powers, or anything else! Doug said, "Yeah, me neither!"

I quickly rolled the window down, and threw that ring into a creek bed we were driving over at the time.

Doug said, "If those powers are real, 'and we saw that they are,' then what I was taught about God, and the devil, in Sunday school when I was little, must all be true too! That means Jesus wins in the end, and I'm on the losing side, and I'm on my way to hell! I'm gonna try and get on the winning side, and find out all I can about Jesus Christ!" (We had seen a very clear picture of good versus evil! I'll always remember him saying that! It made me feel better, because I was scared, and wanted nothing more to do with any of those evil powers!)

In the weeks and months ahead, we moved to a small house and had nothing to do with the bikers, or my girlfriend and her mother, or any of our drug dealing, and criminal friends. Doug studied the Bible constantly.

He told me, the thing that convinced him of the truth of the Gospel was ~ "the Resurrection" of Jesus! He said, "All the Disciples were tortured to death, just for saying they had seen Jesus alive after He rose from the dead." He was convinced that they were telling the truth! "Why else would they stick to their story, and go through all that, . . . if it was a lie? What would they get out of it?"

He had been reading in Luke 18:13, "But the tax collector stood at a distance. He would not even look up to heaven, but beat his breast and said, 'God, have mercy on me, a sinner'." Right then, in his heart, Doug sincerely prayed that simple prayer, "God, have mercy on 'me' a sinner!" Though he really didn't even realize it at the time; he had become "Born Again!"

Nobody had 'witnessed' to Doug, God Himself had called him through His Word alone. "For the Word of God is quick (alive), and powerful, and sharper than any two-edged sword, piercing even to the dividing asunder of soul and spirit, . . " (Hebrews 4:12)

We had both recently turned eighteen years old, and from reading the Bible, Doug realized that 'living together' wasn't right according to God's Word. He decided we needed to get married because God ordained marriage, and he wanted 'God's blessings.'

We had a beautiful small chapel wedding. (Some said, it was the most beautiful wedding they'd ever been to!)

God was with us in many ways, and blessed us, with many people donating their services for our wedding day!

Over the next few months, I watched Doug; and something inside of me became very angry, seeing him filled with so much peace from God! Doug wasn't working, so I got a job at a restaurant which would at least pay the bills.

One day, the bikers found us through some old friends. They came by our house and brought Doug a 'Harley' ~ they were 'giving' it to him! They said it was stolen, with no numbers on it, with a 're-built' title, so you could stamp in the new 'serial numbers' ~ and it'd be, "street-legal." Doug was used to making money through 'illegal' channels, but he had stopped all that. Doug had learned from studying the Bible in Proverbs, "If a man steal, even if he is hungry, he will pay it back seven times!" (Proverbs 6:30,31)

They dropped the Harley off in our front yard and left. Doug knew he couldn't keep it, and be 'right' with God. So he prayed, borrowed an old van from his Dad, loaded up the bike, and took it back. (He knew taking it back could go bad, but he was determined.)

As we had figured, . . the bikers cussed him, and told him 'he was crazy!' Doug said, "Thanks anyway." He left the bike, walked back to the van, and got out of there!

Doug hadn't lived a good or honest life at all, (putting it mildly,) and he had a saying, "If it wasn't for bad luck, I wouldn't have no luck at all!" He was finding out though, it wasn't 'luck' ~ he was "reaping what he sowed." When he was doing evil things ~ it was all coming back to him! He had been keeping God's blessings away from himself, by going against God's Word!

Since he was reading his Bible ~ a lot was changing for the better in our lives, and we liked it!

I was observing Doug's actions; he wasn't just reading his Bible ~ he was 'obeying' God's words. (He wanted God's blessings!) He was trying very hard to get to know Jesus, and His teachings.

All the while, I was having increasing anxiety and anger inside.

At one point, I yelled at him, "All you do is sit around and read that Bible!" In my frustration I slugged him 'hard' on the shoulder! (Normally ~ this would have triggered an immediate 'physical' response!) But instead, I witnessed a 'miracle.' Immediately ~ I saw a 'shining aura' over Doug's head! ~ I saw a peace, that I knew was from God, shining from his face! I also knew, (because of what I'd just seen,) not to ever do that again! I immediately felt ashamed I'd hit him.

Doug told me to, "Pray, and ask God to show you, that He's real." I said, "I believe God is real. I just don't think He cares about me!"

He said, "Charlie, you are miserable inside. Go look in the mirror! You need to pray and ask God to show you He's real, and that He cares about you too."

I went in the bathroom, and looked in the mirror ~ my eyes were full of sadness, and anger. I was still smoking weed, and doing some speed, and I was telling Doug, "I'll be partying in Hell with all our friends!" ~

He said ~ "You're wrong Charlie, there won't be any 'party' in Hell!"

"How do you know?" I asked.

He said, "God's Word tells us what Heaven and Hell will be like, ~ and Hell won't be a place anyone will ever want to be!" He said, "God says Hell is eternal darkness, no hope, no peace, no love, and a 'worm that dieth not' ~ "Eternal" torment, (There won't be any party there!) . . . "

The words "No Hope" ~ stuck in my mind! (I had been through some horrible times where I felt very hopeless, and I didn't think things would ever change.) I got to thinking about being stuck in Hell and never, ever, being able to get out!! I didn't like that idea at all! I already felt miserable, and I didn't want to feel that way forever!

So, I said ~ "Okay, what does the Bible say Heaven is like?"

He said, "God says Heaven is going to be a beautiful Kingdom, where Christ Himself will rule ~ 'And God shall wipe away all tears from their eyes; and there shall be no more death, neither sorrow, nor crying, neither shall there be any more pain: for the former things are passed away.' (Revelation 21:4) And, 'Eye hath not seen, nor ear heard, neither have entered into the heart of man, the things which God hath prepared for them that love Him'." (I Corinthians 2:9) He said, "So just imagine the most beautiful thing you can imagine and it's gonna be a million times better than that!!"

He had my attention by now!

So, at this point I was willing to pray, and ask God to "prove to me" ~ He was real, and cared about "me." Doug just said, "Don't put a 'time limit' on God, and tell Him ~ 'Let me know 'tomorrow' God,' just pray ~ and He'll show you that He's there."

So, in my sad state of mind, I said a sincere, but sarcastic prayer. ~ I said, "Okay God, if You're there, and You care about me ~ prove it to me! I don't know what it will take for me to believe, because I'm stubborn, but if You're God ~ You'll know. . . . Amen."

Doug told me, "Now ~ just be willing to wait on God."

I said, "Okay," and I went on to work.

Doug giving up crime, had depleted our finances and he had been praying for God to ~ "Please help us get some food."

We couldn't even afford to have a phone.

Our house was so tiny ~ the bedroom was bigger than the living room. We couldn't fit any furniture in the living room, so we just sat on pillows. The whole house looked like a doll house.

When I got to work that day, I was glad to have a meal ~ (we were all told ~ that waitresses, cooks, and bus boys, all got one free meal a day.) We could have whatever we wanted; including dessert!

I had been working there about a week, and that late afternoon, as I was finishing my shift, the owner asked me to come back into the kitchen, and step into the walk-in cooler with her! I knew I was doing a good job, but somehow ~ I felt being pulled aside ~ I was going to be in trouble!

She walked into the cooler ahead of me, turned around, looked me in the eye and smiled endearingly, "I've been watching you honey, and you're doing a great job. ~ But I've noticed when you're at lunch ~ you look very hungry, and I've noticed you eat like you're starved! Can you use this?" She motioned to four sacks on the counter and said, "I've packed up four sacks of food, and I want you to take them home for you and your husband. Please don't feel bad ~ I just feel you could use this. Am I right?" I looked at her and smiled and said, "Yes, we sure can! Thank you!!"

She smiled and said, "Good! You're welcome to it!" She began to pick through the groceries and show me what all she had packed in there. There was a huge, long brick of cheese, a huge block of ham, so many veggies, and potatoes, and canned goods, and even a baked pie! She helped me load it all in my little Morris Mini-Minor car. I waved good-bye and thanked her again for everything!

On the way home I kept smiling ~ I can't begin to tell you how excited I was ~ to tell Doug how God had answered his prayers! I wanted to thank God for all of it, but I didn't really know how?

I remember feeling very awkward saying out loud, "Thank you (God?)" With a question mark like, (are you listening?) Again, I said, "Thank You God, for all this food, and for that nice lady." This was a direct answer to Doug's prayers, and I was in the middle of this very personal miracle! I felt full of joy, and couldn't wait to show Doug all this food!

When I got home, Doug's face was beaming as I told him what happened!

He could hardly believe that my boss had given us so much food!

We were both thrilled, and brought in all the groceries together. He had a prayer of thanks, and I can tell you, I did feel God's love and care over us!

The Lord Jesus was showing me that He is a very personal God, and we were both experiencing God's Joy! We also knew God was blessing Doug ~ for taking that Harley back to the bikers!

A few days later ~ I looked out our front door, and a friend of ours was walking up our drive. His hair was cut very short! I told Doug he looked like he'd turned 'Narc,' (a narcotics agent,) and I wasn't going to let him in! (He had been dealing drugs to us in the past, but we hadn't seen him for a while.)

Doug immediately said, "Go ahead and let him in. I want to talk to him and see what he's been up to." So, we let him in. We said 'Hi' and talked a few minutes.

Then he said, he 'came by to tell us something.'

We said "Okay?" . . (He looked pretty serious.)

He started out saying, "You know I've always enjoyed my drugs." We both said, "Yeah?" He went on and said, "and I've never had a 'bad trip'!"

We said, "Right." (He had always looked so happy; he was the reason I started using them!)

He told us, "Last night I took some 'acid,' (LSD,) and I got so far out of my mind, that I only knew one thing, and that was, . . I was 'never' coming back to reality!" He then said, "My parents took me to church as a kid, and I was taught to believe in Jesus Christ. So, I got down on my knees, and prayed ~ 'Dear Jesus ~ if You bring me down off this acid trip, I'll serve You and tell everyone that You're truly the Son of God, . . and I'll start with Charlie and Doug'!" He immediately looked 'me' straight in the eyes, and said, "Charlie, I came down like this!" (And snapped his fingers!) He looked at me and said ~ "So I'm here to tell you Jesus Christ is real! He loves you, and He has a plan and a purpose for your life!" (Now, I knew that no one comes off of 'acid' instantly!)

I also knew ~ without a shadow of doubt ~ that God had sent him, and that this was Jesus Christ Himself saying, "Charlie, I'm real! I do care about you! I love you, and I have the Power to Save you! ~ Just pray, and ask Me to be your Savior!"

Our friend handed me a Christian tract called, "The Four Spiritual Laws" by Campus Crusade for Christ. He said, "I'm leaving this with you, and I've done what I promised Jesus I'd do.

I'm gonna leave now ~ but my mom's baking chocolate chip cookies ~ and if you wanna talk more ~ come down to my parent's house, and we can have chocolate chip cookies and milk!" He smiled real big, and he left.

I couldn't wait for him to leave so I could get down on my knees, and pray, and ask Jesus to be my Savior and Lord! I was physically shaking! God had answered my prayer to prove to me, He loved 'me!'

The feeling in that room was powerful! Right after God giving us all this food, our 'dealer' comes over to tell us this! God was showing me that He is truly a very personal Savior!

I knelt down and prayed, and asked Jesus into my heart!

Amazingly, I immediately felt like a great 'weight' was lifted off of my shoulders, and the Peace of God flooded that room! (And my heart!) Doug was very happy, and thankful to Jesus for answering my prayer!

Now, I finally 'knew' and 'believed' that God cared about me!! I wanted to give Him a chance to show me what He wanted for my life, and 'why' He created me? I was very curious to know what God had for me. . . . (I was about to find out!)

"He that heareth My word, and believeth on Him that sent me, hath everlasting life, and shall not come into condemnation; but is passed from death unto life." (John 5:24)

"I am come a light into the world, that whosoever believeth on me should not abide in darkness." (John 12:46)

"As far as the east is from the west, so far hath he removed our transgressions from us." (Psalm 103:12)

17

III. {Lost and Found; Against All Odds!}

I was unsure my whole life as to 'why I was here' ~ but since I'd prayed to Jesus, I was now willing to give Him a chance to show me!

Doug said he wanted to go see our friend at his parent's house. I wasn't so sure I wanted to go, but I went along to hear what he had to say. I knew his parents and they were very sweet people.

We rang the doorbell, . . (and yes, we could smell home baked cookies!) . . . He answered the door along with his mother, both of them smiling ~ that we had dropped by.

Doug and our friend talked about God as we enjoyed his mom's homemade cookies with milk. (After the lives we had been living, we could hardly believe we were both sitting there enjoying 'cookies and milk!') We thanked them both for asking us over.

Just as we were getting ready to leave, . . the doorbell rang. Our friend's mom answered the door, and a tall, handsome young man stood there smiling. He told her he was the new pastor at their church, and he was just coming by to meet them.

He introduced himself and said his name was, "Pastor Tom." He reached out to shake hands with our friend's mother.

I ducked around him and said, "Excuse me, we were just leaving."

He said ~ "Oh, let me shake your hands before you leave."

He asked us our names and invited us to his church.

(We had no idea at the time, that this was a 'divine appointment,' ordained by God Himself, that would soon change our entire lives!)

He seemed very sincere ~ and his face just shined with the love of God!

When we got back home, Doug told me, "I'm going to that young pastor's church this Sunday!" I was still very much wanting to 'stay to myself,' and not get involved in any 'organized' church.

Of course, I had no idea what to expect.

I had been brought up Lutheran, but I never learned much about Jesus at 'our' church. ~ I had never heard that I could 'know' Jesus personally as my Savior

I'm sure the week before attending this church was probably the longest week Doug had ever spent. Each day that went by, I became more negative and agitated. I was stubborn beyond reason! I didn't even understand what was happening in my soul!

I decided I had 'prayed' and asked Jesus as my Savior, but I didn't want to "go to church" and "get involved!" I didn't want my life to change ~ that much!

I was voicing my strong opinion, telling Doug, "I'm 'not' going to church!" Each day, that feeling got stronger.

I saw that it wasn't phasing Doug!

He just stayed quiet, and that made me even angrier!

He seemed at peace with his decision that he was going "with or without me, no matter what!" I became increasingly argumentative ~ and told him, "We aren't going!"

He said, "That's where you're wrong Charlie. If you don't want to go ~ stay home. But I think there's something there for me, and I'm going!"

That made me feel like he didn't care at all about my feelings. I was hurt that he was putting God over me! I saw that our relationship was changing, and I didn't like change! I continued to argue my point that, "all churches are full of hypocrites!"

Doug looked frustrated with me, however, he just kept quiet.

When I realized that he was convinced, I decided to say, "Okay, if I go, I'm wearing my blue jeans, boots, and jean jacket!"

He just said calmly ~ "You can wear your jeans, boots, and jean jacket."

I said ~ "Well, when we walk in, we're walking down the center aisle, and going to the front pews ~ and if anyone so much as 'looks at me cross-eyed,' we're leaving!"

He said, "That's where you're wrong Charlie ~ you can leave, but I'm staying. I think there's something there for me."

Well, I felt very alone in this decision; and very nervous, . . and yet, I didn't want to be left out.

When Sunday came, I reluctantly went along with Doug ~ feeling that things would happen just as I said, and we'd end up seeing all the 'hypocrisy,' and we'd both be disgusted and leave.

Well ~ we entered the church, and it was a beautiful old church with breathtaking stained-glass windows. (It was the first time we'd gone to a church in years, except for getting married.)

We stood in the back, gazing at a huge stained-glass window of Jesus that was so beautiful, and loving, and inviting!

We started to walk down the center aisle, and yes, . . I was in my blue jeans, jean jacket, and boots! We walked slowly, and you can't imagine the peace in that church!

But I was looking around, waiting for someone to look at us, 'like we didn't belong there.'

To my surprise, the people were mostly elderly, and everyone was either reading, or their heads were bowed like they were praying. Not one person even looked our way!

I was shocked, and taken back.

I felt embarrassed, . . having tormented Doug over something he wanted to do. I can only tell you that my anger was leaving, and I was feeling God's perfect Peace.

We sat up near the front, staring up at that beautiful stained-glass window of Christ praying, and I began to feel more of God's presence as we sat there. Doug reached over and held my hand. I felt okay now being there. I was feeling, "maybe there 'is something here' ~ for both of us."

When Pastor Tom came out to the podium, he acknowledged us, told us he was glad to see us, and told everyone that he'd met us the week before.

He said he hoped that we felt at home, and that we'd come back. He made us feel very welcome, and we were anxious to hear what he had to say.

His sermon was about "Knowing Jesus," as our Savior and friend.

He said, "We don't need 'long, flowery prayers' for Jesus to hear us ~ but we can just talk to Him any time." The more he spoke, the more I felt Jesus was sitting right there with us! His love was present ~ that's for sure!

When the service was over ~ several older women came up to us, their eyes filled with tears, and their faces were shining! One lady said

~ "We came to welcome you kids, and we want you to know, you're an answer to our prayers!"

She said, "We've been praying for two years that the youth would return to the church! We just want you to know you are very welcome here, and God loves you, and so do we!" That meant everything to us! What sweet, sweet ladies, and genuine Christian Love!

We felt very much at home there ~ like a new extended family that actually cared about us! (My thoughts and fears of meeting up with 'hypocrites' all seemed pretty foolish now, and I felt ashamed of myself!) I was very humbled at this point, but also at peace when we left the church.

Doug and I had a nice talk all the way home.

We both felt we needed to go back and see what God had for our lives. We had been lost for so long, going our own crazy way, not caring if we lived or died, living fast, . . . and being led by evil. We needed God's arms around us now, and needed to feel safe, and close to Him. We both wanted to know more of His power and love for us, and we couldn't wait to go back that next Sunday, . . . and feel God's Holy Spirit all around us again!

That next Sunday, Pastor Tom came to the podium ~ smiled at us, and again welcomed us. He remarked that they were all glad we had come back again.

In his sermon, Pastor Tom preached on "Heaven and Hell." ~ He spoke of how the enemy, (the devil,) tricks people, and how many people were believing they were, "running their own lives," when really ~ they were being led by the devil! (We could relate to every word he spoke, remembering all of the evil we had witnessed hanging around with criminals and bikers.)

He said, "God is looking for people He can use to reach others. If we are surrendered to Him, and obedient to His Word, there's no telling what God can do in and through our lives for the Glory of His Name!"

Doug and I had led a lot of people astray, and they went the wrong way because we were not living right.

We both wanted to do better ~ and we wanted more of God in our lives. God's Spirit was speaking through this pastor straight to us! It was like he was reading our minds, our hearts, our lives! That was God's Holy Spirit, and we know that now!

We knew that God was speaking right to us, and when Pastor Tom gave the "altar call," ~ I was feeling pulled to go forward, and acknowledge my Salvation in Christ. I started to stay in the pew ~ but then I felt like God Himself walked me up toward the pastor!

Suddenly, Doug was right there too!

We both told him we wanted to give our lives totally to Jesus, and become members of the church. Pastor Tom was very loving, and we felt like we belonged there!

That day was the beginning of a 'New Life,' and a 'New Start' for Doug and I. We both wanted to be baptized and follow the Lord, . . one day at a time. It was a wonderful feeling to know the love and guidance of Jesus Christ, and now to be a part of this sweet, sincere family of believers.

Shortly after that, we went to our pastor with a problem.

We told him that the bikers had come by, and we wanted nothing more to do with that life. He said, "I'm not telling you what to do, but if it were me ~ I'd move from your little house, and find something else ~ even just a couple of miles away ~ and 'I wouldn't tell anyone' where you moved." We followed his advice, and that was one of the best things we ever did for ourselves!

We saw one of the bikers at a gas station one day. We turned right around and left! We made that break from all our old friends, and we were able to have peace with God, and see His blessings in our lives!

We went to church every Sunday, . . and began Wednesday night Bible Studies. God really blessed us to grow in His Spirit, and His Word. We felt led to get involved in the Hospital Calling Team, to visit the sick and pray with them, and to 'let God use our lives.'

However, our church, our pastors, and Doug and I, had no idea what God was about to do there very soon, (to bring hundreds, and even thousands, into God's family,) through that local church!

There were around two hundred and fifty, to three hundred people there when we began to attend, and then, God answered those dear elderly lady's prayers, and sent 'Revival' upon that church like you wouldn't believe ~ unless you saw it!

Eventually, they had to have three different morning services, and they were offered their own television program! There were so many people coming and going ~ that people had to park blocks away ~ and walk to get to the church! We were all receiving good, solid, Biblical teaching, and bringing all of our friends and family there. Then they would do the same. God's love was being poured out on everyone!

This was a true Revival, in the early nineteen seventies!

Doug and I, and our new Christian friends, were being invited to give our testimonies at other churches in small towns, and we were on the television program with our church.

Doug sang and played guitar in church, and also on the television show. Then we were even asked to be in a Christian movie, which we accepted, and I was also interviewed on Christian radio. Eventually, the church grew so big, that they bought a large vacant junior high school, and moved the church there!

We brought in many 'hippies,' drug addicts, and criminal types, who were wanting to 'get straight.' Many of them received Jesus into their hearts, and were Saved, and completely changed!

Jesus doesn't care how big a sinner you've been. . . "He came into the world to save sinners," and He has surely shown His great mercy and love to us in every way! He's always been here for us, patiently working with us, showing us His grace, and helping us through all of our problems.

God had a 'plan,' and a 'purpose,' to Save two wild teens, named Doug and Charlie, and He had this wonderful plan even before we were ever born! We hope you will be encouraged by our story.

And just remember, no matter what your problems are, or how deep you're in, Jesus is right there . . waiting to help you too, . . "Against All Odds!" May God bless you all, . . just as He has us. Keep praying and let Christ have a home in your heart too!

"For I am not ashamed of the Gospel of Christ: for it is the power of God unto Salvation to everyone that believeth; . . " (Romans 1:16)

"Now when they heard this, they were pricked in their heart, and said unto Peter and to the rest of the Apostles, Men and brethren, what shall we do? Then Peter said unto them, Repent, and be baptized every one of you in the Name of Jesus Christ for the remission of sins, and ye shall receive the gift of the Holy Ghost." (Acts 2:37,38)

"Being confident of this very thing, that he which hath begun a good work in you will perform it until the day of Jesus Christ:" (Philippians 1:6)

2. THE 'JAIL RUN'

We have seen a lot, . . actually too much! ~ But we know that God has let us experience these things to equip us to reach others for His glory! Many times, we feel we have been given hardness as a 'gift' ~ to help bring others into the Kingdom of God!

This was one of those experiences.

~ After we had first become Christians, we both enrolled in a new government school, that paid us to learn a trade.

There were only four white people who attended the school, (two other friends of ours attended as well.) There were a lot of 'students' from rough backgrounds (just like us.)

On the very first day, Doug and I made friends with a black guy who asked us for "a ride home." (We soon found out that "home" was the county jail!) ~ He came to school on a 'work release program,' and came for the paycheck, (as most of us did.) We had been hanging with bikers before this, and he just seemed like one of our old friends.

We were just starting out with faith in the Lord . . . and we were trying to come out of a very dark, and violent lifestyle.

Well, Doug and I kept taking this guy 'home' to jail every day, and we became good friends, and got to know each other over the months.

Then one day, during a 'school assembly,' this black girl I didn't even know, decided to fight me because I was white, (and that was the only reason!) She jumped me from behind, in a room full of what we soon found out, were all 'Black Panthers!' She grabbed my long hair, and immediately, I felt her thumbs digging into my eyes!

Trying to pop my eyes out!

The only real trouble I had in fighting back, was when this big teacher (a white man, fearing for his life, in the middle of this huge crowd of Black Panthers,) came up behind me, grabbed me, . . and held my arms behind my back! ~ He was shouting for us to, "Stop This!" Unfortunately, nobody was holding her!

At this point I started to pray!

I later found out that Doug was praying too! The crowd all started to press in around us, while the teacher held my arms! Suddenly, I felt there was no hope!

I couldn't see! My eyes were being shoved from the middle of my nose out, and her hands were entangled down to the roots of my hair!

She was a seasoned fighter, and I was calling on God to help me!

I suddenly felt strengthened by my faith, and my trust in God, and I drew off of my experience as a gymnast. ~ I was very limber, and could use my feet as weapons!

I'm a survivor, and I was determined I was not going to lose!!

I leaned back ~ resting all my weight on the teacher, and began to do what I could, kicking for my life, with no arms!

Then the whole room began moving in around Doug and I!

Doug wanted to help me, but knew if he did, they might all jump in! We were all ready for a riot!

Everyone was pushing in, and shouting loudly, and it seemed they had all decided to 'Go for blood,' and finish me off! They wanted us to fight to the death!

Just then, like a scene out of the movie, "Blackboard Jungle," the guy we had faithfully taken 'home' to jail every day, stepped forward, and put his arm up in the air with a clenched fist! He held it up, and kept it up! Suddenly, all of them were looking to him like a 'Sergeant' to give them their next orders!

(Even the girl that had jumped me stopped fighting!)

What was eerie, was like a rehearsed play ~ they waited, . . . and you could hear a pin drop!

Then, . . he quickly brought his arm down, and it meant "Stop!"

The entire crowd backed away from us, and moved back toward the walls! ~ They all stood there waiting quietly, like robots! (Doug witnessed all of this, and he was in fear for our lives!)

Our friend, then made the teacher let me go! I was barely able to see! My eyes were totally damaged, and blurred. I had fought the best I could before the teacher grabbed my arms!

I had given my attacker two black, swollen eyes, and pulled a few things out of joint! (Her bra was hanging outside of her clothes!)

All of a sudden, several black teachers came in, and took her by the arms, and grabbed me too! They put us both in a room, and said we were going to tell them "what this fight was all about!" I said, "Go ahead, ask her! She started it! She jumped me from behind!"

The minute they let go of her, she was 'air-borne' over the table at me! I said again, "See?! Ask her, she's the one who started this!"

They held 'her' arms now, and she finally told them her boyfriend went to the school, and had been telling her about, the "pretty white girl" in one of his classes!

She was jealous because of her boyfriend! (She didn't even go to this school!!) Then, they told 'me' I was kicked out, even though she had started it!

But here is the part that is just so miraculous!! We had befriended a guy, to help him out. He trusted us, and knew we cared about him. We had witnessed to him about Jesus, as we talked on the way back to jail each afternoon.

We had no idea that he was the head of the Black Panthers!! They did exactly what he told them to do! (With his hand gestures!)

Who would have ever thought that God would use him to deliver ninety-nine-pound Charlie, from a room full of Black Panthers that wanted me killed for no reason!!? ~ But it sure happened . . . just as I am writing it!

We were warned to break off visiting our friend at school, (and told to "Never come back!") The teachers were all scared!

Well, we never held any of that against the black race. We were never racists, and we never will be! Eventually, God used this in our lives to help us understand some of the fears of our inner-city kids in the black churches, that God later led us into. We worked with many dear Christians there, and got to know and love them all so much!

It is only our great God that gets the glory for sparing my life; and especially ~ for the 'secret miracle' He had ~ riding in the back seat of our car – going 'home' to jail every afternoon!

Much time went by after leaving the school and we had no contact with our friend.

Months later, he called us! He had just been released from jail and surprisingly, he wanted to introduce us to his parents! We gladly went to meet them, and they were very dear Christians! They were both so sweet, and they were glad we were friends with their son!

He came to our apartment a few times and visited, and listened to Doug play guitar and sing his Christian songs.

Later we got a call that he was very ill ~ his appendix had burst, and he had developed gangrene! Doug went to the hospital and prayed with him, and, in time, God healed our friend. Praise God!

We can only hope he will always remember what God did in his life; to bring him closer to Jesus.

Even though the school had told us we could not come back, and to cut off our contacts with our friend, God had a different plan!

He brought him to us! God 'always' accomplishes His Will.

We will never forget our friend 'standing up' for us, in front of all of his friends; and we will always be thankful that we were willing to make, . . . "The Jail Run!"

"And when the children of Israel cried unto the LORD, the LORD raised up a 'deliverer' to the children of Israel, who delivered them." (Judges 3:9)

"The LORD is my rock, and my fortress, and my deliverer;" (II Samuel 22:2)

"For My thoughts are not your thoughts, neither are your ways My ways, saith the LORD. For as the Heavens are higher than the earth, so are My ways higher than your ways, and My thoughts than your thoughts." (Isaiah 55:8,9)

"Be not forgetful to entertain strangers: for thereby some have entertained angels unawares." (Hebrews 13:2)

3. WE NEVER KNOW

We went to school with a guy everybody knew, named 'Terry.' We'd known Terry since Jr. High ~ and then on through high school. We lived in the same neighborhood.

He was an outrageous prankster! (Movie material!) If he wasn't performing an intricate prank, he was usually deep in thought planning the next one! He played no favorites!! Even if you knew him, and were really close, you were just as much a target of his twisted sense of humor, and pranks . . . as the many victims who were complete strangers.

Some of it was funny, although much of what he did was not respectful to say the least! He got lots of laughs from pulling pranks on people, and then 'lived' to tell the stories to all his friends. He was an early groundbreaker for what is considered 'bullying' today!

One evening, (after Doug and I became Christians, and had given our testimonies on television and radio with our church) ~ we ran into him at the mall. We were always a little cautious when we ran into Terry!

He said he wanted to get in our car and talk to us. We said, 'sure.' (To our surprise, he was very serious, for the 'first' time ever!) We talked a little while, and he told us he had been watching us.

Terry said he wanted us to know, that of all the people he knew, who said they had become Christians ~ he knew we were serious about the Lord. He had seen how much our lives had changed, and he believed us! He had tears in his eyes, and he looked very convicted by God's Spirit ~ (we were humbled to hear him say that.)

We told him, we appreciated him telling us that. Then, with tears still in his eyes, he said he was wanting a better relationship with his dad, and wanted them to be 'friends.' He said he finally had a good job. (He felt his dad would be pleased he finally got serious about a job.) ~ We assured him, we would pray for him, and his relationship with his dad. He was different in his mannerisms, and his feelings were 'real,' for once in his life. ~

When he said goodbye ~ and got out of our car, he was looking at us with a very serious and genuine smile. As he walked away, he said, "thanks." Doug and I sat there, feeling like we had just been through a very 'surreal' experience!

It was a lasting feeling that stayed with us all evening. It seemed like God was speaking to his heart and soul.

The thing many of us never realize, is how powerfully our lives shine through to those around us! We need to continue to do our best to be a 'good witness' to everyone, and never compromise our faith. Always remember ~ 'You are the only Bible some people will ever read.'

~ Little did we know, that about a year later, Terry's mother and father would go to California to visit him and see where he worked. They were finally going to have the relationship we were praying for, that Terry wanted so much.

As Terry and his father walked across a main street together, his mother was still on the side-walk. All of a sudden, two cars sped up over the hill! Tragically, the first car hit both Terry and his father as they crossed the street!! Terry was thrown up into the air, and came down sitting 'straight up' in the back seat of the second car, which was a convertible! Terry was killed outright, and his father laid in a coma for quite some time, and died months later. It was so very, very sad!!

At his funeral, all of Terry's friends paid their respects and tried to comfort his sweet mother. It was such a shock for her to lose both her husband and her only child!

It was a shock to all of us!!

We never imagined that the talk we had with Terry in our car that night, would be our 'last!'

We never know...when we see someone ~ if it might be the 'last time.' We need to make the most of our opportunities ~ to show others the love of Jesus Christ.

We really believe Terry made a decision to know Jesus as his Savior. And even though we'll never understand why this tragic situation happened, we believe that Terry, and his father, are both in Heaven with God, and they are 'friends,'. . . now, . . . forever.

God knows everything, and we know that He will somehow use even this tragedy, for everyone's eternal good.

If I can encourage anyone today ~ it would be to ask Jesus to forgive you, and Save you, and take you to Heaven when you die! The Bible says "Today is the day of salvation, Today if you hear His voice, harden not your hearts." (Hebrews 3:15)

~ Jesus is waiting for you. Talk to Him, and pray to know Him . . 'Today.' Take care of 'your eternal soul' ~ it's your choice, . . and remember, we may not have tomorrow!! ~

"Man that is born of a woman is of few days, and full of trouble. He cometh forth like a flower, and is cut down: he fleeth also as a shadow, and continueth not." (Job 14:1,2)

"And the world passeth away, and the lust thereof: but he that doeth the will of God abideth forever." (I John 2:17)

"In hope of eternal life, which God, that cannot lie, promised before the world began;" (Titus 1:2)

4. THE TWO MEN WAITING

An older Christian friend of ours, named 'Buck,' took us under his wing when we were young Christians, (just 18 years old.) He started to take us with him to 'Gideon's Lay Witness' meetings, to speak at various churches. Buck had heard our testimonies of what Jesus had done to change our lives, and knew God could use our testimonies to encourage others.

He asked us to go with him to a church in northern Iowa on one of these ~ 'Lay Witness Missions.' We would stay the weekend in the home of a wonderful Christian couple, who were members of the church we would be attending. We had no idea that God would place these dear people, our "Host Family," in our lives to be good friends, prayer warriors, and a great encouragement to us in the years ahead.

~ We were treated like angels by this dear, sweet, and humble couple, 'Tony and Sophie.' She was a wonderful cook, and they were both so loving, and seemed honored to have us in their home, in spite of our backgrounds.

Sunday came ~ and we were nervous as we sat in their church, waiting for their pastor to call us up to the podium.

As we waited, fear struck my heart ~ like I used to get in school when taking a test, and I was always scared to get up before crowds.

Unfortunately, this fear was greater than I had ever experienced before! I became panicky, and reached over and tapped Buck on his arm in childlike fear. I said, "Buck, I don't think I can do this! I'm feeling very sick, and I feel like I'm going to be sick to my stomach!"

To my surprise, he smiled brightly and blithely told me, "you'll be fine." He then said, "you see? The devil knows you're going to give your testimony, and there's someone here ~ Jesus wants to save!"

He then added a comment that totally devastated my heart. He said, "you've got to be strong and pray, and I will too, that God will put the words in your mouth, because you'll be on the radio, and many 'all over' will hear your testimonies!"

(His face still shining brightly).

At that point, I felt very faint, and I only imagined myself going down the aisle and fainting, and I felt so sick! Before I could think any faster, (to leave,) . . . the pastor called our names, and lovingly asked us to come up, and tell everyone what Jesus had done in our lives, and what Jesus meant to us.

Well, I couldn't turn and walk out then, besides I had nowhere to go! And I sure didn't want to deny what Jesus had done in our lives! I waited for Buck to get out of the pew and go with us.

When I motioned for him to go ahead of us, he whispered, "no, they want to hear from you, but I'll be sitting here praying for you."

At that point I was petrified! I felt paralyzed! As we walked down the aisle, we were asking God to put the words in our mouths. I was glad Doug gave his testimony first ~ but I was faint the whole time. Now, . . it was my turn!

Well, Jesus was faithful (as always) and helped us with His power and strength! I felt great boldness; so much so, that after I had given my testimony, I asked the congregation if they would join us in an "altar call," with a hymn called, "Just as I Am." Buck was a man of great faith, and I believed him when he said that someone was going to get Saved! What I didn't know was, this church had 'never' given an altar call before! I didn't know this until later, or I'd have never felt comfortable in giving one, ... or doing what I did next! . . . .

No one came forward after the first verse, and I asked, "could we sing the second verse."

You can't imagine the looks on everyone's faces, as the second verse ended, and . . . yes, then the third, and finally, the fourth! Still no one came forward! I spoke up boldly and said, "I believe God sent us here for a reason, for someone very special, and you're holding back. Please come and accept Jesus ~ just as you are." . . And with that, we then went to the 'fifth' verse.

Suddenly, this young military man stood up in the back of the church, and bolted down the aisle, sprinting with long legged steps! When he reached me, he grabbed my hands. ~ He was visibly shaking, saying, "It's me ~ I'm the one -- Jesus is calling me!"

As he stood there in his military uniform, shaking, he already had tears flooding down his face! I knew then Buck was right, and he was the one!

The congregation stood silent, (almost in shock!) You could have heard a pin drop!

We then prayed the 'Sinners Prayer' with him, asking Jesus to forgive his sins, and to come into his heart and life. He was so happy and thankful!

The pastor came up to the podium with a look of surprise, and yet a loving acceptance of us, and what I had boldly been led of the Holy Spirit to do.

Everyone received the service well, and told us they were very happy we came along to be part of the 'Lay Witness Mission.' They said they had 'all been praying' for this young man, and they were thrilled that he found Jesus as his Savior!

Now, Tony and Sophie had some very good neighbors next door, who wanted to meet us, and share a few refreshments with us before we traveled back home. They told us their neighbors were not able to meet us at church, and could not attend because of their son being "special-needs." We were glad to go over and meet them all. Their neighbors apologized that they weren't able to come to church and join us; however, . . they'd "heard us on the radio!" I looked over at Doug, and again, I was getting 'butterflies' in my stomach. We both thought we were just being recorded for the radio. We had no idea we were on 'live!'

We all visited, and enjoyed some lemonade and cookies together, and had a nice chat. ~ As we were just getting up to leave from this sweet circle of new friends ~ I noticed their special needs son was beginning to tear up, and his face became very red!

I asked him, "what's wrong?"

He began to weep, and couldn't answer me! His parents looked shocked! Buck put his hand on the man's shoulder, and asked him what he was feeling?

He looked at Doug and I, and pointed at us and said, "I want . . . what they have!" As he continued to weep, his face looked like he knew exactly what we came there for, and he was not going to miss out on knowing Jesus!

Buck asked us all to stand and join hands, and we all prayed for this sweet man with heartfelt empathy.

After we prayed the Sinners Prayer with him ~ we all looked up, and this man's face was absolutely shining! ~ He was smiling, and so happy! He looked completely content and at peace.

It was beautiful to see, and the room had filled with the presence of Christ's peace and love!

We knew then, that Jesus had a purpose for us to be there at just that moment. (And if we hadn't been 'live' on the radio that day, this dear man would have never even heard our testimonies!)

Jesus is real! And He had a special gift for this special-needs man! His parents were overjoyed, and so thankful that we stopped by, and that God had a 'divine appointment,' for 'two men' that day!

~ We all rejoiced and praised the name of Jesus! Our Savior was gloriously present, and it was such a wonderful feeling, that none of us wanted it to end!

We were both saddened, to realize that we would probably never see these two men ~ and all our new Christian friends again—until Heaven. (And we're certainly looking forward to that wonderful day!)

Later, Buck was able to visit that church and he reported back, "Since the 'Lay Witness Mission,' that church is 'on fire' for Jesus!"

"They are witnessing, and bringing in new members, and many of the men there have joined the Gideons Society. and other Christian associations!" (Praise God!)

(Even though we thought that we would never see these Christian friends again, God had other plans.)

Our wonderful host family, Tony and Sophie, and their neighbors, Charley and his dear wife, Janet, remained our good friends until they went to be with our dear Lord.

Even after we moved to Phoenix, they would visit us every year on their annual 'missionary journey' to volunteer at a small Spanish church in Yuma, Arizona.

What a beautiful Savior, who answers when we pray!

God Himself had strengthened us, given us His power, (and His Holy Spirit,) to witness in this church, and to bring these two precious men into His Kingdom!

God brought forgiveness, peace, . . and Jesus, into their hearts and souls; and it was very clear to us ~ that God Himself had sent us there, for . . . "The Two Men Waiting"

"He giveth power to the 'faint;' and to them that have no might He increaseth strength." (Isaiah 40:29)

"take no thought beforehand what ye shall speak, neither do ye premeditate: but whatsoever shall be given you in that hour, that speak ye: for it is not ye that speak, but the Holy Ghost." (Mark 13:11)

"All that the Father giveth me shall come to me; and him that cometh to me I will in no wise cast out." (John 6:37)

5. PASTOR PETE ~ AND THE ANOINTING

We were Saved in early nineteen seventy, and we'd been going to our new church for several months, when I became very ill with a very serious bladder infection. I was bleeding every time I went to the bathroom! It was so frightening! I was only eighteen, and I had never experienced anything like this before.

I had been to the doctor ~ and to the ER, and they prescribed medications several times. I finished the medicines they gave me, and there was no change! The doctors discouraged me even further ~ by telling me, they had 'done everything they could,' and there was nothing more they could do! I was scared, and so was Doug.

We had been learning more about God's Word at our church, and Doug was faithfully reading his Bible and praying for me. After the doctors gave us that discouraging news ~ Doug called one of our new pastors, "Pastor Pete," and told him what was happening.

He asked Doug if we believed in 'anointing with oil,' or had we ever heard of it? Doug told him, "No, we've never heard anything about that." ~ Pastor Pete told him what the Bible says in the book of 'James' about sickness. He said, "If you want me to pray and anoint Charlie ~ I'll come right over." Doug said, "Yes, please come over as soon as you can!" (He came right away.)

He read to us what it says in (James 5:14,15) ~ "Is any sick among you? Let him call for the elders of the church; and let them pray over him, anointing him with oil in the name of the Lord: And the prayer of faith shall save the sick, and the Lord shall raise him up; and if he have committed sins, they shall be forgiven him."

~ I was very weak, (from the constant loss of blood,) and I was lying on our big antique couch when Pastor Pete prayed for me. I confessed my sins, and he anointed me with oil, (on my forehead,) said a prayer, and after praying he said, "in the Name of the Father, and of the Son, and of the Holy Ghost! In Jesus Name, Amen!" . . . .

I remember looking into his eyes, at his strong faith, and serious countenance. I could see he believed every word of the Bible, and was convinced that this anointing, mixed with God's Holy Words, and our faith, would heal me!

37

Even though this was all new to us ~ Pastor Pete's resolve and concern, to come right over, gave us the faith and hope, that Jesus was leading him to pray for me. After he prayed, moments later, I felt like I was in a semi-conscious state. I had never felt like this before!

I can't explain it any other way except, "a ton of peace engulfed me" ~ like a deep sleep, yet I could barely hear voices. I was aware of God's Holy Peace all around me. It was so thick, that I couldn't even open my eyes. I was just basking in "God's Perfect Peace and Love," as I laid there. What a wonderful experience!

I had no idea how long I was lying there, however ~ I was aware that someone sat on the edge of the couch near my stomach. Still weak and unable to open my eyes, I didn't know who it was, but I felt the weight, and the couch cushion pressed down, and 'indented' right next to me.

After some time, when I was able to open my eyes again, I looked around, and I actually saw a golden hazy look in the living room. It was so peaceful!

I called for Doug and he came right out of the bedroom and asked me if I was okay? I said, "Yeah Honey, were you just sitting here beside me?" He said, "No, I've been in the bedroom reading my Bible since Pastor Pete left."

I asked him, "When did Pastor Pete leave?"

He said, "Right after he anointed you Honey. He said he would be praying for us ~ and then he left."

At that point, I knew 'the Angel of the Lord,' (or Christ Himself,) was sitting beside me on that couch! I felt the cushion indented; I felt the Peace of Christ so strong ~ I was not even able to open my eyes!

And then, when I was able to open my eyes ~ I saw a golden brightness in the room that I had never seen before!

There was absolutely no logical explanation!

What a wonderful experience God Blessed me with! We can only believe, our Savior Himself was showing us His Presence, and His Love for me!

As I got up and moved around, I was stronger than I had been. I told Doug I had to use the bathroom. He asked if I needed help, and I told him, "no thanks honey." I felt I could make it without any help.

Then, when I went to the bathroom, there was no more blood, and everything was completely clear! (For the first time in a couple of months, and several medicines later!!) I yelled out to Doug, and he came to the door. I told him, "Everything is clear!"

He said ~ "Jesus answered our prayers, and our faith, and Pastor Pete's anointing, and He healed you Charlie!"

Later, I told Doug I believed that Jesus was the One sitting next to me on the couch and he said, "It must have been Him!" This was just the beginning of the Lord growing us up in His Spirit, and allowing us to see His mighty power, and what He could do ~ if we just prayed, and 'believed' God's Word!

This was the first 'anointing' we had ever experienced!

And after this beautiful, powerful, miracle; from that evening on ~ the bleeding completely stopped. I was Healed ~ and I was never sick with that bladder problem again!! Praise God!!

This prayer of faith, and anointing with oil, would not be the last we'd experience ~ it was only the beginning of greater faith in our dear Savior!

The next day we called Pastor Pete, and told him we wanted to see him. He said, "come on over."

We told him what had happened and he was so happy and excited to hear our story! He agreed that the Lord must have visited me in His Spirit, and healed me! We rejoiced together and praised God, and had a sincere prayer of thanks!

We both decided right then and there; we wanted to start going to the hospitals along with Pastor Pete, and praying for those who were sick, and needed healing.

We watched what he said and did, and learned our Bibles, and it was so exciting seeing others being healed through prayer too! Every time we walked away from praying with someone in the hospitals or nursing homes, we felt good, and full of faith, and expected Jesus to answer our prayers, . . and He did! ~ We saw so many miracles!

Jesus tells us to, "Pick up your cross and follow Me." He also tells us in Matthew 25:40 ~ "Inasmuch as ye have done it unto one of the least of these my brethren, ye have done it unto me."

We praise God for our early training and guidance, and that our pastors taught us to "Lay down our lives for our brethren!" After all, (reading Christ's teachings,) isn't that what 'Christianity' is all about?

"And, behold, a woman, which was diseased with an issue of blood twelve years, came behind Him, and touched the hem of His garment: For she said within herself, If I may but touch His garment, I shall be whole. But Jesus turned Him about, and when he saw her, He said, Daughter, be of good comfort; thy faith hath made thee whole. And the woman was made whole from that hour." (Matthew 9:20-22) Praise God for such wonderful miracles!

"yea, I thoroughly washed away thy blood from thee, and I anointed thee with oil." (Ezekiel 16:9)

"And they cast out many devils, and anointed with oil many that were sick, and healed them." (Mark 6:13)

"And the rest of the oil that is in the priests hand he shall put upon the head of him that is to be cleansed, to make an atonement for him before the LORD." (Leviticus 14:29)

6. THE ONLY CHILD THERE

Our dear older Christian friend, "Buck," who was a member of the "National Gideon's Bible Society," invited us to attend the "Annual Gideon's Meeting," at a big hotel one evening. ~ He had asked us to give our testimonies, to encourage these men in the service of the Lord Jesus.

We were still just young Christians and Buck knew we came from rough backgrounds, and had experienced a dynamic turn around when we asked Jesus to be our Savior.

Buck had told us that, because it was a Gideon's meeting, it would be "all men," and there would be "no women or children there." We sat and waited in the main meeting room for everyone to arrive.

Most of the meeting room had filled up, and we were all waiting for the main speaker, . . . and in he walked . . . with a little blonde girl about eight years old.

He told us all that she was his little daughter, and he apologized that he, "could not find a baby sitter."

He explained that, "My wife had a meeting tonight also."

His daughter was ~ the only child there.

Buck had a prayer with Doug and I in the car before we came in, asking Jesus to use us, and to bless the meeting with His Holy Spirit.

~ When we were called to give our testimonies, this little girl was sitting up on the stage, and smiled shyly at us. Her long blonde curls were perfectly coiled, and she had on a lovely little green dress with a big white bow in front.

Doug and I both gave our testimonies, and we were received with great kindness! After the meeting, we all went into the main lobby to talk, and greet one another.

Suddenly, I felt an arm come around my shoulder. I looked over and this little innocent girl reached up and whispered in my ear ~ "I want to know Jesus, just like you do!"

This was a new experience for me. However, I was eager to talk to her. I asked her if she wanted to talk to me 'privately' and she said, "Yes, let's come in here!" She grabbed my hand and pulled my arm, and headed for the restroom, leading me.

Once in there, I said, "Wanna just sit up here on the counter and talk?" She said, "Yes," and we both smiled. ~ We sat up on the long bathroom counter, and I had my Bible with me.

She looked at me so lovingly, and began to tear up! My heart went out to her! I asked her, "what's wrong?"

I asked if she knew Jesus as her Savior? She said, "No, that's the problem! I want to, but my dad says I'm too young, and I need to wait to be sure I know what I'm doing." She said, "but I want to know Jesus 'right now!' ~ I want to ask him as my Savior like you!"

To reassure her, I told her that Jesus told His disciples to, "let the little children come to Him." She asked me, "Where is that?"

She seemed to want to know 'specifically,' and wanted to read it for herself. She was a very bright young girl. At this point, I panicked a little ~ (we were young Christians.) I knew Jesus said this, but I wasn't sure where the verse was. I prayed in my head, "Lord Jesus, You know this little girl wants to know You, and also wants to know where this verse is, please Lord ~ show me where it's at."

I opened my Bible to search for it and miraculously opened to that very verse in Luke 18:16! "But Jesus called them unto him, and said, Suffer little children to come unto me, and forbid them not: for of such is the kingdom of God." I said excitedly ~ "here it is!" Her tears stopped, and she listened intently.

She was so serious, and knew exactly what she wanted. She said, "can you pray for me to receive Jesus into my heart now?"

She smiled humbly, and reached out, and grabbed both my hands, as if we were sisters or best friends. She had a very loving heart, and a sweet, sweet, spirit!

I told her, "Yes, let's pray to Jesus right now."

She smiled and looked so excited as she bowed her head.

I was so blessed to pray with that little blonde angel with the long curls that evening.

After we prayed, she looked up, and was so thrilled to now have Jesus in her heart, as her 'personal' Savior! We were both still holding hands and smiling these incredible smiles. She was perfectly content, and so happy she was no longer 'alone.' Jesus was going home with her tonight!

She thanked me, and hugged me, and we went out to the lobby. Everyone was still talking. She went up to her dad, and excitedly told him she had "accepted Jesus" into her heart! He smiled lovingly at her and said, "Praise God!"

She and I exchanged addresses, and she wanted to be "pen pals." She was so sweet to send me letters, and tell me how happy she was.

She was telling all her friends about Jesus, and we were thrilled to know how she really took God's Word, (and His hand,) and ran with Him!

Some years later, she wrote and said she was a leader in "Campus Crusade for Christ." Along with the letter, there was a picture of a grown young lady, and I wondered whose picture it was.

Then, at the end of her letter ~ she thanked us that years before, I had led her to know Jesus as her Savior, and she said, "I love Jesus so much, and I love you too, and I just wanted you to see what I look like now ~ this is my Senior picture." Praise God, she was so grown up and beautiful, I just didn't recognize her without her long blonde curls!

I often think of that first night we met her, and how the creed for Campus Crusade for Christ is, "God has a plan and a purpose for your life!" He has a plan and a purpose for all of our lives. God knew that sweet little angel would be there to hear our testimonies that night, and He had a plan, . . to Save ~ "The Only Child There!"

We're looking very forward to seeing her in God's Beautiful Kingdom! I know she'll be looking for us ~ Praise God!

We will always thank Jesus for this sweet, 'divine appointment!!'

"And said unto them, Whosoever shall receive this child in my name receiveth me: and whosoever shall receive me receiveth him that sent me:" (Luke 9:48)

"Whosoever therefore shall humble himself as this little child, the same is greatest in the kingdom of heaven." (Matthew 18:4)

7. HE IS GOD; AND GOD ALL BY HIMSELF

Doug and I were still just new Christians, and we had only been married for a year. We were living in the neighborhood near our new church, and just getting to know our three dear pastors.

We had taken our Pastor Tom's advice and moved a couple of miles away, and didn't tell any of our old 'criminal' friends where we'd moved. We were staying away from old temptations and habits, and we were making a good attempt to 'start over' ~ with Jesus.

We had been regularly attending our church and learning all about the Bible, and Jesus, and how to live the Christian life. One of the first great lessons we learned, and experienced, about God's Holy Spirit was through our dear pastor, "Pastor Pete." He regularly visited the sick in their homes, in hospitals, and in nursing homes.

He was a sincere man of God who truly knew how to let God's Holy Spirit lead him, as we'd soon find out in a very personal way.

We had rented a small house, and we had no phone. Back then there were no cell phones.

Doug was at home, and I had driven over to see my grandmother, who was very ill, and close to dying. I had no idea how close, until I arrived and went into her bedroom. She was lying in bed, just staring, with a glazed, far-away look in her eyes. (In my heart I knew she was dying, and I wanted to be with her if she was.) I whispered one of my first big prayers, asking God for "a few miracles." I had never seen anyone die before, and I was nervous and scared. I wanted Doug there with me, and I wanted our Pastor Pete with us.

Our pastors had recently taught us, "If you need anything, pray to Jesus ~ because, 'All things are possible with God'!"

So, I prayed — "Dear Jesus, I know You are listening to me, and You know how sick my Grandma is. I want to be here with her if she's going to die. If she is going to die, please give me a sign by keeping me busy somehow, so I'll know to stay around. And if she's going to die, I ask You to please give me a miracle, and send Doug and Pastor Pete over here to be with me and Grandma.

And dear God, I also ask You to please let me 'know' that my Grandma is with You! Lord I know if anyone else was hearing me pray this, they'd think I was crazy, but You tell us to 'ask and you shall receive.' I'm asking You right now ~ to help me Lord Jesus, and I believe You can. Amen." (Well, . . our God soon proved to me that He hears and answers sincere prayers!)

What I'm about to tell you will take faith to even believe what our Savior did to answer my prayers.

Immediately after my prayer, my aunt who lived with Grandma, told me that my Aunt June from Davenport, Iowa, had just pulled into the driveway. Aunt June asked me if I would help her in with her suitcases, which I gladly did. (Now, I didn't forget what I had just prayed about "keeping busy," to let me know to "stay around.")

She then asked if I could move my car into the street, so she could get up closer to the house with the rest of her luggage. She asked, 'if I'd help her carry some things in,' and I was glad to help her.

When I got inside, we talked a little and she asked me to drive to the pharmacy down the street for some mouth swabs for Grandma.

I drove to the pharmacy. I thanked God for the errands.

When I got back, Aunt June got a glass of water to use with the small sponges, (on tiny sticks,) to swab Grandma's mouth when she got thirsty. She asked me to help. I'd never done this before, but I listened, and again, I was glad to help Grandma any way I could (and also, to 'stay busy.')

I knew God was telling me to ~ 'stay.'

I noticed Grandma's forehead was beaded up with sweat. So, I got a cool, wet cloth and wiped her brow. ~ I asked Jesus to "cool her brow," and I pulled a chair up to her bedside. The room was dark, so I raised the window shade beside her bed.

I was remembering the times I slept in that bed with her as a child. I stayed there a lot with her and Grandpa when I was little. They were both Norwegian and they were very kind, and quiet, and steady. They were always having the family over for meals, and we had wonderful family reunions, (and delicious dinners) there!

Grandma always snuck me one of her big, crispy sugar cookies when all the other kids were outside playing. She made me feel very special, and as I grew up, she always appreciated my artwork, and my sense of humor, throughout my younger years.

We had made lots of cookies together, and I watched her and my Aunt June make Norwegian Kringle, potato cakes, and lefse. I always helped to set the table for lunch and dinner, and I helped wash and dry the dishes. I remembered picking apples with her and Grandpa, and I picked tomatoes, onions, radishes, and green beans from their garden. I loved being with them!

They would both lovingly watch me as I practiced gymnastics in their big back yard.

They had an old record player there, and I loved playing a certain record over and over, called "Que Sera, Sera." They must have been so sick of that song—but they never let on.

All these endearing memories went through my mind as I sat there holding her hand. One of my favorite memories is that she always sent me a birthday card every year in the mail. Each card she sent had a beautiful little girl on the front with cute little baby animals. Some sparkled with sweet sayings, that I was "a 'Dear Granddaughter,' and so sweet to know and love." She always remembered me, and I loved that.

I looked over at her bedroom dresser, and I saw an eight-by-ten picture of my dear Grandfather, who had already gone to Heaven. I spoke up and told her I loved her.

Just then, my other aunt walked in through the bedroom and said, "You're just wasting your breath, because she can't hear you." (I felt very embarrassed, and hurt.)

Our pastors had always told us, (from their experiences in hospital calling,) that people could hear our voices right up to the moment they died! They had told us of their experiences and said, "Their hearing is sometimes even sharper than ever, even if they couldn't talk." So, I told my aunt on her way out, "I just want to talk to Grandma a little," and I shut the bedroom door.

I began to tell my Grandma, "I just want you to know that I love you very much, and I always have, and I know you'll be going to be with Grandpa soon." I took Grandpa's picture closer to her bedside— and told her "I love you both so much!"

All of a sudden, her head and shoulders strained to sit up, and she said out loud, "I love, . . I love, . . You!" Instantly, I got tears in my eyes. I moved closer to her and held her hand and said, "I know you love me too Grandma and God is right here with us."

I had asked the Lord to cool her brow earlier, and as I sat there, I put my hand gently on her cheek. She was not feverish anymore and her cheek felt cool. God had answered my prayer.

I was so happy that she heard me tell her I loved her, and I was shocked ~ when she tried to lift herself up, to tell me she loved me too!! God was real in that room! I knew then ~ I was staying right there beside her.

Before I had left home, I told Doug, "If Grandma's real bad, I'll stay over there a while, so don't get worried if I'm gone long. If she's okay, I'll come back in a little bit." He had thought about going along but decided to wait. We had no idea how bad Grandma was.

(In His loving and miraculous way, our great God was about to answer my three-fold prayer!!)

Across town, our Pastor Pete was on his way to the library with a friend, (a missionary man, who was just home for a visit) when he felt God's Holy Spirit suddenly urge him to, "Stop by and see Doug and Charlie."

When he knocked on our front door, he told Doug he wanted to introduce us to his "good friend." He asked Doug where I was, and Doug told him I had gone to my Grandma's house.

He told them, "Her Grandma isn't well, and she's been gone quite a while." Pastor Pete quickly said, "I just have a feeling we'd better go over there." He offered to drive Doug over to see me, and Doug gladly accepted the ride.

(This was the second part of my prayer being fulfilled!)

They parked out front on the street and walked across the front yard. My aunt looked out of the big picture window and said in a loud voice, "Charlie! Doug is here! And he's with two strange men I've never seen before!" I looked out the window and told her, "that's our pastor, Pete, and I don't know the other man."

She opened the door and greeted them. I hugged Doug and teared up and said, "Grandma isn't good."

Pastor Pete introduced himself and his friend to my aunts. He told them they had been on their way to the library when the Holy Spirit urged him to "go see Doug and Charlie." When he stopped and found I was with my grandma, and that she wasn't well, he felt they should bring Doug and come over. He then asked to see my grandmother.

As we all went in, my aunt gently grabbed my arm and whispered, "I don't know if I like the idea of two strange men in my mother's room while she's dying." I walked on in with our pastor!

At this point I was taking in every bit of the moving of God's Holy Spirit. I felt like I was in a dream—that was being lived out in real life.

Pastor Pete spoke to my grandmother but she couldn't answer.

He asked me her name. I told him, "Nettie." He said he would like to pray, and told me, "She looks like a dear saint of God." I nodded and smiled through my tears.

He began to pray, and he spoke to Jesus like he knew Him as his best friend. He thanked Jesus for being there with us all, and thanked Him for the leading of His Holy Spirit to stop by.

He prayed a beautiful prayer, and asked God to 'send His angels' to "accompany Nettie home to Heaven." He asked Christ to be close to her and comfort her, and said, "In Jesus Christ's Name we pray, Amen."

As soon as he said "Amen," my grandmother took a loud breath in, and then softly let out a quiet sigh, and peacefully passed away instantly!! (Right in front of us!!)

We all felt a powerful "rush" sweep through the room, that sent 'chills' all over our bodies! Pastor Pete and his friend looked at all of us, and their wide eyes mirrored ours! Pastor Pete said, "Do you feel the peace that just filled this room?"

We all quietly nodded "yes." (This was all very new to us.)

He said, (with a serene, Godly look on his face,) "We were just in the presence of God's Holy Angels!"

He then prayed a beautiful prayer of thanks to Jesus, for letting us be there for "Charlie's grandma."

(It was the answer to all my prayers!) Our God is so personal!

Afterwards, as we talked, I told them exactly what I had prayed (what I've just told you), and as I write this, I am still thrilled each time I relate this story; ~ how God was faithful to answer 'all' of my prayers!

We didn't need a phone! We didn't have to call our pastor! All I had to do was pray to our Lord Jesus with a sincere heart, and believe He would answer my quiet cries, and the quiet prayers of my heart.

When we all saw how God's Holy Spirit answered my threefold, childlike prayer, with such 'perfect timing' ~ it was so incredible, it was almost unbelievable!

He brought little errands for me to run, to keep me around.

He let Grandma tell me she loved me, and I knew she heard me too! And then, to bring my prayers all together, He brought our Pastor Pete, his missionary friend, and Doug over with no way of getting in touch with them!

Then, within a couple of minutes of entering her room, Pastor Pete prayed a beautiful prayer, and God's angels lifted her up to Heaven! These are awesome miracles, that we will never forget!

I had no doubt, my Grandma was with Jesus!

My aunts shook Pastor Pete's hand, and the missionary's hand, and thanked them both for being there. By their sincerity, I knew they were comforted too, (and also in shock, from what we had all just experienced in Grandma's room!)

That "Perfect Peace" was real ~ thick ~ and full, and it stayed with us! It felt surreal; and we were all still in awe!

What a Faithful, Loving Savior!

Please remember ~ even a small whispered prayer can be heard by our Heavenly Father, and never forget; . . He will answer, because ~ "He is God; . . . and God all by Himself!"

~ "If ye shall ask anything in My Name, I will do it." (John 14:14)

~ "Call unto Me, and I will answer thee and show thee great and mighty things, which thou knowest not" (Jeremiah 33:3)

~ "Precious in the sight of the Lord is the death of His saints." (Psalm 116:15)

8. MISTAKEN IDENTITY?

Doug and I served on hospital calling teams for seventeen years, which began through our Evangelical church back in Iowa. We grew to love doing that work for our Lord, and for the people in our church who had gone into the hospital. It was pretty scary at first, until our pastors taught us how to call on the patients.

We were taught to introduce ourselves, and tell them that we were with the hospital calling team from our church. We then asked if they were a member of our church; or a relative, or friend, of a member?

We would talk a little while, and then ask them if they would like us to pray for them.

They were always happy to have us pray with them.

They were eager to get well and wanted to go home!

Well, one day Doug and I were given a lady's name; "Elizabeth Smith." I looked at the door to her room before we entered, and the nameplate said, "Elizabeth."

We knocked lightly and then went in when a lady's voice said, "Come in dear!"

We introduced ourselves and asked if her name was Elizabeth, and she said, "Yes," (she had been crying.)

I said, "Elizabeth Smith?" And she said, "No, Elizabeth Nelson."

"Elizabeth Smith was my roommate, but she just went home."

We excused ourselves for making a mistake, and bothering her. We smiled and were getting ready to turn and leave, when she blurted out crying, "It's not a mistake! You aren't bothering me at all! I need to talk to you!! See?" (She lifted up a 'Yellow Pages' phone book ~ that she had just laid face-down on her chest when we knocked on her door.)

She then said, "I was just looking for a church, a pastor, someone ~ who can pray with me! I need to talk to God about my life!!" (Crying very hard as she spoke!) She said, "God sent you, I know He did!!"

Needless to say, we gladly offered to talk with her.

We asked if we could share our testimonies with her.

She looked eager to hear them and she said, "Please kids;" she was crying and very emotional. We told her our testimonies, and then asked if she would like to pray. She was so happy, she reached out, and held our hands as we prayed for her.

We could see the 'brightness' of "Jesus" in her face ~ the minute we all looked up from that prayer!

'Instantly,' Jesus was with her! His presence had filled the room!!

It reminded us of the Bible account of the thief on the cross next to Jesus! The thief believed that Jesus was the Son of God, and said to Him, "Remember me, when You come into your Kingdom."

Instantly, Jesus said to him, "I solemnly promise you, 'today' you will be with Me in Paradise!" Hallelujah! ~ Jesus is Real, dear people!

Well, we told her we were convinced too, that God had given us her name, and that this was definitely, a 'divine appointment.' (We were supposed to go see this 'Elizabeth' all along!)

Even though the last name was different, (and that lady had already gone home,) this dear lady was the 'Elizabeth'~ that needed to know Jesus!

She was the one waiting, and the one that Jesus was calling!

She said, "I hadn't even found a number in the phone book ~ and I didn't even know where to begin looking!" (But God knew!) His timing is always 'perfect.' We are so thankful that God was able to use our lives, to 'Save' Elizabeth! She found forgiveness, peace, and her Savior that wonderful day!

I would like to ask 'whosoever will,' . . to "Go in faith and ask God to lead you to others, in the Name of our precious Savior, Jesus Christ of Nazareth!!"

Jesus said, "Follow Me ~ and I will make you fishers of men." (Matthew 4:19,) and also, "If any man serve Me, him will my Father honor." (John 12:26)

Pray, dear friends, . . and see where you can serve God in your church, and in your everyday life! There just may be someone who's waiting, . . 'for you!' . . . (And Jesus!) ~ Amen!!

"Also I heard the voice of the Lord, saying, Whom shall I send, and who will go for us? Then said I, Here am I; send me." (Isaiah 6:8)

"When I sit in darkness, the LORD shall be a light unto me." (Micah 7:8)

"At the voice of thy cry; when He shall hear it, He will answer thee." (Isaiah 30:19)

"He that goeth forth and weepeth, bearing precious seed, shall doubtless come again with rejoicing, bringing his sheaves with him." (Psalm 126:6)

9. IN MY FATHERS HOUSE

My folks owned rental houses, and they had just bought a big old house, that had been made into three separate apartments.

The side door to this house opened into an 'entryway,' with doors to all three apartments. There was one door that led to the upstairs apartment, the other two doors to the apartments on ground level.

My sister's boyfriend lived upstairs, and a nice young couple lived in the big front apartment downstairs.

Doug and I lived in the small back apartment.

It was very small ~ no dining room, and no 'eat in' kitchen. We had a small living room, one bath, one bedroom, and a small kitchen.

We had explained to everyone that Doug was a musician, and he played guitar and sang. We told them all, if it was ever too loud, or annoying them, to just 'knock,' and let us know, and he could turn it down. They all said, "We love music" and said they might even come over and listen sometimes. We told them, "You're welcome anytime."

It was really fun living there and we all became close friends, like a big family. We'd go to one another's apartments and hang out, and talk, and laugh. When Doug played guitar and sang, they asked if they could come in and listen. We said, "Sure," and invited them in. (This was the beginning of many miracles to come!)

Well, what eventually took place was pretty unusual, and one of our favorite memories of living in that big apartment house! Everyone loved Doug's original Christian songs, and his singing, so much ~ that we all just opened our apartment doors to the main entry and left them open! Everyone just listened, or came in and hung out, and requested their favorite songs. ~ The Lord had given Doug the gift of writing some powerful Christian songs, and very inspiring words about Christ and Heaven. The Holy Spirit eventually used these songs to draw all these young people to want to know Jesus.

None of them were Saved, however, they all felt the Holy Spirit when he sang about Christ. We ended up having little music concerts every night. They all crunched into our small apartment and took their favorite spots. The couple who lived in the front apartment told her brother about an opening for a roommate in the upstairs apartment, and he moved in. He started bringing friends over to hear Doug sing too.

One night the young couple in the front apartment ~ asked us if she could bring her mother, and her little brother, over to hear Doug's music. We just said, "Sure, we'd love to meet them." Everyone was 'squashed' inside our tiny apartment ~ but the closeness, and the love of Jesus, and His Holy Spirit was felt there, and we all had some of the most wonderful times together.

Eventually, they all began to ask questions about our faith, the Bible, and the turnaround in our lives. We would talk to them and share how Jesus worked in our lives; how He had brought us away from drugs, crime, and gangs, and how He gave us His peace, and 'forgiveness.' All of them wanted to attend our church, and it was really encouraging to see Christ working in their lives, to bring them closer to Him.

Eventually, the young couple in the front apartment, and her mom, and her two brothers, and even her dear grandmother, were attending our church regularly. Our dear pastors welcomed them all.

Doug would take his own 'P.A.' (sound system,) and play his songs for everyone in our church.

The Bible says, God's Word does not return void, (empty.) All we have to do is speak and teach the Words of God, and His Holy Spirit brings His power ~ into people's hearts and lives!

(Isaiah 55:11) says, "So shall My Word be that goeth forth out of My mouth: It shall not return unto Me void, but It shall accomplish that which I please, and it shall prosper in the thing whereto I sent it." We truly witnessed this!

We opened our lives, and home, and spoke God's Words to these dear people. We saw the Lord bring this entire family, (and all their friends) ~ not only to hear Doug sing ~ but also to attend our church, wanting to hear more about our Lord and Savior Jesus Christ!

We never pushed any of them, but let the Holy Spirit draw them. We were honored to be able to invest our lives and our time into their lives, as our pastors had done for us.

The Holy Spirit moved each of these dear people to walk forward in church, to repent of their sins, and to ask Jesus into their hearts. We watched their lives change as they grew in their faith, and they all wanted to dedicate their lives to Jesus Christ!

Thank God for His wonderful Holy Spirit!

~ We continued Doug's 'mini-concerts' in our apartment. We'd cook meals and share, and if cars stalled, or got stuck in the snow, we were all there to help each other out! One night, we even had a house fire, that had started in the electric upstairs!

We were both sound asleep, in the back of the apartment, when we heard a faint knock on our door. Then, we barely heard the sweet young lady from the front apartment calling in her soft, gentle voice, "*Charlie! . . Doug! . . The house! . . It's on . . . F—i—r—e!!*" It was a miracle that we even heard her!

Everything inside the apartment upstairs was burned ~ but the two young men got out with their lives, even though one foolishly, ran back in, 'to get his pool cue!'

The Firemen were able to put it out quickly, before the actual 'structure' was damaged! But it was an experience that shook us all up, knowing what could have happened! We praise God for watching over all of us; and in His plan, using this incident, to make us all think more seriously about life and death!

It brought us all even closer together, . . . and made us think about our souls, and getting closer to Jesus!

We had all been called, and we were now being educated by our Lord Jesus. We were receiving wonderful, solid, Biblical teaching, spiritual guidance, and healing, that has continued to carry us all forward to this very day.

Later in life, the young couple from the front apartment had two beautiful children, and raised them in Christian schools. Both children are sweet Christians, and successful business people.

They now have their own families ~ and are also raising their children in the love of our Lord Jesus as well.

What we didn't know, back in those early days, when we were all keeping our apartment doors open to enjoy Doug's music, was that God had a much bigger and richer plan ~ than just enjoying Doug's music together. We can see now, that there is so much more He was doing! Jesus was on a mission, to "leave no one behind!"

One of our biggest blessings is that the young lady in the front apartment, "Kathy," became our lifelong best friend! The kind made of purest gold! She has been used to help us through some very tough times. She has spent most of her life loving, and praying for us, and we so often thank God for our dear Christian sister, and 'Soul Mate,' in Jesus Christ!

God's Holy Spirit is always working, in and through our lives and circumstances. Many times, we are not even aware of how much He's doing!

We have learned that we can never out think, or out guess God. We've also learned that He blesses us abundantly, when we obey His commandments, and truly love one another.

God gives all of us the opportunity to be a true and loyal friend, to help each other in a time of need, to remain faithful, and to someday hear, . . . "Well done, thou good and faithful servant" on that great Judgement Day!

Let's open our hearts dear people ~ to love others with Christ's pure love!

Let's 'open all the doors,' and let them witness Christ's love in our lives, and tell them that Jesus died to save 'them,' and to cleanse them from all their sins. For our God has a Kingdom that shall never end!

The glorious mansion doors of His Kingdom will always be open, and we will go in and share the beautiful music there together, forever and ever, . . . and for all Eternity!

"Behold, how good and how pleasant it is for brethren to dwell together in unity!" (Psalms 133:1)

"And Jesus said unto them, Come ye after Me, and I will make you to become fishers of men." (Mark 1:17)

"In My Father's house are many mansions: if it were not so, I would have told you. I go to prepare a place for you. And if I go and prepare a place for you, I will come again, and receive you unto Myself; that where I am, there you may be also." (John 14:2,3)

10. DON'T GO IN THERE!

Doug and I always felt blessed to belong to the Hospital Calling Team through our church, we visited the sick in hospitals, and the elderly in nursing homes.

We had thought when we first joined the team, that we would be encouraging many people, which I know we did. However, the more we visited these dear people ~ the more they ended up encouraging us, and we walked away feeling uplifted and praising God! So much so ~ that we stayed with this great program for over seventeen years. (If you want to see Christ's miracles, join a program like this.)

We were always welcomed by the nursing staff, and really felt like they appreciated our service to the patients. Many nurses greeted us with a smile, and a nod of encouragement.

Surprisingly ~ one day an angry looking nurse came out of the room we were heading into. We had never seen her before.

She looked at us like she was in a very bad mood, and for those who know who "Nurse Ratched" was in the movies, well, she donned that look!

She abruptly stopped in front of the door, as if she did not want us to 'cross the line,' and said, "Don't go in there!"

I said, "Oh, is there a nurse with him?"

She glared back at me and said, "No, he's depressed, and crying. He just found out he is full of cancer!"

She looked at us like we'd better do what she said, or else! This nurse was obviously not a believer, and she was a 'crepe hanger' as they say!

We waited for her to walk away, and then went ahead and went in, knowing that ~ "We have a different 'Boss'!"

We had a quick prayer ~ asking God to give us His power, His words, and His strength, to go in and pray with this poor man.

We knocked on the door and peeked in, and told "James" we were part of the calling team from our church. He said, "Oh please, come in!" He was sitting on the side of the bed crying, and we asked if we could pull some chairs up, and talk with him. He said, "Yes, I really need to talk to you right now."

He was so happy we were there, and the timing was Gods timing! This was definitely, a 'divine appointment!'

We asked him about his health. He was quick to share that he had just been told by his doctor, (who had just left his room,) that he was "full of cancer."

We asked him if he knew the Lord Jesus as his Savior, and he looked ashamed and said, "I don't go to church."

We explained that he could still ask Jesus as his Savior, and even if he didn't go to church, if he believed, he could still be 'Saved.' He seemed to take comfort from that.

He was then eager to talk to us, and we spent some quality time with him. He then confessed that he would probably never be able to go to church. He looked up at us and waited for us to ask him why? He was embarrassed.

I asked him why he felt that way? He began to tear up and he said, "every time I go to church, . . I cry!" He then bowed his head and teared up even more.

I told him I had heard many times that crying was a sign of God's Spirit upon people! It could be the way God was working in his soul to bring him closer to Him, and it wasn't a bad thing.

Our hearts went out to him. I couldn't help but think "If this was my daddy, I would want someone reaching out the love and mercy of God to him in a crucial time like this."

We continued to talk with him and encourage him. We told him a short version of our testimonies and how we came to know Christ as our Savior. We told him how Christ had done miracles for us, to turn our lives around. We then read a few verses to him from God's Word.

As we were finishing the beautiful time God had given us to visit with him, we asked if we could pray, and confirm his Salvation, and ask Christ for a miracle to heal him of all cancer.

We told him, "All things are possible with God."

He was very eager for us to pray for him, and he mentioned how happy he was that we came to visit and pray with him.

We held hands and prayed with James, and when we all looked up from our prayer with him ~ his face was beaming with hope, (as ours were too!) We were all feeling lifted up. We could 'feel' Jesus present with us!

He reached out his hands ~ to shake our hands, and we smiled and told him, "We would love to have you visit our church, and no one will judge you for your tears." I said, "You just look for us. You can't miss us. We sit down in the front rows and you just look for my long hair." (We all giggled because my hair was down to my knees.) He actually started to laugh with joy that we might see each other again! (We were all smiling and giggling.)

What a difference Christ Jesus makes; He took us from fear, and sorrow, and tears, to a wonderful memory of God's sweet Spirit, that we will never forget!

We both walked away reluctantly, leaving him there, but believing Jesus was in that room with him now. (And also, in his heart!)

We were believing God for a miracle after we prayed!

As Doug and I were walking down the hospital hallway, we could feel God's presence surrounding us, as we had experienced so many times before ~ feeling as if we were walking on clouds!

I cannot emphasize enough when you are visiting the poor and sick ~ Jesus says you are really visiting Him! "In as much as you have done it unto one of the least of these my brethren ~ ye have done it unto Me." (Matthew 25:40)

A couple of months later ~ we were in church, 'down front,' and I heard a man yell, "Charlie, Charlie!"

I turned around and there was 'James,' rushing down the aisle to greet us. We smiled and welcomed him, and were so happy he finally came to church! ~ He looked at us and said, through his tears, "I'm crying again!" (Only these were tears of joy!)

I said, "Well nobody here even cares!" We all giggled, and his tears disappeared!

He said, "Will you please come and meet my wife and daughter?"

We said, "We'd love to!"

When we met them, James looked at us and excitedly said, "Guess what? We have great news! . . . I'm healed of all cancer! The doctors can't believe it!!" His wife and daughter, then had tears in their eyes!

We were all thrilled, and so happy for James' healing miracle!!

He grabbed my arms, and turned me around, and said to his wife and daughter, "See, I told you she had hair down to her knees, isn't it beautiful? She's the one who prayed, and she healed me!"

As excited as we all were, I had to correct him.

I told him lovingly, "Jesus is the only one who heals us." I told them, "We can only pray to Him, for His mercy, and His miracles!"

He was so excited about his healing, and being new to all this ~ we had to direct him back to Jesus.

We told them, "Jesus alone gets the praise and glory!" We knew they understood.

His wife and daughter were so thrilled that James came to church! They said they had been praying for years that he would attend church with them. We found out they had been attending our big church, and they were the ones who put James' name on the calling list when he became so ill. We saw this dear family many times, in the weeks, and months, to come. And we will never forget that emotional day we sat in the hospital room, sharing Jesus with this dear man.

How often we've thought about that nurse saying ~ "Don't go in there!!" and thinking, "What if we hadn't gone in there?

What if we hadn't knocked on James' door that day, and had the boldness, to go on in and introduce ourselves ~ in spite of that nurse's orders?!" ~ James might have never received his 'miracle healing,' if we had listened to that mean nurse!

We must remember ~ Jesus is our Savior, Commander, and Chief, and we must always listen to His Holy Spirit, and 'His Voice.' Amen!

We thank our great God for hearing and answering the prayers of His people, and we are certainly looking forward to seeing James and his family in Heaven some day!

I know, we will 'all' be crying tears of joy on that Glorious Day!!

"And Jesus looking upon them saith, With men it is impossible, but not with God: for with God all things are possible." (Mark 10:27)

"Let us therefore come boldly unto the throne of grace, that we may obtain mercy, and find grace to help in time of need." (Hebrews 4:16)

"He will be very gracious unto thee at the voice of thy cry; when He shall hear it, He will answer thee." (Isaiah 30:19)

"for I am the LORD that healeth thee." (Exodus 15:26)

11. HIDE ME BEHIND THE CROSS

A relative of ours went through a very sad, and tragic situation.

When she was nine months pregnant, toward the end of the ninth month, the doctors couldn't find the baby's heartbeat!

They decided to induce labor, and found that the little baby girl had died inside of her!

This was, of course, one of the saddest, and most traumatic events in this mother's life. The whole family was devastated!

It was winter time, and the snow was all over the ground. The idea of putting that tiny little baby in the cold frozen ground was almost too much to bear!

What sadness! . . Instead of bringing her home to her warm crib, and all her new little clothes, and baby gifts; and all the love and cradling that was anticipated and expected, we would all be gathering in the winter cold ~ for her little funeral!

What was the mother and family to do? Everyone's thoughts and hearts were totally broken; the pieces laying here and there, and all feeling like they'd never come together again!

None of us had ever had to bury a tiny little baby before!

The doctor's report said that the baby had been perfect in every way, but that the 'cranial bones,' at the top of her head, had not developed properly.

As the enormous stress and sadness mounted, Doug and I knew we needed to pray and ask God's help for everyone involved.

We thank God, that we had a wonderful young pastor who we often turned to for help. We asked him if he would help our family through this great sorrow, and if he could give the funeral service.

He lovingly accepted and he prayed with us for God to be present at this funeral in His power and strength.

"Pastor Pete," (as we all called him,) graciously prayed with Doug and I in his office. He prayed, "Dear Lord Jesus, we ask for Your help and consolation for this dear family. Please be with us all, on this sad occasion. Please Lord, comfort this family with Your presence, and Peace, and let everyone know that You are there with us.

Please let the weather clear, and let the sun come out to melt the snow away so everyone can get safely to the grave site, and Father ~ 'Hide me behind the cross.' In Jesus Name we pray. Amen."

We would soon see God answer that prayer in every way ~ and more!

The day of the service, the funeral director, (a big, husky man,) had a very somber look on his face, as he carried the very tiny, white satin casket to the grave.

Amazingly, the sun had come out in all its brightness, which we hadn't seen in months! We were all relieved that we were able to get to the little grave site, far back in the cemetery.

Everyone was commenting on how the snow had melted!

As we all huddled together, Pastor Pete lovingly and humbly gave a beautiful message. We will always remember his sermon.

He spoke about God giving us all gifts on earth, and God also had gifts 'waiting for us in Heaven.' He mentioned their tiny baby's name and said, "this is now one of her parent's gifts, waiting for them in Heaven."

"This will be a gift that, every time they think of her, God will pull their heartstrings up to Heaven ~ until that wonderful day, when they will receive their little girl." ~ He said to her parents, "God Himself will be keeping her safe for you ~ until you enter His gates to be reunited with your beautiful little daughter."

"This gift will always keep you both looking forward to Heaven."

After he had finished his sermon, we all felt a beautiful peace and great strength, that we knew was only from God's Spirit. It seemed as if all the sadness and sorrow had vanished in a cloud of Peace!

The strange thing was ~ my aunt, and a long-time neighbor, and another friend, were asking each other, "Were you able to see the pastor when he gave his sermon?"

We asked them, "Why?"

They all acted a little taken back as they tried to explain it. They said, "Well, we kept trying to see him. ~ We even moved over and shaded our eyes, but the sun was shining so bright behind him; the sun rays were in the shape of a 'cross,' and we couldn't see him, he was behind the cross!!"

We told them, "We saw the same thing!"

They all remarked that they, "felt a strong peace!"

We said, "Yes, . . that was Jesus!"

What a beautiful Miracle to behold, and we have never forgotten that day!

When Pastor Pete had prayed "Hide me behind the Cross" ~ we knew he was only asking for the people to 'see Jesus' and not himself, so that only God would get the glory.

But God took it a step further, and actually let the sun's rays form a 'cross' blocking everyone's view!

Jesus had answered every word in Pastor Pete's prayer, and 'Jesus even decided to show up Himself!' ~ And He indeed, "Hid Pastor Pete behind the Cross!"

(What an unforgettable Miracle!)

Thank You Father for answering all our prayers, and giving our family Your perfect peace and strength when we needed it most!

"Rejoice not against me, O mine enemy: when I fall, I shall arise; when I sit in darkness, the LORD shall be a light unto me." (Micah 7:8)

"For the LORD shall be thine everlasting light, and the days of thy mourning shall be ended." (Isaiah 60:20)

"But unto you that fear My name shall the 'Sun' of righteousness arise with healing in His wings;" (Malachi 4:2)

"Then shalt thou call, and the LORD shall answer; thou shalt cry, and He shall say, Here I am." (Isaiah 58:9)

12. WONDERFUL!

One day my dear Mama told me her long-time friend, 'Betty,' was in the hospital, and asked me to please go and visit her.

I hadn't seen Betty for years, as we didn't live near each other.

I was told she was very ill, blind, and close to death. Mama also told me, "They're saying that she doesn't know anybody." I prayed to Jesus, asking for 'His will,' and went right down to the hospital.

When I arrived, I saw that she was terribly swollen, and sadly, she was unconscious.

Two relatives were sitting in her room, and discussing what they'd do with her little dog, . . and who they'd give her deceased husbands clothes to! It made me nauseous!

I had to leave. I was sick to my stomach, and sick to my soul.

I was always taught that people can hear very clearly, even when unconscious ~ right up until they pass away. I felt so bad she might be hearing that! (This is why I believe we should never talk about crude and heartless things around people who are gravely ill ~ or even in a coma!) We have seen many examples, which prove that they can hear us! Let's always try to be sensitive, and speak words of hope!

I knew I couldn't pray with her ~ with those relatives in the room! (So, I left!)

All the way home, I prayed and pleaded with our Lord Jesus to forgive me ~ and give me another chance to talk to Betty, and pray with her alone. (And thank God, He heard my hearts cry!)

I was moved to go back that evening. (Just a few hours later.)

I walked into her room and sat beside her bed. ~ As always, I took my Bible in with me. ~ I said, "Betty?" and much to my surprise, she answered, and asked who I was? I told her my folks names, and that I was 'Charlie.' She remembered me!

We talked a little, and I asked her if I could pray with her?

She told me that I could pray for her, but she sadly admitted, "I haven't been a very good person." She said she had been an alcoholic all her life. I told her that Jesus loved her, and would forgive her, and accept her right now.

I then gave her my testimony.

She hung on every word, and understood everything I was telling her! I was being encouraged every minute I was sitting with her, . . that she wanted to accept Jesus into her life! (And to think, just a few hours earlier; she had been completely unconscious!)

After I was finished telling her how Jesus had Saved Doug and I, and helped us, and rescued us from a very rough lifestyle, she seemed relieved.

She seemed full of hope for 'her' life, and for God's forgiveness.

I asked her if she'd like me to pray with her, and she said ~ "Oh yes honey ~ I sure would. Please pray, and help me to know Jesus too!"

I held this dear lady's hand and prayed with her. I asked Jesus to "forgive her and cleanse her of all her sins," and asked Him to, "come into her heart and life, as her Lord and Savior."

She was squeezing my hand the whole time, and her eyes were tightly closed. Then she said, "Thank You!" ~ "Thank You so Much Honey!" She said, "I'm so glad you came to visit me and pray with me!" I told her I was very glad to do it. I said, "God loves you and I do too, and you are in 'God's Family' now."

She asked me to, "please come back." I promised her I would, and I read to her out of the Bible. She just kept on thanking me.

Well, I needed to get home, so I hugged her, and kissed her good-bye, and told her I loved her. I left her room, and began to walk down the hallway of the hospital. I had my purse, but then I realized, 'I'd left my Bible!' (I'd never left my Bible before!) I had to go back!!

When I quietly peeked into her room ~ I heard her saying loudly ~ "Wonderful! Wonderful!!" . . . I waited a minute ~ and then I walked in. I told her I had accidentally left my Bible.

She said, "I am just 'So Happy' that you came to see me! And now I'm Saved, and going to Heaven!" The Holy Spirit of God had filled her room ~ I could feel Jesus there! She was praising Him, over and over! (One of Christ's names in the Bible is "Wonderful") (Isaiah 9:6!) Her face was just Shining! She was truly enjoying the presence of Christ!

She asked me before I left ~ if I could read her something else out of the Bible. I was so happy and blessed, to share the Scriptures with her again. (When I had promised her I would come back, I had no idea ~ God would have me keep that promise so soon!!)

It was evening, . . and I hated leaving her, but I knew Jesus was with her now! (She thanked me again for coming to visit her.)

I went home, and told Doug all about what happened.

We had a prayer for Betty, and for God's will, and thanked Jesus! We went on to bed a little while later.

Then, in the middle of the night, I sat straight up in bed and heard the name "Elizabeth!" I didn't know what it meant? I heard the name "Elizabeth" two more times! The next morning, I called my mom to tell her about the visit and she told me sadly, "Betty passed away last night."

I asked her, "When?" She told me the time, and it was the exact time I had heard the name! I told her, "Last night, I heard the name 'Elizabeth,' three times in the middle of the night!"

She said, "Well, that was Betty's 'given' name!" (I hadn't even thought about that!)

I told her how Betty had accepted Jesus as her Savior the night before!

Mama was so very happy to hear that, and we rejoiced together!! I thank God that He heard my prayers, and gave me a second chance to go back to see Betty! What a miracle that she had been 'conscious,' and 'able to comprehend every word I told her!' (Just as I had prayed in my car!) Hallelujah!

We are looking forward to seeing 'Elizabeth' in God's Kingdom someday, along with all who have given their hearts to Jesus, our "Wonderful" Savior!

(She was blind; but now she sees!)

It's never too late to ask Jesus to Save you, and be 'your' Savior! (That's why He came into the world!) 'Betty' is proof of that!

"For God so loved the world, that He gave His only begotten Son, that whosoever believeth in Him should not perish, but have everlasting life. For God sent not His Son into the world to condemn the world; but that the world through Him might be Saved." (John 3:16,17)

"Behold I stand at the door and knock: if any man hear My voice, and open the door, I will come in to him," (Revelation 3:20)

"Whosoever shall call on the Name of the Lord shall be Saved." (Acts 2:21)

"And he said unto Jesus, Lord, remember me when thou comest into thy kingdom. And Jesus said unto him, Verily, I say unto thee, Today shalt thou be with Me in paradise." (Luke 23:42,43).

13. GRANDMA KNEW

When I was just a young Christian, I was working for a very nice women's exercise salon. I sold and processed new memberships, and ran exercise classes in the afternoons, and evenings.

I loved the job, and was very successful in helping many ladies, and younger girls, to lose weight. I had developed 'a following' so to speak, because I gave a good workout, and many told me ~ I gave a "tough workout;" that they really felt the difference, and were "seeing results." I went over their meal plans with them, showing them where they could make improvements. We all became good friends.

Some of the ladies would ask me to lunch each day, as I had a split schedule, and we'd meet for a nice salad and an iced tea together. I really enjoyed my job, and because I had been a gymnast, the daily exercise was something I loved as well!

As time went on however, we began having problems with a man calling our salon. We were trained to answer the phone; say the name of our salon, say our name, and then ask, "May I help you?"

The stranger's calls started slowly, maybe once or twice a week, then became more frequent. It quickly got to the point where we all dreaded answering the phone. (This was before, "Caller ID.")

Each day we were confronted over the phone, and this stranger was getting more personal! The calls began getting more sexual, and perverted! It was very unnerving to say the least! We told the couple that owned the salon, but they didn't seem very concerned at all. They told us, "Just hang up on them."

Well, their 'solution' ~ only seemed to escalate the calls. The fact that he knew our names, and which staff member he was talking to, was much like being in a 'scary movie!'

Each day was more intense, and these calls were now getting out of control! (The owners of the salon were just "sticking their heads in the sand" about this!)

They trusted us enough to let us completely run their business, and they only came in to pick up the cash, and payments for new memberships. They never stayed there, they just took the 'lock box' and left.

We were told at the end of the night, we were to carry out the big trash bags, down the outside cat-walk ~ down the stairs to the ground floor, and put the trash in a big outside bin (behind the building.)

I made the personal decision that we stop that routine at night. It was so dark behind that building, that we couldn't see anything back there! The owners weren't at all impressed with my new rule! Anyone who knows me, knows that I am very protective of all my family and friends. (I don't like anyone getting hurt, or being in harm's way!)

The owners made a couple of comments, that they did not want us "to tell any of the ladies about these calls." (They were afraid their business would fall off I'm sure!)

The staff all continued to fear the phone calls.

One night, a staff member was run off the road as she was nearing her house! She was alright ~ but she was very 'shook up.' At the time, it was passed off as "just college kids."

Another night, as I was on the way to my car, I happened to see a lit cigarette tip, lighting up under a big pine tree across the street, (at the funeral home!) I was of course more aware, and looking a little harder at what was going on around me.

(We were all on edge ~ because of the trouble we had been having with the phone calls, which had intensified!)

As I got into my car, locked the doors, and started to leave, I saw a man take a last drag off of the cigarette, and he quickly threw it to the ground! Several guys then ran out from under that big pine tree! Because of the streetlight, I could see three men hop in a car, which quickly tore out of the funeral home parking lot!

Within seconds, I quickly realized that I was their target, and in a "living nightmare," and was being chased home!!

I knew I had two things going for me.

God was with me, and also, I grew up on five acres, where we had our own race track! We would race cars and trucks around that track as fast as we could, just for fun! I will say, I was very good at quick turns! I was also very 'street smart,' due to my background, and my husband playing music in nightclubs for years! I knew not to trust many men, (or even women sometimes!)

The guys in the car behind me were very fast; right on my tail lights! I was in a chase for my life ~ and I knew it!

I prayed, and kept my confidence in God. I knew because of my faith in Him, and His Love for me, He would get me home safe!

Eventually, with my heart almost beating out of my chest, I finally out ran these guys! I went down a few streets, backtracked on a few other streets, and finally flew into our driveway!! I quickly turned off my headlights, and ran into our apartment!

There were no cell phones back then, and Doug was just waiting for me to get home from work. I told him I'd been chased home and to "shut off all the lights," which we did, and to "pull all the shades down!" This made these guys really mad, that I outsmarted them!

We peeked out under the shades and saw them searching through the neighborhood! We were shocked to see them shining a penlight on my license plate! We just left our lights off for the evening, as if no one were home, and watched television.

The next morning, Doug went out to take our Great Dane, and our German Shepherd to the park, but I stayed home. About eleven a.m. I heard the front entry door open, (it opened to the apartment upstairs, and to our apartment downstairs.) A man knocked on my apartment door. I asked, "Who is it?"

He said, "I'd like to talk to you,"

I asked through the door, "What about?"

He said, "About some business."

I told him, "I've got no business to discuss!"

He then said, "I'd like to talk to you about some insurance."

Then I saw the door knob move, (which showed me he was up to something!) I told him I didn't need any insurance!

He said, "I'd just like to explain it to you."

(Now, I 'knew' he was up to no good!) So, I told him, "If you don't leave right now, I'm calling the police!"

He said, (as if to give in,) "Okay, I'll leave."

I was so leery ~ I laid down on the floor and watched under the door, and I saw his feet! He opened the entry door and let it bang shut. (My fears were confirmed because, . . his feet never moved!) I knew then, he was hoping I'd come out!

(He was Wrong!)

I wasn't ignorant! I kept watching under the door, and he was just standing there, not realizing I could see him!

Finally, I got really mad and said, "That's it! I know you're still there! I'm calling the police!"

Immediately, I heard the door bang shut again. I looked under the door and he was gone! He knew I meant business! I was so angry!

Later that night, I got the idea to look up the phone number for that funeral home across the street from the salon.

Around ten p.m. I called the number, and I couldn't believe a man answered! (As a matter of fact, he sounded just like one of the guys that kept calling the salon!) In shock, I quickly hung up!

But then, I quickly decided to call right back and act a little 'wild.' I changed my voice, and I said, "Hey, I just called there and I realized I got the wrong number, but I decided to call back and ask why you're answering the phone so late? I mean, 'It's a funeral home'!"

The guy chuckled, and started telling me, "We baby sit the 'stiffs' at night, and we go to college during the day." Surprisingly, I got a lot of information out of him about the place.

We decided to run the whole story past a good friend of ours, and he thought something weird was going on at that funeral home too!

He gave me the phone number of a police detective he knew.

I kept it on file.

A couple of days went by. The next night Doug and I were both at home, when suddenly, we heard our back windows being rattled! Our big dogs woke right up and started barking! There were several guys talking, and we heard one of them say, "There's big dogs in there, let's go up this fire escape and see if we can get in up there!"

We stayed quiet, but the dogs went wild, . . barking furiously!

(We weren't sure at the time if they had gotten in upstairs, as our dogs were making such a racket!)

The next day ~ our upstairs neighbors told us they were "broken into," and some things were taken!

That next morning, I left for work a little early, as I often did ~ to stop by and check on my Grandma, who I loved dearly. My Grandma was tough! She looked part Indian, and had long gray braids down past her waist!

She and I were really close, and we'd always talk. I hated to worry her, but felt I had to tell her what was going on at work.

She listened very intently to all I told her. Then she surprised me when she said, "I want you to quit that job! Call in and quit!!"

I told her "I'd have to give notice." She was not happy about that at all! She asked me, "Why?!" I told her I had "commissions" coming from new membership sales ~ and I knew they wouldn't pay me if I just quit without notice. She said, "You might not get it if you stay!"

Grandma had a 'fearful' look on her face!

She said, "Your life isn't worth that money! I want you to quit!"

My Grandma was known for having a 'sixth sense' (and I ended up with it too!) I knew in my heart, she was right, and I decided to get out of this job!

I told the owners I was quitting that day. They immediately ran an ad, and asked me to help train the new girl. I promised them, whoever they found, I would train her the best I could.

I was very honest with the beautiful young lady they hired. I told her we were having problems with men calling on the phone. I also told her that one of the other girls had been chased off the road on her way home, and I had been chased home as well!

She smiled, and assured me she'd be fine. She said she knew to be careful. I said, "Well, I wouldn't feel right if I didn't tell you." She thanked me, and again assured me, "I'll be fine."

One evening shortly after, when all the customers were gone, we had an after-hours management meeting at the salon with all the staff.

As always ~ the owners, and all the staff, sat on the carpeted floor, in a big circle. We discussed new memberships, commissions, and our schedules for the coming week.

All of a sudden, we heard a lot of heavy footsteps coming down the long, metal cat-walk toward our business door! It was frightening because it was after nine p.m. and very dark out!

I looked over at the managers and immediately got the feeling that they were, 'clueless.' They didn't seem to have any sense of concern, or responsibility, for any of us!

As the footsteps kept coming closer, I jumped up, and noticed the keys hanging in the front door lock.

I ran toward the door, and the owners said, "Oh you don't need to lock that ~ we're fine." I literally flew to the door, and quickly locked it, as if I was locking out the devil himself!! (I found out later, I was!)

Immediately, I saw three tall men outside!

They had on hooded sweatshirts, and they were glaring back at me in anger, for locking that door! Their eyes were evil!

They tried the door! I thought, "Oh Lord, I hope I got it locked!!" Then a couple of them went further on down the cat-walk, and looked through the plate glass windows, to see if there might be another door they could try! I looked over at the owners! Both of their faces were beet red, and they looked scared!! I spoke right up and said to them, "Are you still convinced ~ 'we're fine'?"

Staying true to form, the owners didn't want to call the police, and risk any "bad publicity."

That night ~ we all waited a long while to leave, and the owner offered to walk each of us to our cars.

The owners looked at all of us, and we were all scared to death!

My heart was beating so fast, and my mind was racing ~ going over and over ~ running to that door, (when my inherited sixth sense kicked in!) I kept wondering, what would have happened to all of us that night ~ if I had frozen with fear, and not acted upon my God given discernment!?

(And, . . I still wonder what would have happened!)

One of the owners did thank me for locking that door! Had those keys not been in the door, (a miracle in itself) ~ we'd have all been 'sitting ducks,' since it was a key lock!

I decided to talk with the owners the next day, and cut my time short on training the new girl! I knew that after such a close call, I'd better listen to Grandma!

Unfortunately, the owners weren't 'that' thankful, and they never paid me my commissions as they'd promised!

Then I decided to call that detective and tell him everything that had been happening. He agreed that they were "up to no good!" ~ but his solution was to have 'me' be the ~ 'live bait!'

He wanted me to "wear a wire" (a radio transmitter,) and act like I was going to go out on a date with one of them. I would get in their car, and the detective would follow us, and then, "they'd get them!"

Doug and I were not going for that plan ~ at all!!

I told the detective, "Anything could go wrong!" I told him these guys were crazy, determined, bold, and after us all! I told him, "I'm not 'Angie Dickinson'!" (a lady detective on television at that time.)

The detective assured me "they'd follow close behind their car."

I said, "Sorry, there are too many things that could go wrong!"

He said, "Well, we'd have to have proof to be able to get them on something." I told him he'd have to "find someone else," because my husband did not want me in a car 'alone,' with those monsters and perverts!! (I have spared telling you the perverted things that they said to us over the phone!)

Needless to say, I was relieved to quit that job and be rid of those phone calls, and the fear of being watched, (and stalked,) every day!

Shortly after I quit ~ we moved to an old farm house way out in the country.

The end of this story is not the nice ending I would like to tell you, in fact it's horrifying, and terribly sad!! Unfortunately, we later found out that the beautiful blonde girl I had trained at the salon, had been run off the road one night, raped, and murdered!

We were so sick about this, that we have never really gotten over it! It was just what my Grandma was afraid would happen to me!

~ This sweet girl's parents were quoted in the newspaper as being "devastated," and "wanting any information at all, from anyone who might know anything." Of course, I contacted them, and spoke to her dear mother, and told her everything that had taken place!

It was a terribly sad conversation. All of our hearts were broken!

I got the idea to watch the want ads in the newspaper.

Shortly after this dear girl's death, there was an ad for that funeral home across the street from the salon ~ looking for "someone to work part-time at night, answering phones when necessary!" I was shocked to see, that 'my fears' were confirmed! I decided to call the number, and I spoke to the funeral director. I told him I needed to get in touch with the guy that had been working there! The funeral director said,

"Oh I have no idea where those (two) went! They left in the middle of the night, and didn't tell me, and didn't leave a forwarding address! They were just a couple of college kids." I immediately called this girl's poor parents back and told them what I'd found out.

She thanked me so much for checking into it, and giving them the information. She was so nice, and told me she didn't want me to feel any guilt at all about any of what happened to her daughter.

She was so sweet to me. Her daughter took after her, and she was just as sweet, someone I would've loved to have had as a friend.

The devil is real dear people, and he has a plan! ~ The Bible says, "the thief (the devil) cometh not but for to steal, and to kill, and to destroy." (John 10:10) In this case he stole this girl's life, he killed her, and destroyed this entire family. I don't know why it was her and not me, I will never understand it!

All I 'do' know, is that "Grandma Knew!" And we know that our Savior, Jesus Christ, spared my life for a reason ~ for His plan!

We never found out if the police ever caught these murderers, but whether they did or not, we know that God will deal with them!

"Vengeance is Mine saith the LORD, I will repay." (Romans 12:19) They have either paid already, or will soon pay for what they have done, because there is a 'higher court,' before which we must all appear! (No one escapes payment for their evil deeds!)

"For God shall bring every work into judgment, with every secret thing, whether it be good, or whether it be evil." (Ecclesiastes 12:14)

"Even as I have seen, they that plow iniquity, and sow wickedness, reap the same" (Job 4:8)

Be sober, be vigilant; because your adversary the devil, as a roaring lion, walketh about, seeking whom he may devour. (I Peter 5:8)

14. I JUST QUIT!

After we had moved to an old farmhouse out in the country, I got a job working at a nursing home in a nearby town, as the 'activity director.'

One day, as I was walking down the hallway, I saw there was a sweet elderly man crying in his room! I went in, put my hand on his shoulder, and lovingly asked him, "What's the matter?"

He answered as he wept, "My wife . . is dying, . . and the nurse said, . . she couldn't take time off, . . to take me over to see her . . at the hospital!"

Well, of course, I went straight to the nurse's station! I asked if I could drive him over to see his wife?

They told me it was "against our rules and policies" for us to take them in our "personal vehicles."

I said, "Get him in a wheel-chair. I'm taking him to see his poor wife!"

The nurse who had told him "No!" looked mad, and told me that, I was "not allowed to!"

I looked her straight in the eyes, and told her, "I just quit!" (And it was one of my favorite moments in my entire life!) She didn't know this, but I have a higher Boss!

I lovingly helped this poor man into my 'Travel-All' truck, loaded up his wheel chair, and drove him to the hospital!

As I was driving ~ I looked over at his dear face; his tears were gone, and he looked happy and peaceful. He thanked me over and over! I told him, "You're very welcome."

I wheeled this dear man into his wife's room, and when they saw each other ~ they both burst out crying, and held each other's hands tight. I got him in a chair next to her bed, and let them have some time alone. They both thanked me!

I told them I was a Christian, and I couldn't of done anything any different!! Amen!

Sadly, I learned later ~ that after their sweet reunion, his darling little wife had passed away. (What a testimony ~ of God's perfect timing, . . and His divine appointments!)

Dear people! ~ Let's love one another ~ as Christ has loved us!!

Later, I got a call and was asked to come in and meet with the director of the nursing home, which I did. He said he'd heard of my resignation and to my surprise, he not only wanted me to come back ~ he wanted to make me a director over all the nurses! ~ (Knowing I didn't have a degree, or the proper credentials.) I mentioned that to him, and he said, "I knew that when I called you in, but you could be 'grandfathered in'."

He said he was impressed with how I worked with the residents in activities, and he saw and heard how they all loved me! He said that he "appreciated my heart," and he thought he "needed some new blood" in there!

I was humbled, and thankful he would consider me . . . however, I had to turn down his offer ~ as the position would require too many hours. I could only work part-time, because we only had one car. (I also knew that the nurses would resent me being over them!)

This taught me though, that when we "love one another" as Jesus tells us to, God can give us favor, and bless us in ways we aren't even expecting!

Dear people ~ Let's all allow Jesus to lead us and guide us with His beautiful Holy Spirit of Love. Jesus is our example!

The Bible says to, "Do your work, as unto the Lord, and not unto men." (Colossians 3:23)

"Honour thy father and thy mother: and ~ Thou shalt love thy neighbour as thyself." (Matthew 19:19)

"And let us not be weary in well doing: for in due season we shall reap, if we faint not." (Galatians 6:19)

"Blessed is every one that feareth the LORD; that walketh in His ways." (Psalm 128:1)

"The LORD is nigh unto them that are of a broken heart; and saveth such as be of a contrite spirit." (Psalm 34:18)

15. KEEP YOUR EYES ON THE SHORE

I'm sharing a very sad story, (however, one that we have learned a valuable lesson from.)

Many years ago, we worked with a very nice young man, (a brick layer,) in new home construction. We really respected him. His name was "Dan." He was very strong and fit, and had a great work ethic. He was a very talented, and sought-after, brick and stone mason!

One winter day, he was on a snowmobile with his fiancée, and they had a terrible accident! They were just out for some fun, blowing across the frozen surface of a lake in Iowa. We saw on the news that they had hit a weak spot in the ice, and tragically fell through!

They became trapped in the icy lake, and were unable to climb out by themselves! A passerby saw them fall through the ice, and drove to a phone, and called for a rescue unit.

A helicopter was sent out, with an emergency 'rope!' (That was all!) When the men lowered the rope, they expected Dan to be able to hold onto the rope, and hold on to his fiancée too!

After being trapped in that freezing water for so long, both their hands were 'numb' and 'frozen,' and their arms were extremely weak, from treading water! As a result, he was unable to hold on to his fiancée, and the rope too, and he barely made it out himself! When he tried to grab for her, it was too late, she slipped away into the freezing cold water, and was gone!!

When Doug and I heard the story we were very angry, and felt at the time, that the rescue team should have had a much better plan!

(Like, one of the rescuers hanging from the rope in a harness, and reaching out to hold on to them!) Unfortunately, that didn't happen.

Dan couldn't come back to work for the longest time. He almost had a breakdown.

When he finally did come back, we were there for him, and we listened with great empathy. He told us his very painful personal story ~ that we have learned a Holy life lesson from.

Dan told us it was his fiancée that had kept him alive!

He said, he was "ready to give up" out of weakness, and didn't think he "could keep on treading water!!" He felt, no one would ever find them! ~ He told us that his sweet fiancée kept telling him over and over, "Dan, just keep your eyes on the shore!" He said ~ "That was the 'only thing' that kept me going!"

He was devastated that she saved him, but he wasn't able to save her! We tried to comfort him, but it all haunted him; that he could not save her, and would never be able to marry her.

We prayed for Dan for a long time, and we hope he has somehow found peace through Jesus. Sadly, we have lost track of this dear man over the years.

However, we did learn a great lesson from his very heartbreaking story.

In this life, we know we will all die of something. But we also know, that we have the promise of "Eternal Life," through our dear Savior! (Jesus alone is our 'life rope,' and Heaven is 'the Shore.')

He gives us 'all' the chance to know Him, but it is 'our choice' to receive Jesus as our Savior, and hold on tightly to Him.

And, no matter what our problems and trials may be, (those trials and 'crosses' are all different;) Jesus tells us to ~ keep holding on to Him, (by reading and obeying His Word!) He also tells us to . . . "Keep Your Eyes on the Shore!"

(When we do, we will all have the victory; and make it to His beautiful Kingdom, where we will be comforted for all eternity!) ~ Dear people ~ 'Keep your eyes on Victory's Shore!' Amen!

"If ye continue in My Word, then are ye my disciples indeed;" (John 8:31)

"And God shall wipe away all tears from their eyes; and there shall be no more death, neither sorrow, nor crying, neither shall there be any more pain: for the former things are passed away." (Revelation 21:4)

"Thou wilt shew me the path of life: in Thy presence is fullness of joy; at Thy right hand there are pleasures for evermore." (Psalm16:11)

16. THE 'ROOKIE'

I was a "rookie" staff ~ (new on the job,) working at a co-ed group home for delinquent kids. One day I was on duty alone with a 6' tall, seventeen-year old boy named 'Fred.' He was infatuated with the 'biker' lifestyle. (Somebody you would call a biker 'wannabe.')

We were sitting and talking in the kitchen of the group home.

Fred and I were the only one's home, and I was telling him about our Savior, and about our past experiences with bikers. I noticed that he kept looking nervously out the kitchen windows, which overlooked the long driveway.

All of a sudden, he interrupted me and said, "There's something I have to 'confess' to you."

I turned and looked at him and said, "What Fred?"

He said, "Well I don't know how to say this, but some guys are on their way over here!" (He looked really scared!)

I said, "And? ~ Tell me!"

He said, "Well they're planning on robbing the safe in the office, and kidnapping you." Then he said, "I like you, and I don't want to see you get hurt."

Right then, I saw these guys fly up the drive in an old car, and jump out in a hurry! I ran and bolted the front door shut, and ran into the office! He said, "What are you doing??"

I said, "I'm lockin' myself in the office Fred! The safe is empty, and I'm lockin' the door, and callin' the cops!" I said: "You're either with me, or against me. Which is it Fred?"

He hesitated, and said, "Well, …"

I started to shut the door, and I said, "Once I shut this door, there's no way I'm opening this door back up to let you in ~ after it's locked! Especially once they start breaking the front door down! ~ So, you better hurry up and decide!!" ~

He said quickly, "I'm in ~ Charlie!"

A male staff member had shown me one night where he kept a 'weapon' hidden in the staff bedroom, "just in case of emergency!"

I ran to the closet and grabbed that.

Fred said ~ "What are you gonna' do with that?"

I said ~ "Use it on anyone who's gonna' come against me!"

(I wasn't sure Fred wouldn't turn on me once we were locked in the office! After all ~ these were 'his' buddies!)

I picked up the phone, and called the cops!

I told them I was a rookie staff, and there were several guys at the door ready to rob us! It seemed like the police were there in about one minute! (That was the fastest reaction time I've ever seen!)

Well, unfortunately, in just that 'one minute' these guys drove off across the yard and eluded the cops ~ but thank God He protected me! (And thank God He convicted Fred's heart to tell me about it!)

We need to be ready, to take action for whatever will come our way, and above all, to depend on Gods protection. But our God would never have us to be ignorant, and not take steps to protect ourselves, and others! ~ "Behold, I send you forth as sheep in the midst of wolves: be ye therefore 'wise as serpents' and harmless as doves." (Matthew 10:16).

Those guys were kicking down the front door, but God was taking care of me, because I was trusting in Him. (But also, because I ran and locked the door, went into the office, dead-bolted that door, and called the cops!) We need to always use common sense dear friends!

But the real moral of this story is, Fred had to decide, "Who's side he was on!" The Holy Spirit had convicted him, that he was in with the wrong crowd, and because he liked me, he wanted to tell me ~ to protect me.

(So, who's side are you on?) God's? or the devil's?

Are you in with the wrong crowd? If so, remember, . . Jesus is here, . . and Jesus is waiting! The Lord says ~ "He that is not with Me is against Me; and he that gathereth not with Me scattereth abroad." (Matthew 12:30) Which is it, dear friend?

I know that Fred learned a good lesson that day about following God, and about choosing good versus evil! We really hope he went on to serve Jesus with his life.

Doug and I are so thankful to our Savior, Who has always been faithful to protect us ~ we love Him, and try our best to serve Him. We give Jesus Christ all our thanks and praise!

He is truly alive, and He walks with us

"But whosoever shall deny Me before men, him will I also deny before My Father which is in Heaven." (Matthew 10:33)

"He delivereth me from mine enemies: yea, Thou liftest me up above those that rise up against me: Thou hast delivered me from the violent man." (Psalm 18:48)

"And the LORD shall help them, and deliver them: He shall deliver them from the wicked, and save them, because they trust in Him." (Psalm 37:40)

17. JUST GET IT OUTTA HERE!

Doug and I have been Christians a long time now, and have run homes for delinquent teens. We have seen a lot! A lot of stress, a lot of bad situations, and also many victories through Jesus Christ! We have also seen a lot of demonic activity in these kid's lives, as they were giving themselves to 'weed,' hard drugs, and the devil. (Like we used to.)

All the kids at our group homes knew that we were Christians.

Doug and I were working for the same agency ~ but at different group homes. One of the toughest kids at my group home was named 'Jason.' He was into the devil, and his girlfriend was into being a witch.

One night, Jason suddenly started screaming out into the hallway after hours! He sounded terrified! (The lady who was on duty with me was also terrified, and stayed in the office!)

I ran to his room, which was only a couple of doors down the hallway. He yelled at me, "Charlie! It's in the corner! The devil is in the corner! Get it out of here!"

"You can get him out of here ~ Please!!"

I said, "Yes Jason, I 'can' get him out of here, because 'Greater is He that is in me ~ than he that is in the world.' . . But I won't do it unless you realize that you should not be messin' around with all this evil stuff!!"

He said, "Anything Charlie, just get it outta here!!" (His eyes, and his face looked horrified!)

So I prayed, and called on the "Mighty Name of Jesus Christ" and cast that devil out of his room, and 'bound it,' by the Blood of Jesus Christ, . . and that devil had to leave! (And it did!!)

Jason yelled, "It's gone!! It's gone!! That was a miracle!!"

In the meantime, the lady in the office, (who was not a Christian,) was standing in the hallway when I walked out of Jason's room. She looked scared to death!

She had taken the large Crucifix off of the staff bedroom wall ~ and was holding it against her heart! She went back into the staff quarters and laid down on the bed, still clutching the Crucifix and holding it tightly to her chest! She was shaken, and frightened from hearing Jason screaming out, and hearing how scared he was, (and from hearing what had just gone on in his room!)

She said, "I sure am glad 'you' were here Charlie, and I wasn't here all by myself!" (God worked it out ~ for all of us that night!)

~ The Bible says, "In my Name they shall cast out demons" ~ and I have done this many times since! We must be bold, and believe in Christ, and His Words, and we will 'see' the power of God! From that night on, Jason told me he wanted "God's power" in his life!

He had seen for himself that, "God is 'greater' than the devil." He wanted to ask Jesus as his Savior, and he did!

He was so sincere, that he talked to his girlfriend, and she asked Jesus into her life too! Jason got away from drugs, cut off his long hair, and started going to our church with his girlfriend!

Our pastor would always reserve seats for our kids from the group homes, in the front pews of the church. Pastor Tom would even ask people to, "please move to another pew," because those front pews were "reserved for Charlie and Doug's kids."

Praise God ~ for such loving and dedicated pastors, and for such a sincere and loving congregation!

So many of our kids were saved there, and dedicated their lives to Jesus! We miss them all! ~ and we're looking forward to an eternity together! ~ Amen!

Remember, there is great 'Power' in the 'Name' of "Jesus Christ," and I sincerely thank Him, for His Presence, His Power, and His Love ~ especially on that strange, and scary night!

"And these signs shall follow them that believe; In My Name shall they cast out devils;" (Mark 16:17)

"Finally, my brethren, be strong in the Lord, and in the power of His might. For we wrestle not against flesh and blood, but against principalities, against powers, against the rulers of the darkness of this world, against spiritual wickedness in high places." (Ephesians 6:10,12)

"And they cast out many devils, and anointed with oil many that were sick, and healed them." (Mark 6:13)

"And the seventy returned again with joy, saying, Lord, even the devils are subject unto us through thy name." (Luke 10:17)

"The LORD is nigh unto all them that call upon Him, to all that call upon Him in truth." (Psalm 145:18)

18. THE MOTORCYCLE WRECK

This is a story that we will never forget. It is forever stored in our memory banks of Gods great mercies. I dedicate it to all who are in need of a miracle. . . Please keep 'hope' in your heart!

One evening years ago, in Des Moines, Iowa, Doug and I were just out for a relaxing drive.

We came to an intersection, and we saw a motorcycle down, and a man lying there in the street along the curb!

There were only two people there, so I turned our car around.

Doug didn't want to stop. He said, "We'll just be in the way for the ambulance" but I told him, "No, I have to!!" (No ambulance was there yet.) I said, "We can pray!"

When we got there, this man looked so much like one of our best friends ~ we truly thought it was him!

We both had a compelling feeling from the Holy Spirit to pray!

I will try not to be too graphic here, but his leg was 'curled up,' smashed against the curb! In the middle of his forehead was a deep gash, that was pumping out blood in a stream high into the air!

The lady there, down on her knees attending to him, happened to be a nurse.

Doug and I raised our hands above our heads and began to pray, (we don't usually do anything like this!) We were pleading to God to let his head be healed, and let the blood stop streaming out!

The nurse kept saying, "I hope the ambulance gets here soon, he's losing too much blood!" So, we kept praying!

All of a sudden, the nurse said in surprise, "I can't believe this, I've never seen this happen! The blood is coagulating!" The stream had just stopped! And it was starting to clot!! We looked down and saw it! Right then a young man ran up with a cloth and said, "I'll wipe that blood off of his head."

The nurse quickly pushed his hand away, and said, "No, Don't!! This is a miracle!!" She looked up at Doug and I, as she was kneeling on the street, beside this young man. She said, "I don't know what you're praying, but whatever it is ~ keep it up! It's working!!" (We kept right on praying!) ~ We could 'feel' the power of the Holy Spirit all around us!

The ambulance finally came ~ loaded him on a gurney, and we all left. As we drove home, we prayed in our car for this man, (who we still thought was our good friend.) He looked just like him!

I dropped Doug off at home, but I felt led of God's Holy Spirit to go to the hospital, and see what was happening. As I was sitting in the lobby of the ER, praying, a tall lady in 'whites,' (nurse's clothes,) came in ~ and sat right down beside me. She was crying. . . I tried to comfort her and asked her, "What's the matter Honey?"

She said, "I was working in the ER tonight, and I can't believe my son was just brought into Emergency, and they think he might lose his leg!"

I said, "Motorcycle wreck?"

She said, "Yes." (I then realized that this wasn't our friend!)

I told her Doug and I had stopped at the accident scene. I also told her about the miracle of God stopping the blood from streaming out of his head, (as we were praying for her son!)

We talked a while and she asked me if I would please come to the hospital the next day and visit her son.

She told me his name was, 'Lanny.'

I assured her I would come and visit him.

The next day, when I arrived at the hospital, Lanny was in a coma. His mother asked 'me' to go into the I.C.U. but I told her, "I don't want to take up your time with your son."

She grabbed my arm, and with a pleading look in her tear-filled eyes, she said, "No, you go in, and please pray for my son!" (I knew I needed to stay beside this dear lady, and pray for her and her son.) So, I did.

Each day she gave up her time with Lanny, and would tell me to, "Please, go in and pray for my son." I felt bad for her (staying in the lobby,) but I went in, and felt it an honor, because she had asked me.

Only one person was allowed in the I.C.U. at a time, and there were very strict limits on visits.

We didn't have a phone back then, so I asked my sister Ginny if it was okay if this dear lady left messages with her. Ginny said it was fine. And because we didn't have a phone, my sister would even drive to our house, and deliver messages to us for this lady. (I was very proud of my sister, for her willingness to help, and for her desire to be a part of God answering our prayers! I couldn't have done it without her!)

So, day after day, I'd faithfully visit this young man. I would talk to him, and pray for him, and I'd read to him from the Bible. I'd say, "Lanny, can you hear me? If you can ~ squeeze my hand."

Then, one day, all of a sudden, Lanny squeezed my hand very quickly! I was so encouraged! I asked him again, "Squeeze my hand if you can hear me," and he did!! Well, this was such a miracle!! It greatly encouraged our faith that God was answering our prayers! However, in the days ahead, the enemy sabotaged our encouragement, when he developed "spinal meningitis!"

The doctors were forced to remove his spleen, and then; (Oh, the disappointment of all of this!) they moved Lanny to a 'special room,' and were basically just expecting him to die!

His dear mother continued to ask me to go visit him and "Pray!" So, I did. I had a dear aunt who warned me against going to visit him because of the meningitis, but at this point, I could not get scared. I continued to visit, asked God to "protect me," and asked Him for more faith! We were required to wear face masks for his sake, and for our own protection, and we continued to pray.

It was several months altogether; and we had all prayed daily for Lanny. His mother was so sweet. (What she hadn't told me,) was at this 'same' time, her husband was in the 'same' hospital, experiencing heart problems. She was dividing her time between going to visit her husband, and sitting in the lobby waiting for me to come out and give her a daily report! . . . I got to know Lanny's sweet grandpa, who came to the hospital every day and laid a little radio up by Lanny's ear and played his favorite 'rock' music for him. (It was just so sad!)

Well, the day came, that my sister drove by to tell us the miracle, "Lanny spoke one word!" It was "Ouch!" (When the nurse stuck him for blood!) We were all so thankful to God!

And so, . . little by little, . . he would say one word at a time. He was getting better, and better, and we kept praying, and thanking God for Lanny's miraculous improvement.

We also thanked Him for protecting us from meningitis!

Now that he was recovering, I needed to concentrate more on my own life, my husband, and my job at a co-ed group home, working with delinquent kids.

Months later, I was at the group home, sitting on the office floor, with papers I was working on ~ all around me.

A man came through the door that I didn't know. I looked up and thought he was a new social worker. He was dressed in a suit and tie. I said, "Hi, can I help you?"

He said, "Hi, I'm Lanny, and it's my birthday!" (And then he said,) "I wanted to come see you first, because I don't think I'd be alive ~ if it wasn't for all your prayers."

I jumped up, so happy, and gave him a big hug!! I said ~ "Lanny! God Bless You!" I told him that it was God that had kept him alive and brought him out of that coma! He said, "and you prayed for me, and I heard every one of those prayers." ~ All I could say was, "Praise God!" (This had all started, because we thought Lanny was our good friend; but now, he looked 'nothing' like our friend! "God works in mysterious ways!")

After we had talked a while, my face hurt from smiling so much!! (Ever done that?) I was so thrilled that he stopped by!

The doctors had fit him with a prosthesis, because he had lost his leg to his knee, but thankfully ~ by God's Grace he was alive!

Now, the really sad thing was, the very day Lanny was to come home, his Daddy had died in the hospital. ~ But he knew, that Lanny was awake, and was going home. There were many prayers going up for that little family!

Lanny and I continued to talk for quite a while, and we had a wonderful time! It was great! Doug and I went to their house to visit his mom after she lost her husband. We prayed with her and tried to comfort her. It was a bitter-sweet situation, and the good Lord helped us all get through it.

About two weeks later, they surprised us and came down the aisle at our church, and sat beside us!

It was just like a movie! "Gods movie!"

Well, they came to our church quite a few times, and then one Sunday ~ Lanny went forward and gave his life to Christ! Praise God!

I'm sure God is still working on Lanny and we know that He has a plan and a purpose for his life!

~ We moved to Arizona, and sadly lost contact with them. I sure hope Lanny is staying close to our Lord Jesus ~ after receiving so many miracles! Thank You Lord Jesus ~ for giving me the faith, the strength, and the boldness to honor a dear mother's request, to take her place, and pray for her son. (And thank you to my sister ~ Ginny, for her encouragement all along the way, . . and for being a faithful messenger!)

~ May God bless this story to inspire anyone who may be going through these great sorrows. Lanny is proof, that coma patients can hear you pray. So please, read the Bible to them, pray for them, and encourage them! And realize that sometimes, we must 'wait on God,' and 'pray through' ~ for our miracles!

(And always, have faith in our Big God, Who loves us all, . . more than we know!) ~ Amen!

"Who comforteth us in all our tribulation, that we may be able to comfort them which are in any trouble, by the comfort wherewith we ourselves are comforted of God." (II Corinthians 1:4)

"And Jesus went about all the cities and villages, teaching in their synagogues, and preaching the gospel of the Kingdom, and healing every sickness and every disease among the people." (Matthew 9:35)

"For this thy brother was dead, and is alive again; and was lost, and is found." (Luke 15:32)

"But without faith it is impossible to please him: for he that cometh to God must believe that he is, and that he is a rewarder of them that diligently seek him." (Hebrews 11:6)

19. THE BURNED BIBLE

"In the world ye shall have tribulation: but be of good cheer; I have overcome the world." ~ Jesus

I want to tell you a story about a miracle of Salvation. This story happened in Iowa, before we moved to Arizona. My memory files are so full, but we will never forget this one, so I believe this is one story the Lord wants me to share.

This story is about a young neighbor lady we had. She was a very sweet person. She wasn't a Christian, and she lived with a man who was 'evil.' He was a control freak, a manipulator, and he beat her! He was not a nice person at all!

(We have been involved with many stories like this over the years. We believe that God picks our neighbors ~ and we also believe, He expects us to help them whenever we can.)

I knew they were having big problems.

We sometimes heard yelling and fighting from across the drive between our houses!

One day I heard yelling right outside my house! I went out, and there he was, in the driveway, screaming at her elderly parents! There she was, staring, . . . in shock, (as her parents were too!)

They were looking at him ~ holding their 'land-line' phone in the air, with the cord swinging around where he had ripped it out of the wall! He was yelling, cursing, and threatening!

He was hollering at her parents, "I'm going to take this cord and strangle you both!" He shouted ~ "Get out and don't come back!"

When I saw her and her poor parents cowering in fear, I was filled with righteous anger! I ran up to him, grabbed the phone, yanked it out of his hands, and said, "Give me that thing! You're not choking anybody!! Not on my property!" God gave me the boldness, (and the supernatural strength,) to grab that phone right out of his hands!

He was shocked! When I looked in his eyes, I knew he was 'high' on something! He looked evil!

He went back inside and her parents quickly left. Then she went back into their apartment and things quieted down. (Thank God I was home that day! They would have had no way to even call the police, since he had ripped the phone out of the wall!)

A few days later, we heard that she had tried to commit suicide!

She had been drinking heavily, and had turned on the gas to her oven! She wanted to die, to get out of the misery of being stuck with this evil, and controlling man! I felt I should get involved, and went to the hospital to see her. She knew I had tried to help her and cared about her.

When I got there, she was still coming out of the fumes she had inhaled, and she was still 'drunk.' I leaned down, and quietly said her name. Suddenly, she turned over, . . and punched me right in the face!

(Of course, it hurt!)

She was mad that she was still alive! I had to shrug it off, because I thought, "Sure, what did she have to live for, with all that abuse?"

So later that week, after she was home, Doug and I visited with her, and told her our testimonies.

We asked her if she would like to go to church with us sometime? She accepted our offer and went with us that Sunday. We bought her a Bible and she was happy to receive it. She wanted to continue to go to church with us.

A few days later, I went over to visit her, and there was a part of a Bible, in a pile of ashes on her doorstep! I just knew he'd burned her Bible! . . And he had! Again, I felt God's righteous anger rising up in me!

I went straight home, took a piece of paper and a magic marker, wrote him a note, and taped it to his door! (I wrote his name out!) I said ~ "Come next door! I want to see you!!" I signed it, 'Charlie!'

When he came over later, he seemed jazzed up on something! He screamed at me, "What do you want?!"

I yelled right back! "I want to know why you burned her Bible?! That was not yours!!"

He started yelling at me, that he didn't want her to believe in that 'crap' (I'm changing his language!)

I said, "We paid for that Bible, and we are paying for the gas to take her to church, and none of this is any of your business! It's a free country, the last time I checked! We'll just get her another Bible, and we'll be there to pick her up for church on Sunday!"

He told me, "No, you won't!!"

I told him, "You might boss her, and try to control her, but you aren't gonna boss me!"

He said, "I'm gonna go get my gun, and kill you!!"

I said, "See? ~ there you go, threatening again! I wish you 'would' go get it, cause when you do, if it's not my time to die, God will let that gun misfire, and explode, and blow your hand off!!"

He looked at me with a wild look, and then, (as he was 'stomping' off my porch,) he looked back at me, and it seemed as if God let him see something about me! He looked surprised.

Then he said, "You really believe that ~ don't you?"

I said, "Yeah, I really do! . . So ~ go get your gun if you want, I'll be waiting right here!"

Well, he immediately changed his tone, and said, "I'd like to hear your stories sometime, and see how you got to be Christians."

He left, and just a few days later, we witnessed to him. I told him, "You ought to come to church with us, it would be nice to see you believe in Jesus."

He got infuriated! He said, "I don't need God!! I have a good job, a nice car, and I'm gonna be a manager!"

I told him, "None of that will do you any good on Judgment Day. The only thing that will count then ~ is a personal relationship with Jesus." He wanted no part of it!

I told him, "If you put anything else in your life above God, (in God's place,) He will bring it all down!"

I told him, "You can 'mark my words' on that one!" I also told him, "If you could give all this energy over to God, instead of the devil ~ there's no telling what God could do with your life!"

He angrily disagreed, cussed at me, and told me I was "Crazy!" (Now, we could hardly believe the miracle we saw with this man later.)

He went home, and we didn't see him for quite a while. (Not long after this episode, his nice girlfriend asked Jesus as her Savior.) She broke up with him, and moved out. She took my advice and didn't tell him where she moved! She got her independence back and happily began her life over with Jesus!

Then, . . some months later, I was calling on a girl in the hospital. It was a friend who was having some emotional problems, and was hospitalized in the mental ward ~ so the doctors could evaluate her medications.

So, there I was, visiting with her, when I heard a voice say ~ "Charlie?" I looked over, but didn't see who was calling my name, and the voice came again, "is that you ~ Charlie Deitrick?"

I turned again, and there sat our neighbor, the man that had burned the Bible; that we had witnessed to! (I could hardly believe it!)

I asked him, "What are you doing in here?" He said, he had gotten drunk, "too drunk," and pulled a gun on his boss! (The boss that was going to give him a manager's position,) and now, here he was in a mental ward, with no job, no money, and his nice car was no longer his! So, what God had told me to tell him that day on my porch, had all happened in one night! ~ Well, he immediately asked me to help him get out of there. I asked him, "How do you expect me to do that?"

He started to tell me to "pray," and 'what' to pray. I said, "Hold it! You don't tell me what to pray, God does!"

I assured him I would pray, but I would ask for 'God's will.' I told him, "If God were to let you out right now, you might get drunk again, and kill your boss next time."

"No," he insisted, he wouldn't. He seemed broken and humbled; Which is where we all need to be, to seek God in our troubles, and we will find He is there, and has been there all along ~ but many times, we just continue to ignore Him!

Well, I told him I would pray and ask God to "get him out when it was 'His will' to let him out."

He said he would think over what I said. I gave him our phone number and he said, "I'll call you when God lets me out." I said, "I hope you do. We would be glad to talk to you," and then I left.

(He must have been thinking, 'as I was,' ~ "What are the chances we would meet up, . . . in Here?!")

Three days later he called, very excited, and told me he was so happy, "God heard our prayers," and he was let out!

(A miracle in itself, since he had threatened someone's life with a gun!)

We talked a while, and he said he "wanted to talk to Doug." I said "sure," (and, because of his past,) I knew he needed to talk to a 'man.'

Doug got on the phone, and in a few minutes, he asked Doug to lead him in the 'Sinners Prayer' to receive Christ as his Savior! Praise God! We never know what God is up to! ~ Sadly, we have lost touch with this man over the years, but we are trusting that God will 'finish the work He started in him.'

Let me tell you, when you are willing to be near the hurting, the sick, and the down trodden, you will "find Jesus there."

Jesus walked with the poor, the sick, and the needy when He walked the earth, this is "where Jesus lives." He was, (and still is,) "a friend to sinners." Hallelujah!!

Jesus is to be praised, and I will never forget the boldness He gave me, to talk to someone that was threatening my very life!

God is always with us, and we can see miracles when we pray in faith each day, to have Christ live His life through us. And if we come up against rebels, God can help us, and protect us!

God worked this all out for the Salvation of two precious souls; and we praise Him for giving us the opportunity to share His love, and stand up for our faith.

Also, the sweet young lady we took to church has been our good friend now, for many years! She has been an inspiration to us!

She loves Jesus, and has strong faith in our dear Savior.

Hallelujah, what a Wonderful, Merciful God we serve! ~ Amen! ~

"For all the law is fulfilled in one word, even in this; Thou shalt love thy neighbour as thyself." (Galatians 5:14)

"Love worketh no ill to his neighbour: therefore love is the fulfilling of the law." (Romans 13:10)

"Hereby perceive we the love of God, because He laid down His life for us: and we ought to lay down our lives for the brethren." (I John 3:16)

20. YOU CAN KILL THEM!

When I was younger ~ we were at a big family reunion. Suddenly, a dear relative started choking on food! He was very overweight, and some family members were holding his arm up in the air to help! I knew that raising his arm, like a child, was 'not' going to help him!

As his immediate family kept trying unsuccessfully to help him get his breath, I was watching in fear and horror! After watching them frantically trying to save his life, (and failing,) I thought I better jump in when I saw him turning *purple*! ~ I gave him a big, hard, 'whack' on the back, right between his shoulder blades, and whatever was lodged in his windpipe flew out!! I was so happy, and he was too!

He shook my hand and weakly said, . . "Thank You!"

Now ~ immediately his family started in on me, about how I "shouldn't have hit him in the back!" They said, "You should never hit anyone in the back when they are choking! You can kill them!!"

They made me feel terrible!

(He was way too big for me to do the, Heimlich Maneuver!!)

My relative finally got enough strength to speak up and tell them, "Well at least she got the job done! She saved my life!! All you were doing was holding my arm up in the air!!" (My thoughts exactly!)

Here is my point ~ we, as Christians, should all try and save people's lives, (and souls!)

Some people are using methods which "baby" people, and don't really get the job done! Some of us might use a little stronger method, but we can't just stand back and watch until somebody dies!

Many time's God has sent me into a situation, to 'personally' use a stronger method than others. I see the need, and jump in, and give it my most, and try like everything ~ to save that person's life and soul.

Had my relative died that day, all the ones who were just 'holding his arm up in the air,' would have felt they should have given it more 'power' ~ behind their efforts.

Over the years I have heard a few people say, that some Christians are being "too strong" in giving the Gospel message! ~ Well, the way I see it, God says "It is appointed unto men once to die, but after this the Judgment." (Hebrews 9:27) (We're not promised tomorrow!)

I am afraid, . . . just "holding someone's arm up in the air," come Judgment Day, . . will not save them from going to Hell!

~ Let's preach strong and hard, . . Now, while there's still time! . . Death waits for no one!!

People are 'choking,' and dying 'spiritually,' all around us. Let's try our best to save them!! ~ Amen and Amen! ~

"And of some have compassion, making a difference: And others save with fear, pulling them out of the fire; hating even the garment spotted by the flesh." (Jude 1:22,23)

"Preach the word; be instant in season, out of season; reprove, rebuke, exhort with all longsuffering and doctrine." (II Timothy 4:2)

"He that believeth and is baptized shall be saved; but he that believeth not shall be damned." (Mark 16:16)

21. THE ONES YOU CAN'T SEE
(Lord I Didn't Know!)

I have a very different story to tell you.

Back in the early 1980's we lived in West Des Moines, Iowa, in a quaint little area surrounded by antique shops called, "Antique Alley."

There were lots of nice older homes. Ours was bright yellow, with a red brick foundation! There were a lot of plain white houses, and there was one on the corner that was old and gray. (At this time God was leading me to meet many of the people in our neighborhood.)

In that old gray house lived a very old man, bent over, and he was our neighborhood paper-man. He walked in sunshine, rain, or snow, to deliver the morning and evening papers, that he carried in a big leather bag. His daughter "Tina," was rarely seen.

Tina began helping her dad with his paper route (because of his worsening arthritis.) Occasionally, I would see her and wave. She was very shy. She would barely respond, and always kept her head down.

Months went by, and I realized that I hadn't seen her for quite some time. I decided to stop by and check on her. I never thought I'd ever go to their house. Her Daddy ~ who was over 90 years old, was out on his route delivering papers.

When I knocked, she came to the back door.

Their dog was chained next to the door, and was barking loudly at me. She opened the door and told me his name was 'Jack.' She told him to "be quiet!" I asked if she was okay, because I hadn't seen her in a while.

She said, "Well, I've been sick for three months, and I can't seem to get well!" The Holy Spirit urged me to ask her if I could come in, and talk to her a few minutes.

(I had never asked myself into someone's home before.)

She said, "Well, the place isn't very clean, and I don't ever have company, but I guess if you don't mind." She opened the door and I went on in.

When I got inside, it was a sight I had never seen in my whole life! The walls had no plaster on them at all, it was just the wood lathe (slats.) All the windows were covered with newspapers! It was very dark, and there was a 'strange' feeling inside. It was rather 'spooky.'

As she turned on a small dim lamp, I was praying in my mind and heart. It felt so 'creepy' in there ~ that I started praying for God's "protection," (and also for just the right words to say to her!)

I tried to act like the surroundings were normal, and that I wasn't at all shocked by them. This set Tina at ease and she began to talk to me, and tell me that she was, "not well at all."

She told me her appetite was gone, and she felt like she "might not ever get well." She coughed, and coughed, the whole time I was there.

I asked if her Mama had passed on, since I never saw anyone but her Daddy and her. She told me that her mother had died when she was young, and she didn't mind, because she was mean to her. "She beat me all the time, and pulled my hair!" Tina had actually prayed that her mom would die! And she did!! She said, . ."life was easier without her."

I asked her if she had any friends? She smiled, and said she had "plenty of friends." They were "Ones you can't see," but that they kept her company, and she liked them.

She said, "I talk to them all the time." She looked around the room and told me, "They're here right now, laying all around us." I tried hard not to react!

Her face was very pale, and she looked so sad, and lost. (I could feel the evil 'spirits' in that room, even though ~ only she could see them!) She told me she 'lived in books,' and she also wrote poetry.

I told her I was a Christian and asked if she would like to hear my testimony. She said, "Sure." She was very intelligent, and because she was an avid reader, she was able to listen with much interest. She seemed happy I was there!

After I told her what Jesus had done for Doug and I, . . I was led to ask her ~ if she wanted me to pray for her to be healed?

She said she would like that, and then, to my surprise, she wanted to accept Jesus as her Savior! . . (Lord, I didn't know!) I told her I would lead her in a prayer to accept Jesus as her Savior. But first, I had to boldly step out in faith, and tell her she would have to repent, and she'd have to be willing to get rid of those 'spirits,' (which were demons.)

She looked sad. She once again looked around the room and said, "They've been with me ever since I was young."

In Christ's boldness, I again told her, she would have to choose Jesus over darkness, and all those 'demons.' I explained that, "Jesus is Light, and He is Life," and that He could give her Joy, and Peace, and Eternal Life! She looked hopeful!

She agreed, she wanted to repent and pray with me.

Now, I'll tell you, when I prayed to cast out all the 'darkness,'. . . you could *feel* the evil spirits 'leave,' out of that old gray house! I heard a loud 'clap!' (To this day, I still don't know what it was, but it was a 'distinct' clap!) I prayed that Jesus and His power would dwell there, and I prayed that Tina would be healed, "In the mighty Name of Jesus Christ!!"

When we were done praying, we both looked up, and the Peace of Christ was there in such power! She said, "I can feel God!"

I said, "Do you feel His 'Peace'?"

And she said ~ "Yes!!" (She was smiling!!)

I said, "Can you feel that those evil spirits, are gone?"

She said "Yes! And it feels 'crystal clear' in here!" (And it really did!!)

I told her, "Jesus is here now," and she could feel it. She knew and believed every bit that He was present, and that His power was there!! (And it was!) ~ We were both 'swimming' in the Peace of Christ! . . Dear friends, it was incredible!! God is Real!

I asked her if I could come back sometime and visit. She smiled and said, "I'd like that."

As I walked to the door to leave, I told her, "Jesus is with you now, and He will never leave you, or forsake you; you will always have Him in your heart, and you can pray, and talk with Him now anytime!"

She smiled, and said, "Thank You!!" We gave each other a hug before I left, and she said, "Come back and see me again."

Doug and I prayed that night, that the Holy Spirit would finish the work He had started in Tina.

The next week she asked me over. I was excited to go.

I took her a "Living Bible," and when I walked in, she was visibly (changed) ~ her face, her whole countenance looked 'happy,' and bright, with God's Spirit!! It was so encouraging!!

All of a sudden, I looked up, and she said, "Look, do you see what I did different?" I was shocked, . . all the newspapers had been taken off of the windows! She had cleaned the best she could, and even showed me her books on her bedroom shelves, and said, "I got rid of all the 'bad' ones!" She looked at me and smiled.

She said, "I want 'God's light' here now." All the windows were open and sunlight everywhere!! (My face must have been beaming!)

But the best part was yet to come. She said, "God healed me the same day you were here! I felt my sore throat leaving right when you prayed, and I got my appetite back, and I can eat now. I'm really healed!" Then she said, "I'm helping Dad with the paper route again." We both rejoiced together!

That was something I never, ever thought I'd encounter, when I went into that old gray house! But I had followed the leading of God's Spirit, and went ahead with the boldness of Christ and asked if I could pray for her. I came away from there, thinking again, . . (Lord, I didn't know!)

I was able to visit her often, and even listen to Tina's poetry as she read to me. It was very good!

Her dear Daddy passed away some months later, but her faith in Jesus helped her to get through it. She had cared for him ~ up until he had to leave her.

She was Irish and her dream had always been "to go and visit Ireland."

Shortly after her Daddy's death, she decided to go for a vacation and she really enjoyed her whole time in Ireland. In fact, she made friends there and went back several times! She sold her house, moved into an apartment, and began attending church not far from our house!

How many times have we said to ourselves, "Oh, they wouldn't listen to my testimony!!"

We talk ourselves 'out of witnessing' about what Jesus has done for us; instead of doing what Jesus commands us to do, ("Go into all the world and preach the Gospel.")

There was holy, precious fruit there, just waiting to be gathered for our Lord. Are we willing to go to work in His vineyards?

We might just see a soul saved, and a life changed completely, and eternally . . . and walk away, saying, (Lord, I didn't know!)

"I am the vine, ye are the branches: He that abideth in me, and I in him, the same bringeth forth much fruit: for without me ye can do nothing." (John 15:5)

"How beautiful are the feet of them that preach the Gospel of Peace, and bring tidings of good things!" (Romans 10:15)

"When the even was come, they brought unto Him many that were possessed with devils: and He cast out the spirits with His Word, and healed all that were sick:" (Matthew 8:16)

"And many that believed came, and confessed, and shewed their deeds. Many of them also which used curious arts brought their books together, and burned them before all men:" (Acts 19:18,19)

22. A JOB ON A RANCH ~ A COWBOY HAT ~ AND COWBOY BOOTS

Doug and I had helped a young man from his boy's home in Iowa.

He wanted us to meet his friend, a man in his twenty's, that was living in a men's mission downtown.

We visited the mission, and he introduced us to ~ "Dave."

Dave was a very nice, and respectful young man, with very good manners. He was on the list of men there ~ who were eligible to work, and then return to the mission at the end of the day.

We asked Dave to come visit our home, and we talked to him about what he would like to do in his life. He looked us straight in the eyes, and with a hopeful smile he said ~ "What I really want, . . is to get a job on a big ranch, and with my first check; buy a cowboy hat, and a pair of cowboy boots."

I asked him if he believed in God? He said, "Yes."

I then asked, "Do you know Jesus Christ as your Savior?"

He said, "No, . . I've done some bad things back in Pennsylvania, and I had to leave because of it."

We explained that if he confessed his sins to Jesus, and asked His forgiveness ~ that He would forgive him and come into his heart, and give him Eternal life! We also told him that God's Word promises, if you put God first in your life, "He will give you the desires of your heart."

He looked very humbled, and tears began to well up in his eyes. He said, "I'd like to know Jesus as my Savior."

Doug and I were privileged to pray with Dave, and we knew God led us to him, and our souls seemed to know this as well, . . . all of us!

We drove him back to the mission, and told him we'd like to pray for a job for him ~ before we dropped him off.

We prayed, and asked Jesus to please find him a job, so he could have purpose in his life, and could get out on his own. We asked our Lord, to allow Dave, "to work on a ranch, and to be able to buy 'a cowboy hat, and cowboy boots,' with his first check!"

After we left, we both wondered, "Where is God going to find a ranch, in Iowa?" There were plenty of farms, but we had never seen a ranch! However, we know our Savior well enough to know, He is 'personal,' and we know how much He wants to show His love for His people! . . Dave was now one of His very own, and one of His lost sheep that had come home. (He was our brother in Christ, and we were praying, and expecting our Savior to answer our prayers for Dave!)

A few days later ~ Dave asked our friend to call us, and tell us to call the mission. (There were no 'out-going' calls for the men there.)

When we called, Dave excitedly told us that a rich man had come to the mission, and told the manager, "I need several real good, hard workers for the next few days," and Dave was one of the men that the manager recommended. He was so excited to get out of the mission ~ and work.

We really encouraged him, and we were excited too! We told him we'd be praying, and we'd stay in touch. What none of us knew, was that ~ Jesus was answering every prayer we had prayed for Dave, through this rich man!

We found out this man owned hundreds of acres in Iowa, and even had buffaloes on his huge "ranch!" (Yes! I said 'Ranch!')

Dave was so thrilled to tell us about his first day at work! Dave was stocky, and looked like a rugged, young 'Charles Bronson,' with steel gray eyes!

When we got together with him again, he had just been paid. He asked us if we could take him to buy his "cowboy hat," and "cowboy boots!" We told him, "we'd be glad to!"

We were all beaming with God's joy ~ as we drove him to the 'western wear' store.

He looked very sharp in his new cowboy hat and boots! We were all smiles, and we had a prayer of thanks to God, who had truly answered our prayers for Dave!

What a blessing, to see Jesus being very 'personal,' to Dave's needs! ("Delight thyself also in the LORD; and He shall give thee the desires of thine heart." Psalm 37:4) We were so happy for him! We were all thankful to Jesus for answering our prayers so quickly, and giving Dave, "the desires of his heart!"

We saw God's plan for Dave's life unfold in the weeks ahead. The rich man kept asking for Dave, and giving him work, because he was such a good, hard worker. Every day was another answer to our prayers, and a financial blessing for Dave.

Soon, Dave was hired permanently! He was thrilled! He mended fences, dug ditches, cut down trees, drove the tractor, fed the animals, and many other ranch duties . . . all the things he had dreamed about, and wished and prayed for!

When talking about his job ~ Dave's eyes would well up with tears ~ knowing God's Sovereign Will over his life. (He couldn't have been happier!) This was a whole new life for him, as he was getting to know Jesus through prayer, and Bible study!

Dave told us he was "no good at saving money." He asked us to keep his money for him, and save it, so he could move out of the mission and get his own apartment. (We did just that!)

He worked very hard, with determination, to be independent. He now ~ had goals. We were very proud of him!

Every Sunday ~ we drove to the mission and brought Dave to church with us and then drove him back to the mission. He loved church! He loved our pastors, he loved God's Word, and he even took notes! He wanted to get to know our Savior better!

Each week we saw him grow in the Lord, and his spiritual gifts were many. His greatest gift was the gift of God's Love! He loved people, and loved helping others! He also had the gift of Joy! (And it was a joy to be around him!)

We had a very nice, (and fun,) retired neighbor lady, we all called, "Mrs. R." ~ who lived right across the street from Doug and I. She had an attic apartment upstairs ~ which was vacant at the time. We talked to her, and she met Dave and liked him, and she decided to rent to him. We had weekly Bible studies in our home, and Dave attended every week.

We all loved Dave, and we all became a close-knit family. We were always having him over to dinner and he rode to church with Doug and I every Sunday. He became close to our immediate family, and even shoveled snow for them, and for all the elderly in our neighborhood, 'without charge.' He loved helping others, (especially the elderly and widows who needed his help.)

One day, after a good snow, we all decided to build a snowman. Dave's landlady, Mrs. R. saw us, and she wanted in on the fun! (We all loved her!) She hollered over and said, "I have a couple of things to donate to this project!"

She was always so happy, and up for anything fun!

We laughed when she came over all bundled up, in her big winter coat, snow-boots, wool scarf, knitted hat, and mittens!

She was also carrying a stretchy polyester dress, and a hat! She wanted to make it a snow 'woman!'

"Why not?" we said. We all laughed until we were crying ~ as we were stretching that dress down over that big snow woman! We put a hat on her and gave her a big smile with rocks from the neighbor's drive. We found long sticks for her arms, and Mrs. R. found a pair of mittens, and before you knew it, the "Snow Woman" was part of our family! Mrs. R. put a silk flower on her hat, we got our camera out, and we all took turns having our pictures taken with our new neighbor, the 'Snow Woman!'

What a fun day we had! We all worked, and played, and laughed together, and made some wonderful, fun memories that day!

God blessed us all with His love and joy, and we all got along great and built wonderful friendships! We played cards, helped each other out, and had so many laughs together!

The spring weather arrived, and Dave bought a bicycle which he rode several miles to work and back every day.

One evening, he came home with a five-gallon bucket (on his bicycle handlebars.) In the bottom of the bucket, was a nest with a baby bird in it! We looked in and saw the baby bird, with no feathers, and Dave looked at us and said, "I brought you a present!" His eyes looked so sad. His boss had wanted him to cut a tree down on the ranch that day, and he said, "I couldn't just leave this baby bird on the ground in a nest." He knew that I had raised a few other wild birds, so he decided that I was the 'chosen one' to raise it, and I would make a good 'mother.'

With a sad smile he handed us the little bird. It was a pretty big baby bird, no feathers, just pink skin, a big beak, and long red legs! None of us had any idea 'what' kind of bird it was, so we were all excited to see what it would grow up to be! We even joked about it being ~ a "baby vulture!"

We sure didn't know it at the time, but this baby bird ended up being a blessing to our whole neighborhood, (except for a couple of people!)

I had raised many baby birds before, they always seemed to find me! (Once, when I was just a kid, God even let me climb an extension ladder, to catch a loose parakeet out in our trees! He came right to me, and ended up being my buddy for years!)

So, I got out my birdcage, my eyedropper ~ and my 'tested recipe' for feedings. I got up every four hours to check on our new baby. We prayed every day for this new addition to our family.

Each day it was exciting to see this little creature of God's, taking its food from me, looking at me and chirping as if I was his "Mama." We fell in love with this little bird, and named him "Adam."

Soon the little guy developed pin-feathers and fluff, (he looked a mess!) ~ He grew bigger, and bigger, until we were able to finally see, . . . we were the proud parents of a beautiful, genuine, full-fledged pigeon! He was gray, blue, and lavender, with a little burgundy wine color! We are lovers of all of God's creatures, and we felt blessed he came to us to take care of him. He grew to be a beautiful, healthy bird!

He grew up in a cage in our house, like a parrot. We saw right away how intelligent he was ~ as he studied us carefully every day. He got to know us both very well, and incredibly, later ~ he got to know the whole neighborhood!

Where we lived, was a very old and quaint neighborhood in an area called "Antique Alley." We loved antiques and collectables, so we would walk and window shop there, and look curiously in all the windows of the shops. We'd look at all the things the shops had set outside on the sidewalks, to get people interested in stopping by. As Adam grew, I held him and took him with me. He loved going along, and he eventually rode on my shoulder. (Everybody loved him!)

Doug being a guitar player and singer, would play songs every night and Adam would quietly listen in his cage. As Doug was calling it a night, he would start putting his guitar away. Adam would get so upset when the music stopped, that he'd start wrestling around in his papers, flitting his wings in his cage, and begin 'cooing' very loud!

I said to Doug, "He's upset you quit playing and singing! He's telling you off!" So, Doug would get his guitar and start playing again. Adam's cooing would get softer and softer, and slowly, his eyes would close ~ as he was trying to go to sleep by the music. This became a ritual every night. Doug would play guitar and sing, and when he was ready to stop ~ Adam threw his 'fit,' cooed loudly, and flit his wings, until Doug started singing again. Adam's cooing would get softer and softer as he fell asleep. We got a 'sweet chuckle' every night, knowing that Adam loved Doug's voice and guitar playing so much! (That little bird loved God's peaceful presence!)

All the neighbors knew Adam and would always ask me how he was? I'd regularly give them the latest update. They'd always smile, (with their eyes shining!) Our friend Dave ~ was in and out of our house often, and he talked to Adam like a pet dog.

Adam even rode around on our German Shepherd's back! Adam loved it! (Our dog wasn't so sure!) But she would always obey me ~ when I'd say, "be nice now."

As we saw Adam growing bigger, we reluctantly decided it was time to give him his 'freedom' and turn him loose.

We never liked turning the birds loose after I'd raised them, but it's a part of nature, and it's necessary. As sad as it was, we knew this day was coming. We sat on our porch and let Adam sit out on the porch with us. I picked him up, and then I gave him a big lift off into the air! He flew in a wide circle, . . . and came right back to us!

He had no intention of going anywhere! He had his own way of thinking! ~ He was a real character!

Well, we left Adam outside and went away for the evening. When we returned, there was Adam ~ perched on top of our porch light! I said, "Doug, do you see what I see?"

He said, "Yes, maybe we ought to bring him in just for tonight. Maybe he's scared."

So 'in he came,' and he was 'so happy' to get inside of his cage!

He immediately went about making himself comfortable as he waited for the evening music concert to begin! At that moment we realized, we had a "homing pigeon!"

As the night went on, Doug began to play his guitar and sing, and when he was ready to quit, Adam heard that guitar stop, and started his fit! "He's training us" Doug said, "I think we might be stuck with him!" I said, "I think you're right!" (we both laughed.)

We continued to let Adam out every day ~ hoping he would feel the wild calling to him as our other birds had. However, we soon found ourselves living in a storybook that played out before our eyes every day ~ and the title could have been ~ "Adam's World!"

My favorite thing, was going outside ~ calling Adam's name, and he would fly down, and slowly land on my arm! I loved hearing the sound of his wings lowering down, and feeling his warm little feet grabbing my arm, and hanging on!

This bird was such a character! Each evening when it got dark, Adam was eagerly perched on our porch light, and ~ in he came!

If we happened to be gone later than usual at night, we'd hold our hand up to him, (to let him jump on to our hand,) and he'd walk up our arm and peck our face! As if he was telling us, "You're Late!"

Each morning I'd let him out, and he'd stay gone, and come back and forth throughout the day. He would perch on my shoulder, and we were great friends. He would often ride on my shoulder down to Antique Alley and back ~ observing everyone and everything; taking it all in and never causing a problem!

We had a big International "Travel-All" (like a Chevy Suburban.) One time, we were sitting inside of it ready to leave, and it began to rain. We put the windshield wipers on, and all of a sudden, Adam flew down and grabbed a hold of the wipers, and rode on them back and forth, and up and down, flapping his wings! He enjoyed it! He gave us a lot of laughs! Many times, Adam would land on our Travel-All when we'd come home, ... to greet us.

One day, as he landed on the windshield, (and slid down) I saw something attached to Adam's leg! ~ I got out and took it off, and it was a little note from Dave ~ asking us if he could come to dinner?

We laughed, knowing that Dave was having fun with Adam, (and enjoying his friendship too!)

Now the really astounding, (and funny) thing was; we found out a little while later that Adam had developed friendships throughout the 'whole neighborhood' ~ that we weren't even aware of!

Apparently, he was making his rounds in the mornings!

One day I checked on our neighbor, Mrs. 'L.' She told me, "Oh, Adam comes to see me and hangs on my screen door every morning until I give him a cracker! I talk to him a bit, he listens, and off he goes!" She smiled at me like it was the highlight of her day. (She had recently lost her husband.)

Mrs. R. ~ across the street, loved Adam so much! She sat on her porch swing, and always laughed about things she saw him do. One time she saw him flying along-side of a city bus, looking in the windows, and gawking at the people "like a wild goose!" She laughed and laughed telling us the story!

She told how Adam was in the street one day, "and the city bus was coming at a good clip." The bus driver slammed on his brakes and came to a dead stop, and waited until Adam flew off! He loved Adam too!

Mrs. R. told us one day ~ Adam was wanting to land on a man's shoulder as he walked down the sidewalk; she was laughing with tears in her eyes as she said, "That big man just hit the deck!"

She was laughing so hard; and then she said, "A grown man afraid of a pigeon!"

Mrs. R. also admitted Adam visited her kitchen window every morning, and she'd come out and give him a graham cracker! And off he'd go! (She just laughed.)

Alice lived alone, (next door to Mrs. R.)

She told me, "Why, Adam comes to see me every morning, and I give him a piece of my toast!" She loved him too! Her face lit up with the biggest smile! She said, "I wait for him."

He would come to her front screen door in the mornings and she'd greet him, and then he'd be on his way!

The biggest surprise of all; we had a very nice mailman named, 'Ollie,' that carried our mail each day with a big leather mailbag over his shoulder! We found out that Adam was riding on his shoulder every day 'helping him,' deliver the mail! We said, "Oh Ollie, if he's bothering you, . . ."

He said, "Oh no! I love him going with me every day! He gives me someone to talk to!" Ollie's eyes and voice were so genuine when he said it, I knew Adam was his friend too! Later, I saw Adam riding on Ollie's shoulder, as they were walking through the autumn leaves, and delivering the mail together! My heart melted!

One day I was at work. I was delivering balloons for a small shop, and was headed out to a children's hospital with a 'balloon bouquet,' when I got a call from Ollie. He knew where I worked, but I'd never had a call from him! I was worried by the tone in his voice. He told me it was "about Adam." I said, "Yes?"

He said, "Well someone from the television news station wants to do a 'live newsreel,' on me and Adam delivering the mail together."

We both chuckled ~ but we were both concerned that this might draw some sick person to do something mean to Adam.

So, after we talked, we both decided to decline the news segment, and just continue to enjoy Adam, and not make him ~ a 'Star!'

We all continued to live in "Adam's World," and each day he brought smiles and laughs to everyone who knew him! Some days, he hung out in Dave's apartment, or on Mrs. R.'s porch.

One day, (a day we will never forget,) Doug came to me and told me to come to Adam's cage. He said ~ "I think we're going to have to re-name Adam!" I said, "Why?" He pointed and said, "I think he's an 'Eve'!" There laid a beautiful egg! She looked at us like she didn't know what to do, and neither did we!

She was finally finding her place in nature, and God's Creation! It was such a shock to all of us. (Especially Adam!) We continued to call her 'Adam,' as we were attached to the name by this time, (and so was she.)

So, Adam continued her rounds and routine of visiting the entire neighborhood ~ cheering everyone up, and helping Ollie deliver the mail. What wonderful and fun times we all had in our, 'storybook' neighborhood!

Some months earlier, we had applied for a new home loan, and eventually we were accepted. It would be our first new home.

We were very happy and excited, but we hated moving from our wonderful storybook neighborhood, where we were all family! It was bittersweet. Everyone hated to see us leave and said they would really miss us, . . and they'd miss Adam too. The feelings were mutual.

Of course, we took Adam with us!

One day, at our new house, I was sitting outside on our front porch cleaning Adams cage. Adam was inside the cage just watching me, when suddenly, a huge wasp flew into her cage! It scared us both terribly!

She flew out the door of the cage and flew way up in the air. I called her name! "Adam, Adam!" She made three big circles, way up in the sky ~ higher than I'd ever seen her fly, and she flew away, . . and sadly, we never saw her again! We were both heartsick and just devastated! Several times we drove back about fifteen miles to our old neighborhood to look for her, but we never found her!

We remained sad and heartsick, and of course, we have never understood why this happened as it did, or where Adam went. But God knows, and He had shown us so many wonderful things through this one loving little bird.

She was happy, content, enjoyed everyone, and cheered everyone up! She was determined, she had a purpose, and her purpose was to make us all feel happy, and loved!

Adam brought us into her 'storybook world,' and everyone who knew Adam had a special place in their heart for her. Looking back, over twenty years of our work with delinquent kids, we can say we have a 'special place' in our hearts, for every one of them too! Each child grew, and many were helped, and each one took their wings and eventually ~ flew away.

Just like Adam, they found their way, and they needed to experience their calling in their own lives, to do what God created them to do. Many of these kids made us laugh, and we enjoyed them, and we wished we could have always stayed in touch with them ~ including Dave. But, as we all know, that's not how life goes.

Even so, . . we also know ~ that when we have Christ in our hearts and lives ~ we will all reunite someday in His Glorious Kingdom!

The Bible says, "And God shall wipe away all tears from their eyes; and there shall be no more death, neither sorrow, nor crying, neither shall there be any more pain: for the former things are passed away." (Revelation 21:4) Thank You, Lord Jesus ~ for this wonderful promise!!

So, let's enjoy each other while we can, as long as we can, and let's learn from even a little bird like Adam ~ that we can make a difference in this world!

We can sure say ~ that God had a plan for Adam's life, and He surely has a plan for each of our lives too!

Let's talk to Jesus, and let's be determined to live for Him, and to be a blessing to everyone we meet!

Dave didn't have the heart to leave that baby bird alone on the ground that day! (And just like Dave found that little bird, Adam,) Jesus finds us . . . when we're down ~ and He just "doesn't have the heart to leave us there alone."

He picks us up and cares for us, He feeds us and brings us in, and brings us up, and sets our feet on solid ground. Let's always stay close to Jesus and always live for Him . . . for He promises, "I will never leave you nor forsake you."

He is our Savior, and Father ~ He is waiting to pick you up . . . Because, 'He doesn't have the heart ~ to leave any of us ~ behind!'

"Be not forgetful to entertain strangers: for thereby some have entertained angels unawares." (Hebrews 13:2)

"Yea, the sparrow hath found an house, and the swallow a nest for herself, where she may lay her young, even Thine altars, O Lord of hosts, my King and my God." (Psalm 84:3)

"I know all the fowls of the mountains: and the wild beasts of the field are Mine." (Psalm 50:11)

23. THE OLD SHIP OF ZION

Our dear Pastor Pete, who was such a Godly influence upon our lives, . . (The most genuine person you'd ever want to meet, and have as your pastor and friend) ~ asked us one Sunday to a black inner-city church, named "Morning Star."

We had never been to one before, and we told him that we'd love to go. We were excited to try it, and visit with them. Pastor Pete said, ~ "You'll love the music, and it'll be like a 'vitamin B shot,' for your spirit." He gave us one of his big, famous smiles, which was always like sunshine to our souls!

When we walked in, we heard the beautiful music. It was unlike any music we had ever heard before! I looked around for a hymnal. They had no hymnals!

These songs were touching deep within our hearts and souls! They were somehow hauntingly familiar, even though we had never heard them before! (You just 'had' to stand up with everyone ~ and 'clap' in beat to the music!) It was like being part of the 'Heavenly Choir!'

These were songs that had been passed down to them, from many generations past; filled with the Spirit of God; . . and somehow, made us feel like we had come home! The Lord Jesus was being glorified ~ in song, prayer, and in the 'Word of God,' in the service.

We were so impressed to hear how sincerely, and powerfully, this dear pastor spoke of the "Love of Jesus," to every soul in that church.

Each person had a different story ~ we were all there for different reasons. Doug and I were there because our pastor had asked us to go hear some beautiful gospel music. We would find out later however ~ that 'God's reason,' was far greater than ~ just the music!

We were enjoying the service, and felt we were not going to make this visit our last!

Upon finishing his sermon ~ the pastor began to sing!

And what we heard was a beautiful song from his heart ~ as if we were all, as a congregation, alone with our Lord, singing and praying for all of His people at the end of the service. . . They had the love of God in their hearts, and His love shined in their faces!

At the end of the service ~ we saw that the custom was; as we all went out through the church vestibule, (entry way,) everyone, 'like family,' would file out, . . one by one, and shake the pastor's hand. The pastor would greet each person individually, and hug whoever needed a hug, (and he hugged all the little children.) It was like we were in a wonderful old movie!

The most important point of this story is ~ we felt accepted, and there was absolutely no 'color' ~ it was solid, wall to wall ~ the pure Love of Jesus!

When we were greeted ~ the pastor shook our hands, and with the proudest smile ~ he invited us back, and said, "We'd love it, if you'd come back and join us again!" We promised him we'd be back.

When we stood outside with Pastor Pete ~ we couldn't have been smiling more! We were lifted up in Christ's Spirit; and we were filled with His Holy Spirit, His Love, and His Joy!

As we drove home, we talked about the overwhelming feeling of God's Love in these dear Christians. They "had Jesus," in their lives, in their music, and in their church service!

We had been there much longer than a regular service (over three hours) ~ due to the music ~ but it only seemed like an hour or so! We were caught up in God's Spirit!

These dear people did not sing from a hymnal, (with each hymn having four verses,) they sang from the Holy Spirit within their souls! If they felt the Holy Spirit move them to sing the song a second time ~ they let 'Him' lead, and everyone there wanted to hear more, it was just so moving!

We discussed how time seemed to be lost, . . it was as if ~ time didn't exist, or matter! That was something we'd never experienced before!

That was what we all felt, and it was like a touch from our Savior, to draw us back to this wonderful little church in the inner-city!

We thanked Pastor Pete for inviting us to go with him. Doug and I decided, we both needed to go back, and receive the blessing of this joyous worship service again. And we did!

That next Sunday, the church members all made their way over to us, greeting us again ~ with the 'true Love of Jesus.'

We sat toward the front and couldn't wait for their choir to sing, and then, for the pastor to preach and sing. We found that same Power of Christ once again in this service, just as full and real as our first visit.

At the end of the service, once again, the congregation filed out in single file, everyone being greeted by the pastor ~ shaking hands, and exchanging hugs. The little children all ran to the pastor for his hugs!

This church had found the most important gift of the Lord; His Love; and they stayed right with it ~ and kept it number one, as the Lord tells us to do. "And this is His commandment, that we should believe on the name of His Son Jesus Christ, and love one another, as He gave us commandment." (I John 3:23)

Love is Real ~ because our God is Real!

We see a hurting world every day ~ and if every church, on every corner, could pray for God's Love to be "number one," in their lives (and church services,) and stay right with it, and 'keep it number one' ~ this world would change for the better!

People would run to the church ~ just as Doug and I were doing ~ to experience God's pure Love!

One thing we saw, was that ~ everyone who walked through those doors, no matter what your background, your culture, your color, or your age ~ you were family! This, dear people, is a duplicate of God's Family here on earth! It reminded us of the words from The Lord's Prayer ~ "Thy Kingdom come, Thy will be done ~ on earth as it is in Heaven." I believe nothing would put a smile on God's face more, than churches working, and functioning within the 'Love of God's Holy Spirit.'

We both talked, and decided we would pray about going to this beautiful little church in the inner-city, 'permanently.' We asked God to show us "His will." We had no idea what God would show us ~ but we just knew He would lead us. He had always shown us His will, and paths for our lives, and we knew God would never let us down, because He is our Faithful God!

We told no one but God, that we desired to know His will about this. The next Sunday ~ we attended again.

We all began to sing. ~ The choir was prayerful, and humming an old "Spiritual" song ~ a beautiful time in God's Spirit, was lifting us all ~ once again! We were sitting there holding hands, and waiting for more beautiful music, . . and anticipating another strong sermon from the pastor.

When the pastor came out, he said a few words, and then looked over at 'us' and said, "Brother Doug, would you please read the Bible verse this morning, and have a prayer for God to bless us all this Lord's Day?" (I can't tell you how absolutely shocked we both were!)

Doug grabbed his Bible ~ opened it up, and the pastor gave him the verse to read, that would go along with his sermon that morning.

Doug was very glad to do it ~ but he was a little taken by surprise, and a little nervous. He read the Bible verse, and had a prayer, and the pastor thanked him and went on to his sermon.

In all the churches we'd ever attended over the years ~ we'd never seen, or heard of a pastor calling on 'new visitors' to read the Word of God, and pray to open the service, and we've never seen it since! We both felt that this was 'the sign from God' ~ that we had been praying for.

(We decided to have a talk with our pastor of the last thirteen years, Pastor Tom ~ and tell him what we were feeling, and planning.)

We loved him and his wife so much, and we wanted them to know what God was showing us.

After we talked with him, we knew he understood we were being led by God's Spirit. We then went on to make Morning Star our new 'church home.'

Every Sunday, "Pastor Alex" gave an altar call, and we decided to go forward to become new members of their church.

We were so happy, and they were too, and we couldn't have felt more like we were right where our Savior wanted us to be! Pastor Alex was now 'our pastor,' and he soon asked Doug to be one of the deacons of his church, which, of course, he humbly accepted.

Doug and I felt led to continue our service ~ of calling on the sick in the hospitals, and in their homes. We had family and friends that dropped in and visited our new church, and they all felt the Love of God, and enjoyed the beautiful old gospel songs as well. Eventually, we too, learned many of these beautiful songs by heart, and God has used them to help sustain us through the years, and they still do today!

One thing that Doug has always said, "We went there with open hearts, to be used of God, to serve these dear Christians any way we could, and to help them in the Lord's work. But eventually, God used them to help us more than they could ever know!"

Each Sunday we attended ~ was another day of Christ's Love and Joy! This is what church should be!

We eventually met on Wednesday nights and prayed together, and saw many answered prayers.

One prayer that we all asked, was that somehow, the Lord would remove a notorious 'drug house,' right next door to the church! Every Sunday there were men standing out on the sidewalk, gathering in groups as we arrived. It was always a scary feeling! There were also many "break-ins" in the neighborhood! (Including our church!) We continued to pray God's will, and asked Him to 'remove' that drug house!

Then, one Sunday, we were all surprised, and glad to see that drug house was closed down! All the windows were boarded up! (This had been a drug house for many, many years!) Now, we could freely walk past that house to get to church, (day or night,) without fear, and we all praised God for His answer to our prayers!

We had many special times with our pastor and the church family.

We had scheduled music programs, with other churches coming in. ~ One program was called, ("The Old Ship of Zion.")

That evening, Doug brought his guitar and sang a 'stepped-up' version of "Swing Low, Sweet Chariot" ~ and when Doug finished the guitar part ~ (his style on this song was to 'slap' the guitar in beat to the song.) ~ He ended it abruptly with a loud 'slap!' Dear "Mother Ruth" hollered out, "Amen Brother Deitrick!" ~ She was laughing as she looked around and said loudly, ~ "He done blowed that ship right outta the water!" She got us all laughing with her!

She was the 'Patriarch Mother' of the church, and was in her late eighties!

She was such a loving, joyful Christian lady! We all got along ~ in Christ's Love, and really had such joyous fun!

The church was now our 'home away from home.' This group of Christians were very special to our hearts.

Pastor Alex had such an appreciation for music! He had grown up in Memphis, Tennessee ~ where he was very familiar with "Beal Street," and the old blues, jazz, and gospel artists like 'B.B. King, Muddy Waters, Louis Armstrong, Albert King, and many others. He sang with a well-known gospel group for years, and was known as 'The Little Man with The Big Voice!' (Yes, he was!) Amen!

A number of those in the congregation, (and the choir,) were also from Memphis, and they all knew and appreciated 'good music.'

So, a lot of people were drawn by our pastor's great Love for God, his love for people, his beautiful singing, and his love of music.

What a privilege it was to be part of this beautiful church, and this family of Christians who truly loved Jesus with all their hearts! ~ We felt many times, like we were in a movie, and it all seemed surreal! ~

The music was exceptional; the best gospel music we had ever experienced! The Holy Spirit was so present in their songs! You never wanted to leave!

We heard years later, from a Christian newsletter from another church ~ that a youth group had attended a church service there at Morning Star. They experienced the same phenomenon we did. They said in the article; that it seemed like "time stopped." They were all lifted up in God's Spirit, and the Gospel music, and they didn't want to leave!

In the article they mentioned how happy they felt there, and how they all felt ~ "full of God's Joy." When they got outside ~ they couldn't believe they'd been in there over three hours! (The same thing we experienced with Pastor Pete!)

God's Spirit is 'Eternal' dear people!

We were experiencing that, and it gave us a vivid glimpse into what the Kingdom of God will be like; which is not bound by time! It was so beautiful, and pure ~ you wanted to cry with happiness!

Now let me say this, we are not wanting to build up a man here ~ but we give glory to God for a pastor that is so dedicated to Him.

He helped us to see Jesus, and to get a clearer glimpse of Heaven; where we all wanted to stay faithful and get there!

He worked a full-time job at a big factory.

He didn't take a salary from the church, (only a one time offering every year around Christmas.)

He raised his dear family, and was always available to everyone in the church whenever they were in need, and even helped people who called for his help from the streets! He is in his nineties today and still serving our dear Savior faithfully!! He has still got more energy than Doug and I put together! (Now that is a faithful servant of our Most High God!) "And let us not be weary in well doing: for in due season we shall reap, if we faint not." (Galatians 6:9).

Another thing we noticed about this little church, ~ was that we all had our personal ministries outside of the church.

There was a seriousness about serving Jesus, in the hospitals, in nursing homes, helping the poor and needy, and helping neighbors.

There were 'get-togethers,' but not a lot of time spent on the 'fun attractions,' that seem so prevalent in many churches today. We were 'about our Father's business' in following Jesus, and what He asks us to do. "This is my commandment, That ye love one another, as I have loved you." (John 15:12)

The sad day came when we had to go to our dear Pastor Alex and tell him that I had been diagnosed with a serious muscle disease.

He asked me if I was in pain? (As he'd "seen pain in my eyes.") I teared up and told him ~ it was "unbearable pain."

I told him I had to give up driving our stick shift car, and it was to the point where I couldn't carry my purse, or even my Bible! We told him the specialist I'd been seeing, suggested "a move out west" ~ because his older patients, who also suffered with 'fibromyalgia,' said they always felt better when they visited Arizona, "in the dry heat." He also said that I had the worst case of this disease he'd ever seen, even in eighty and ninety-year old people! The doctor told me I was "too young" to suffer such great pain, and a vacation out west would definitely let me know if I could have a better life there.

Our pastor was very concerned, and sympathetic, and said he'd be praying for us. He told us, "I'd sure hate to lose you from our church family," but said that he'd seen a difference in my countenance, and knew I was suffering a lot of pain. He said they'd be praying for a healing, and for God's will!

This was a very sad time, as we had just seen my Daddy through his cancer surgery, and Pastor Alex had been so faithful to visit him at home and in the hospital! They had become good friends. We had all become good friends!

Life has taught me that time is not merciful! Time marches on, and doesn't hold up, and wait for the sick; for their dreams, or needs ~ it is like a 'Drill Sergeant,' enforcing strict rules! We move on, or we get trampled! That's just the nature of time! That's why we need to get in line with God's Will for our lives ~ 'now,' and find out why He created us, what He wants for us, (and from us,) . . . before time runs out! (Let's work for our Lord, while there's still time!)

The days ahead would be a test of our faith in God, and in trusting Him with our entire future. Sadly, we had to go and tell our pastor that I was not getting the healing we were all praying for.

There was great sadness in his face as he assured us, that Doug needed to "do everything he could" to get me well, and out of pain.

He also told us that the deacons would have a special service to "pray over us" ~ to ask God to "direct and keep you safe on your journey." We felt he was guiding us as a father ~ to put all our trust in Jesus, to expect Miracles, and to believe that God had something for us to do ~ "in Phoenix, Arizona." (That would eventually prove to be very true!)

We attended the special prayer service a few days before we were to leave for Phoenix. The deacons all laid hands on us and prayed for us, anointed us both with oil, and asked God to lead, and protect us.

That was a night we will never forget.

The Holy Spirit was so powerfully present, and the Love of God surrounded us with His Great Peace!

There was great sadness as well. We knew that they would miss us, as much as we would miss them!

However, one great comfort was, directly after the service, Pastor Alex told us, "If you have any trouble along the way, you call me, and I will personally come and get you!" The sincere look in his eyes told us ~ that he meant every word he said!

We never doubted his promise!

Again, we could feel God's Love reaching out to us, comforting us, and guiding us ~ as we were traveling off into the 'unknown.'

We were leaving everything we held dear ~ in God's big, loving Hands, and we were seeing God's will unfold for us.

However, as we left the church, and drove away, . . It was like our hearts were being torn out! We didn't want to leave!

~ We were carrying with us so many good memories from Iowa, (and thanks to the teaching and guidance from Pastor Tom, Pastor Pete, and Pastor Alex,) we had a solid Biblical foundation to sustain our faith through the days, months, and years ahead.

Praise God, the move proved to help me! I was relieved of most of the immense pain I'd been dealing with for so long, and I could move freely again ~ I even went on hiking trips! (All thanks to our Lord, for this wonderful miracle!)

Pastor Alex promised us that he and his dear wife would come out to visit us, . . and they did just that! They stayed with us, and we had a wonderful time!

They had prayed in that special service, that we would be directed by the Lord to a church that would love us, and help us.

We found an inner-city church in South Phoenix where we felt the Love and Presence of God, and we grew to love the dear people there as well.

We were both led to teach Sunday school ~ and served as deacon and deaconess for the church.

We were very involved with the children and the teens there. We took them on hiking trips to the mountains, and had a lot of fun with them all. When Pastor Alex and his wife visited our church, he was asked to preach that Sunday!

Everyone loved his preaching, (and singing,) and that helped our new church ~ to get to know our 'Iowa pastor' and his wife, (and a little more about us ~ as well.)

It was just like our Savior's great love, to settle us in a new church home, and make sure that we had a good start there.

We had many years of service with this church, and worked to witness in the community, in the hospitals, in 'the projects,' and we were able to encourage our Sunday school kids, and their parents, in the Lord. They certainly encouraged our hearts, and our faith as well!

What a wonderful plan God had for our lives!

It all started with Pastor Pete asking us to visit a little church in the inner-city, to be inspired, and to hear the wonderful music there!

God greatly used this little church (and Pastor Pete) in our lives to bring us closer to Him, to help us, to guide us, and to become our dear 'Forever Friends' and Christian family!

God has a beautiful plan for our lives and a wonderful Kingdom where we will all be together, and never have to say good-bye again!

Doug can sing "Swing Low" for all of you then ~ and we'll all sail on that "Old Ship of Zion". . . Forever! ~

"And when they had ordained them elders in every church, and had prayed with fasting, they commended them to the Lord, on Whom they believed." (Acts 14:23)

"That He might present it to Himself a glorious church, not having spot, or wrinkle, or any such thing; but that it should be holy and without blemish." (Ephesians 5:27)

"Saying, I will declare Thy name unto my brethren, in the midst of the church will I sing praise unto Thee." (Hebrews 2:12)

"I Jesus have sent Mine angel to testify unto you these things in the churches. I am the root and offspring of David, and the bright and 'Morning Star'." (Revelation 22:16)

"Now the Lord had said unto Abram, Get thee out of thy country, and from thy kindred, and from thy father's house, unto a land that I will shew thee:" (Genesis 12:1)

24. IN A DREAM, IN A VISION OF THE NIGHT

I'm going to tell you about an experience I had, that might seem unbelievable to the human mind. It was a 'miracle,' and you have to believe in miracles from our Lord and Savior, Jesus Christ, to really know, and understand, His great love for us!

Hopefully it will encourage many of you.

A dream came to me one night while we were in Iowa, over 30 years ago now. At the time, I was suffering with the worst pain I'd ever experienced in my life, due to fibromyalgia. On the other hand, we were happier spiritually than we had ever been in our lives. We were members of a wonderful 'Spirit filled,' inner-city Baptist church, and God was truly present and moving in our lives!

Doug and I did hospital calling for our church; and I was about to find out, that God had one very special call . . . waiting for me!

That morning, I woke up after having the most vivid dream I've ever had in my life! I sat straight up in bed, and Doug was there next to me. I told him, "I just had a dream, but it was as real as a vision!"

"What was it?" he asked.

I said, "Well, when I tell you, if it comes true, we'll both know that it was straight from God Himself!" . . . (And, it was!)

I explained the dream to Doug. I told him, "It was a black man, lying in a sick bed, and he had 'bright blue' eyes! He had someone else there in his room, and when I told him my testimony, that person sitting beside him ~ just about laughed me out of the room, and I felt sad! I know I'm going to see this man, and I know I'm going to witness my faith in Jesus to him."

Doug told me, "Honey, you don't need to convince me, I've seen enough to know and believe, what you say is from God!" That made me feel good!

Well, around two weeks later, we went to church and got a couple names of people who had gone into the hospital, and who needed a visit. No other information.

I had gone by myself this time, and as soon as I walked through that hospital room door, . . I was totally in shock! There was this black man, (a big man,) lying there looking at me ~ and yes, . . . with those "bright blue eyes,". . . (from my dream!!)

I was a little taken back, because I knew the rest of the dream! I looked over to the side of his bed, and there was a woman! (Who I now know, was his daughter.) She looked like she was going to 'have fun' with me ~ (when I told them I was from the church.)

She started snickering under her breath.

I told him, after introducing myself, that I had never seen him at church. She put her head back and laughed, and then spoke up and said, "My Dad? He don't go to church!"

(I immediately asked the Lord to give me strength!)

Well, I knew it was going just like my dream!

I asked him his name, and he said "Johnny." I smiled at him, and asked him, "Johnny, do you mind if I tell you my testimony, and how I came to know Jesus as my Savior?"

His daughter almost laughed me out of the room, (again, just like my dream!)

All of a sudden, he became protective of me, (that was Jesus!)

He said to his daughter, "Now, come on, let her tell her story. You go ahead baby, and tell your story to Johnny, I want to hear it."

I was thinking, (Thank You, . . Lord Jesus!!)

So, I told him how Jesus had saved Doug and I; how we had been mixed up in drugs, and running with the wrong people, and how Jesus proved His love to us. ~ Finally, when I finished, he grabbed my hand and with the sweetest look on his face, he thanked me and said ~ "I needed to hear that."

I looked, and he had tears in those big, sad blue eyes! I glanced over at his daughter; she was humbled, and tears were flowing down her face too. I asked if I could pray with him, and he said, "Sure baby, sure you can pray with Johnny." So, I prayed, and his daughter closed her eyes too!

My heart beats fast right now ~ because here is where the Holy Spirit of God really began moving. . . After the prayer, Johnny asked me, "If I ever get out of this hospital, will you come and visit me? I'd like to hear more."

I said, "Sure I will" and I asked for his address.

Well, Johnny 'did' get home, and I 'did' go visit him . . . as I had promised. When I knocked, one of his sons answered the door, and I heard Johnny's voice ask, "Who is it?" His son said, "It's a white lady Dad." He came right to the door, and thanked me for coming.

His wife came to the door and I had seen her at church! She sat in the deaconess section of the pews. I hadn't met her, so I introduced myself, and she seemed so happy to see me.

Well, I went back quite a few times, and kept visiting Johnny. We sat on his porch swing together, and I read the Bible to him, from the 'Living Bible.' We were really being blessed in God's Spirit, and I knew from my dream, it was going just like the good Lord had shown me. I knew nothing more about Johnny than what I have just told you. (but Jesus knew!)

Then one Sunday, at the end of our church service, we heard some people whispering excitedly during the altar call. I looked up, and saw that Johnny had walked down the center aisle of the church!

He was walking to the altar to receive Jesus as his Savior! He had come to church apart from his wife, and sat in the back pew.

Everyone was shocked that he was there, and especially that he had come forward to the altar! There were lots of tears that day, dear friends! Tears of Joy!

Then Pastor Alex made a small and humble announcement, and said that the "whole church" had been praying for Johnny for years, hoping that someday God would answer his wife's, (and the church family's,) prayers! I had no idea about any of this! (But, Jesus did!)

God loved Johnny so much, that ~ "He gave His only begotten Son, that whosoever believeth in Him, should not perish, but have everlasting life!" (John 3:16)

Now, I didn't know when I had that dream, that it wouldn't end with me just sharing my testimony; . . No, it didn't. Jesus wanted me to be obedient to His Spirit, and I thank the Lord I was! . . . Jesus kept working, and kept walking next to Johnny ~ and also with me!

The Holy Spirit blessed it all! We give our Lord all the Praise!

If you could have heard the cries, and the prayer from Pastor Alex, and seen everyone shaking Johnny's hand, and rejoicing in our church that day, it was like a wonderful old movie!

Like a 'Heavenly Homecoming!'

We know, the Angels sang in Heaven that day!

Johnny came back every Sunday, and came right up to Doug and I and shook our hands, and we couldn't be more proud of our Savior, than when we tell Johnny's story. We are just so blessed to have this story, and to have witnessed this experience ~ from beginning to end!

~ We can't wait to see him and his dear wife together in Heaven someday! What a glorious day that will be!

This is what I need to ask you ~ "How far did Jesus go to Save You?" (Maybe some of us will never know, but we hope and pray, and ask God, to lead 'you' to others who need to know about Him.) I can tell you, I called on people even though I was in terrible pain!

I had to go alone many times, (when Doug had to work at his home for delinquent boys.) I can only thank our Lord Jesus ~ that He graciously blessed my efforts and faithfulness.

Pray dear friends, and just tell Jesus that you are ~ 'willing' to go tell others that He loves them. . . You may not have a dream. . . (You can't duplicate what the Holy Spirit of God decides to do!)

However, we can trust Him to use our lives for His glory, and we can always trust Him to accomplish His will, (when we pray in faith.)

Again, please think about this ~ "How far did Jesus go to Save You,". . . and to show 'you,' . . His Great Love?

"For God speaketh once, yea twice, yet man perceiveth it not. In a dream, in a vision of the night, when deep sleep falleth upon men," (Job 33:14,15)

"And he dreamed, and behold a ladder set up on the earth, and the top of it reached to Heaven: and behold the angels of God ascending and descending on it." (Genesis 28:12)

"How beautiful are the feet of them that preach the Gospel of peace, and bring glad tidings of good things!" (Romans 10:15)

25. GOD SENDS ANGELS

I grew up as a 'painter's daughter,' around a lot of rather rugged painters, who were unbelievers. Most were likable characters, and we learned to accept everyone as "family," and love them just as they were! We were especially fond of a couple, who were like my second parents, (Mr. and Mrs. 'C.')

They had a lot of problems, and fought a lot due to their drinking, and both were very stubborn! However, they were always good to us, and loved us very much, and we all loved them.

I was the closest to them out of all the kids in our family, and I used to stay overnight once in a while with their kids. They knew we loved them, in spite of all their drinking and fighting.

After many years, our friends were divorced.

Mr. C. was very bitter.

He told me ~ "If you want to be friends with her, you can't be friends with me!" He was so angry, he told me, "You're gonna' have to choose, now!"

I put my hands on his shoulders and said, "I can't do that! I'd never stop loving either of you!" I said, "You're like second parents to me, and I'll always love you both! You can't take that love away from me!" He looked so sad and ashamed, because he knew how much I loved them.

Years went by and he remained bitter. Later though, I heard Mrs. C. had received Christ as her Savior and was running a mission downtown for abused women! I had not seen her for many years.

The story I am going to tell you, is quite an emotional one for me. It is one of my biggest miracles of God hearing, and answering, my 'tears,' and my 'cries.'

My dad and I were best friends. (Everybody knew that.)

(Only God knows what my Daddy meant to me, and what he helped me through. I don't believe I would be alive if it weren't for his constant love and friendship.)

Doug and I had just bought our first house, when we found out my dear Daddy had developed cancer of the larynx! I can't explain it any other way, except that I was devastated beyond belief; beyond what words could express! Doug was too! The most dreaded fear of my life was to ever have to live without my dad's love, his sweetness, and his laughter!

At this time, our car had broken down, and we had spent all our savings to buy, and move into, our new house. My dad's surgery was to be performed in Minnesota, two hundred and fifty miles away; but there was no way we were going to let him go through this cancer surgery alone!

I was trying to keep faith, and yet I weakened when we asked some close relatives, (who had four vehicles,) if we could borrow one of their cars to go to Minnesota to be with my Daddy and we got a firm, cold, "No!" They had no feelings for us at all! We had no idea why!

It hit both of us like a brick wall, and I began to lose hope and crumble. As Doug and I sat on our couch, I laid across his lap, (crying in a miserable heap,) asking Doug, "What can we do?"

Doug said, "We need to pray, and ask God to help us get there."

I asked, "how?"

He said, "We don't know how, but we know God can make a way where there is no way, and, All things are possible with God."

I told him he'd have to pray ~ I was too upset to pray! So, Doug prayed that somehow, God would give us a miracle.

He talked to God and said, "Dear Lord, You know how close Charlie and her dad are. We ask You Lord, to please hear our prayers and provide us a way there. We love you dear Father, and we are going to give this burden all over to You. Please help us to leave it in Your hands and not worry. Thank You Lord Jesus. In Your Name we pray, Amen."

Well, we can never repay our Savior for His compassion, and faithfulness to us. He honored our love for Him, (and our love for my sweet Daddy.)

After Doug prayed ~ I became very peaceful and, like a child, I asked, "When do you think Jesus will answer us?"

He said, "Let's just trust Him, and not put any time limits on Him," and he rubbed my back, comforting me as I wept. (What I am going to tell you, is still a heart pounding miracle for both of us to this day!)

The Bible says, "Before they call, I will answer; and while they are yet speaking, I will hear." (Isaiah 65:24)

As I was laying there across Doug's lap, weeping like a baby, our phone rang, and I answered it crying. The voice on the other end was 'Mrs. C.!' (We had not seen or heard from her in years!)

She said, "Hi Honey! It's me, Jo! Are you okay? I've had you on my mind, and felt something was wrong! What's going on?"

I got my mind together enough to say, "I guess I'm just sitting here having a pity party, . . . with me, myself, and I." I was still crying and she knew it, she said, "I knew something was wrong! Honey, what's going on?"

My voice was shaking as I proceeded to tell her about my Daddy. She knew how much we loved each other, and she told me, "Well you just dry your tears, I'm going to talk to 'Mr. D.' (her new husband.) We'll have a talk, and he'll come up with something to help you and Doug, Honey!"

We hadn't talked to Mrs. C. in years, and now she told me she had me on her mind, and knew something was wrong! (That was God's Holy Spirit, laying me on her mind!)

All of a sudden, I was filled with hope, and my tears were gone. We had no idea what they could do, but we had just been sitting there on the couch like children, waiting for God to help us somehow. It couldn't have been ten minutes later; and the answers to our prayers could be coming through a dear lady (I loved like my second mom,) and hadn't seen in years, and her new husband, who we'd never met! (But we were sure to meet him within the hour.)

She called us back within ten minutes! She said, she told Mr. D. all about us; how we had become Christians, and how close I was to my dear Daddy, and how good my dad had been to them ~ and to everyone else she knew.

She said, "Honey, I no more than got half of the story out, and when he heard your car was broken down, he said, You call those kids back right now, and tell them they're taking my new truck up there, to be with her dad!" He said, "I'll wash it up, and gas up both tanks, and it won't cost them a thing!" They told us to take a cab to get to the women's mission, as she had to stay with the women there, and he was getting the truck prepared. Now, that was God!!

When Doug and I got there, Mr. D. was just drying off his brand new ~ shiny red truck!

They were so happy to see us, and we loved seeing them, and getting some of her famous hugs and kisses!

Mr. D. was so sweet and kind, and it seemed like we'd always known him! We talked quite a while, and Mr. D. told us, "Kids, both gas tanks are full, and there's a box of snacks in the front seat from the food pantry here to eat along the way." (There were granola bars, juice boxes, candy bars, and chips, crackers and cheese.) And there was even a gift card with fifty dollars in it! This was all Our Great God, working through these dear Christians!!

We could hardly believe it was all happening, as he handed us his keys! We were all smiling, and they hugged us good bye, and told us their prayers would be going with us!

We 'knew' they'd be praying for us!

As we began to drive away, we were all waving. They had tears in their eyes, and we did too! We felt humble, thankful, and hopeful, (just like Jesus was carrying us.) We thanked the Lord over and over!

We were driving away in faith to a city we'd never been to, and we were feeling God's Mighty Strength as we neared the hospital where my Mama and Daddy were waiting. It felt so good to be able to be there for support, and we wouldn't have wanted it any other way. Thanks be to God! He was so faithful in answering our hearts prayers!

We were able to pray with my parents, and see them through this great trial. We never prayed so much, or so hard, as we did then!

We stayed in Minnesota over a week.

Daddy's surgery was a reconstructive surgery of the neck and throat. His voice changed; things were different; however, we were so thankful he could still talk, and also eat, and so very thankful that he was 'alive,' and still in our lives! (We didn't think it was possible, but we loved him even more!)

We all had our prayers answered, and when they came back to Iowa, Doug was able to drive him to each of his cancer treatments, and waited for him, and prayed for him. Doug loved my dad so much!

Everybody loved Daddy because he helped everyone, . . and loved everyone; being around him made you want to be a better person.

Whenever we pray, and receive answers from our loving Savior, we believe we should stay 'thankful,' and 'prayerful,' and continue that closeness with Him. We never want to be "fire escape Christians" ~ (only coming to God in the middle of our trial, yelling for help on a fire escape, and then forgetting all about Him after He helps us!)

We all know people in our own lives, who only want to come around and be friends when they need something, and then when you help them, they disappear. Think how that makes Jesus feel?

Our time with my daddy after his cancer surgery was quality time.

Our church in the inner-city was very faithful to my parents, and to Doug and I.

Our Pastor Alex, from Morning Star church, came to visit my dad and also sent his "Angel Choir" to sing for them in their home. The little children sang so filled with God's Spirit, that my dad, mom, my sister, and Doug and I, all had tears in our eyes after they finished several songs!

Daddy commented, "Boy! Those little kids were so bold, and sang right out, they weren't shy at all!"

He asked my Mama to get them some candy, and give them some money to take back to the church. It meant so much to them to have the Angel Choir come and sing! What a blessed time we had in God's Spirit!

We saw a glorious picture of how God's love 'should' work, to support the weak, and comfort the sick. When we as Christians stand with the poor, the weak, and the sick, Jesus says, "When you have done it unto the least of these my brethren, you have done it unto me."

~ This 'great love' is what we saw in Mr. and Mrs. D., loaning us their new truck ~ and I saw this in Doug, taking my Daddy faithfully to his cancer treatments. Daddy said to me, "Doug is a good man." (Which meant so much to us.) He loved Doug like a son. We saw it through our Pastor Alex, and the little ones in the Angel Choir too!

The Bible says, "In a wealthy home there are dishes made of gold and silver as well as some made from wood and clay. The expensive dishes are used for guests, and the cheap ones are used in the kitchen or to put garbage in. If you stay away from sin, you will be like one of those dishes made of purest gold ~ the very best in the house ~ so that Christ Himself can use you for His highest purposes." (II Timothy 2:20,21) TLB.

Let's make the decision today ~ to draw closer to Jesus, through reading His word, praying to Him, and asking Him each day, to use our lives for His highest purposes!

And always remember to pray in times of trouble, because "God Sends Angels," . . . and sometimes God's Angels ~ are . . . you and I!

"And Jacob went on his way, and the angels of God met him." (Genesis 32:1)

"Are they not all ministering spirits, sent forth to minister for them who shall be heirs of Salvation?" (Hebrews 1:14)

"For He shall give His angels charge over thee, to keep thee in all thy ways." (Psalm 91:11)

"Then the devil leaveth Him, and, behold, angels came and ministered unto Him." (Matthew 4:11)

26. AS THIS LITTLE CHILD

When our little niece was about seven years old, she came to stay the weekend with Doug and I. We always loved having her come and visit us. She was always good for us, and fun to have around.

It was Sunday, and she was sitting in the living room, watching a church service on television.

The pastor was giving an excellent sermon titled "Who is the Holy Spirit?" He was explaining the Triune God ~ the Father ~ the Son ~ and the Holy Ghost. She was really listening intently. In the Bible ~ God says, His Word does not "return void," (empty.)

After the sermon we went about our day, and later, while we were driving her home; she was sitting in the back seat of our car. She spoke up and asked, "Uncle Doug, how do you know the Holy Spirit is there?"

Doug explained as he was driving ~ that the only way he could describe it was, "The Holy Spirit is like the wind ~ you can feel the wind, but you can't see the wind." He said, "That's the way I'd describe the Holy Spirit."

"The wind bloweth where it listeth, and thou hearest the sound thereof, but canst not tell whence it cometh, and whither it goeth: so is every one that is born of the Spirit." (John 3:8).

He went on to tell her, "When we believe, and decide to ask Jesus to be our Savior ~ His Holy Spirit comes into our heart. He will always stay with us and He will never leave us or forsake us ~ He promises that to all, who believe in Him."

She looked at me and smiled, and said, "I'd like to be Saved!"

She wanted to ask Jesus into her life, and have His 'Holy Spirit' in her life too!

We should never underestimate what God's Holy Spirit is doing through His mighty Words being spoken, whether it's on television, the radio ~ or when just talking with others about Jesus.

In the secret of her heart ~ the Holy Spirit was calling our sweet little niece, and she wanted her questions answered.

As Doug spoke about the Holy Spirit ~ and when he explained the Holy Spirit as Jesus does in the Bible, she understood it, and she immediately made up her mind right there in the car. I asked her if she would like to pray?

She said, "Yes," and we all prayed right there.

She asked for the forgiveness of her sins, and asked for Jesus to be 'her' Savior, and asked the Holy Spirit of God to come into her heart and life. She was so happy when we finished praying, and you could see it, in her eyes and smile! ~ She was just serenely staring out the window of our car, and she looked 'satisfied,' with her decision, and with the prayer of faith she had just prayed.

She loves Jesus to this day! She is married to a good Christian man; they have five children ~ and we are very proud of her and her husband. They take their children to church, and teach them the Bible, and are serving our Lord today.

We thank God that He stays with us. He works with us, and grows us up in His Spirit, and He promises He will never abandon us in life!

He will never leave us! Praise His Holy Name!

Thank You dear Lord Jesus, for loving and calling 'little children' to Your side. (And Father, we give You all the thanks and praise, for calling our little niece to love You, that wonderful Sunday afternoon!)

"And Jesus called a little child unto him, and set him in the midst of them, and said, Verily I say unto you, Except ye be converted, and become as little children, ye shall not enter into the Kingdom of Heaven. Whosoever therefore shall humble himself as this little child, the same is greatest in the Kingdom of Heaven. And whoso shall receive one such little child in My name receiveth Me." (Matthew 18:2-5) . . . "Jesus loves the little children!"

For whosoever shall call upon the Name of the Lord shall be Saved." (Romans 10:13)

"All that the Father giveth Me shall come to Me; and him that cometh to Me I will in no wise cast out." (John 6:37)

"For there are three that bear record in Heaven, the Father, the Word, and the Holy Ghost: and these three are one." (I John 5:7)

27. HE JUST DISAPPEARED!

We had recently moved to Altoona, Iowa, and had just bought a new home there. ~ We now had to take the 'Interstate,' 15 miles home each evening from our work in Des Moines.

This particular evening, I was late leaving to go home, and it was freezing out, and 'sleeting' snow.

It was scary being out in the storm! I was on the Interstate all by myself; and it was now night time!

This was before cell phones.

We used to travel in the music business, and Doug's grandfather had bought us a 'C.B.' ~ (Citizens Band, 2-way radio,) but it was in our other vehicle. So ~ I had no communication!

The 'old method' for protection, (when driving in a storm,) was to stay close behind another vehicle, preferably a 'semi-truck!' (Many of you can relate, I'm sure.)

I had noticed a semi was traveling behind me ~ and I kept looking in the rearview mirror, to make sure I could see him.

It made me feel safer since I was alone; I figured I could pull over, and maybe get some help through him if it got too slick for me to go on. As the sleet kept falling, I kept my eyes nervously looking back, and praying I could get home safe!

Just as long as I could see his lights in my rearview mirror ~ I felt safer! This piece of Interstate was a 'straight shot,' with no curves.

On my next look back, to my surprise, the headlights were gone!

(I felt sick to my stomach! A fearful feeling came over me, and I 'knew' something was wrong!)

No one was with me, but our Lord Jesus. (It's great to know He is always there with us!) So, I prayed to Jesus, and asked Him to protect me, and to help me find that trucker!

There had been no 'turn-offs,' so I knew he didn't turn off on an exit! I slowed way up, thinking that I might have gotten a little ahead of him, but that was wishful thinking!

I knew the Holy Spirit was letting me know that something awful had happened to that trucker!

When I finally made it home, I told Doug what had happened. I told him I had to call ~ 911!

Doug said, "Oh, don't do that, he probably just turned off on an exit."

I looked him straight in the eyes, and said ~ "Doug, there 'was' no exit!" I told him, "If he exited, it was off of the road, and he could be hurt!" Doug believed me then.

You would not believe the run around I received on the telephone on that snowy night! . . No one wanted to check it out. It was horrible! Everyone re-acted like Doug did at first, and just said, "This trucker probably just turned off the Interstate!"

Well, you don't know me, but, . . when someone is trying to discount what I'm saying, and I 'know' what God is telling me ~ deep in my soul, something rises up in me, with a 'can do' attitude! . . . So, I kept pursuing this!

I called the Highway Patrol, and finally told the officer, "If I can't get anyone to believe me, . . I'm going to get a flash-light, and go back and see for myself!" He advised me, "Oh no, don't do that!"

He said it was "too dangerous." He told me to just stay put, they would send a patrolman out!

When I had slowed down on the Interstate, I noticed the highway mile-marker. I told him that number, and said it was "before they get to that marker." ("That helps," he said.)

Now, I made this patrolman promise me, that they would give me some information back ~ if they found out I was telling them the truth! He said he'd sure try. (Of course, they never called back!)

I believe he might have even thought it was a prank call . . by the way he sounded in his voice.

(But he did send someone out,) because, the next morning I was reading the paper, and 'there was this man's story!' (The trucker God helped me to save!) I believe his hometown was Greenfield, Iowa.

Well, 'sure enough,' this trucker had gone off the road on 'Black Ice,' (very dangerous ice, that you can't see.) They didn't find him until the early morning hours. He had his seat belt on, hanging upside down in the cab; hurt, and was not able to move to free himself!

The newspaper article went on to say that he thought he was going to die! He knew there was no one out there that saw him. (Or so he thought!)

The next part made me feel horrible; he said that his head was in a ravine that had water in it, and each minute he was in that ravine, the water kept getting higher on his face! He just knew he was going to drown!!

(Oh my, I was in shock as I was reading his story, because there was no mention of our Lord in it!) The man finally said, "Maybe there 'was a man upstairs,' watching over him."

Well, I couldn't stop myself from writing him. I have always been one to write letters to people, so I sat down and wrote to this man. (I prayed, and asked God to help this man to get 'Saved' as he read my letter!)

I told him the story ~ and told him that the 'man upstairs' is 'Jesus Christ,' and that 'He' had been watching over him! I told him, "That's why I pursued finding you; because I am a Christian, and I knew God was telling me that you had gone off the road, and needed help!"

I told him, "Jesus died to save you from your sins, and now, He's also saved your life after this accident; just so you could know Him and be Saved!"

I told him, I didn't want him to write me back, (or get me in the news!) so I wasn't going to give him my return address. I just wanted him to know Jesus, and who 'He' is . . . and know that we would be praying for him; and hopefully, he would remember how much Jesus loved him, and we hoped he would ask Him into his life as his Savior!

I called the hospital, and asked for his room number and sent the letter there. I mailed it in time for it to be delivered the next day.

Now, I knew when he received the letter, . . he would be reading the other half of his miracle!

Only God has the whole story, and one day our lives will all be pieced together, and we will see how far God has gone ~ to prove to each of us; that He is here, and that He loves us so intensely, . . and eternally!

~ Let's love others as He has commanded us to do, (pay attention to the 'mile-markers,') and always ~ 'go the extra mile.'

"For thus saith the Lord GOD; Behold, I, even I, will both search my sheep, and seek them out." (Ezekiel 34:11)

"Therefore all things whatsoever ye would that men should do to you, do ye even so to them: for this is the law and the prophets." (Matthew 7:12)

"For I am persuaded, that neither death, nor life, nor angels, nor principalities, nor powers, nor things present, nor things to come, nor height, nor depth, nor any other creature, shall be able to separate us from the love of God, which is in Christ Jesus our Lord." (Romans 8:38,39)

28. GODS SURPRISE TOUR

In my earlier story, I told you about reuniting with our longtime friend, "Mrs. C." (nicknamed, "Jo.") ~ She and her new husband, Mr. D., had loaned us his brand-new truck, so we could be with my Daddy through his cancer surgery in Minnesota.

Jo, had been a severe alcoholic for many years, but she had found Jesus Christ as her Savior and Lord and was now Saved, and healed! She was supervising a mission for abused women, and also women transitioning from jail back into the community.

A few months after we had reunited, and God had used them so mightily in our lives, she called me and asked me, "Honey, what are you doing tonight?" (She sounded scared!)

"Why?" I asked.

She said, "Do you think you could do me a 'Big Favor,' and help me out this evening Honey?"

I said, "Sure ~ anything."

She said, "There's something I know God has, . . . just for you!" ~ She was busy preparing for it, and told me, "Just come down to the mission at six pm, and I'll be 'forever grateful to you'!"

I was more than willing to do her a favor, since she was like my 'second mom,' and her and 'Guy,' (her new husband) had done such a big favor for us! ~ So, I rushed around, and drove the fifteen miles to be there at six pm.

When I arrived ~ "Sister Margaret" ~ (a very sweet nun,) greeted me at the door. She worked as a counselor for the women who were blessed to be housed there, and she also answered the phones and the door. Sister Margaret smiled sweetly and told me to wait in her office, . . she'd go and find Jo.

(Accepting to do this 'favor' ~ would eventually lead to an opportunity for God to reach many for Christ in the months ahead.)

When Jo came through that office door ~ she looked pale, and scared!

I asked her what was wrong, and she grabbed my hands and said, "There's a tour in there for the mission." She said, "I can't do it, I'm not good at these! Please help me and don't say no, Honey!" She nervously smiled, (I knew she was scared.) She asked me to follow her to see what was going on in the living room.

As we looked in, she had tears in her eyes, and she whispered, "Charlie, I think you'd better see this for what it is!"

I looked into the big living room, and there stood around fifty young girls, who looked curiously back at Jo and I. They looked like they might be in the sixth grade. They were with their church leaders ~ who wanted them to "see what a mission was really like."

Jo looked at me, . . . still with tears in her eyes, and said, "Honey, all I kept thinking is, these kids need to hear your story, and what Jesus did for you and Doug! I'm not good at speaking to groups!" (What she didn't know was; . . . I wasn't either!)

So, I asked to have a prayer in the office beforehand with Jo and Sister Margaret. I asked God to give me the courage, and the strength, to speak His Words, and to bless our story and testimony.

After we prayed; as I walked out of the office door and into the living room, I could feel God's strength in my spirit. I was instantly comforted with the thought, that there were a lot of kids in there that Christ could help, and maybe keep them from a sad, and dangerous lifestyle!

As I entered the room, Jo introduced me as her "good friend," and simply said, "I want you to hear her story."

With that, I told them my name, and told them that they could all sit on the floor and get a little more comfortable. I was very nervous as each child's innocent eyes were looking up at me, and listening very intently ~ not one child acted out as I spoke; their heads were leaning on their folded hands. I just remember their innocent eyes, and I was thinking, "If only one of these kids can be helped ~ it will be worth this whole night!"

I looked over to the couch and saw Jo and Sister Margaret sitting there, with tears in their eyes.

I knew without a doubt, they were praying for me, and all those young girls! This was a very serious, and 'Holy' opportunity, to let these children know how important it is to make 'right choices' in life, and stay on the 'good path,' ~ close to Jesus!

I was still very nervous inside, but I introduced myself, and began to give our testimonies. I started by saying, "Even as children, we all know right from wrong. The Bible tells us that God has placed a 'conscience' inside each of us, and our conscience tells us when something is 'right' and also, when something is 'wrong.' When we go against our conscience, we feel 'guilty,' and we know we have sinned against God. What do we do then?

That's when we need to stop, turn around, and ask Jesus to forgive us. We can 'always' ~ ask Him to cleanse us, and give us the strength to turn away from our sins, and He will! ~ Jesus paid for our sins on the cross and He is the only one who can forgive us, and change us, and take us to Heaven when we die."

I went on to tell them, "There are many roads people take in life that lead them into trouble, jail, and even death; from hanging around with the 'wrong crowd'."

I told them, "When I was a child my life was very hard, and I was very unhappy. I began to run away a lot, and my life went from bad to worse. I met a lot of people who led me in the wrong direction and I followed right along! You will all have these same temptations to do wrong. When that happens ~ you need to ask Jesus to help you, and open up and talk to someone." I told them, "never try to run away from your problems, or run away from God. I wish now, I hadn't done that."

I explained to them, "The 'devil' will give you more and more opportunities to sin, because sin separates us from God, and the devil wants to keep us away from Jesus and His power to save us! When we sin, we begin to lose our loving relationship with Jesus."

I had to tell them, "I made the wrong decision and started drinking alcohol as a child, and later I went on to 'weed,' and other drugs. We hung around with the people who sold us the drugs, and eventually we really got off the track ~ and began to sell them ourselves."

I told them, "I felt totally lost, sad, and miserable, even suicidal at times, but I didn't know Jesus as my Savior. I had gone to Sunday school, and was 'confirmed' in our family church, but that didn't help me at all, because I didn't really 'know' Jesus.

I only prayed to God when I got into a jam, and I'd run out on the 'fire escape' of life, yelling ~ 'God please help me!!' And amazingly, He was always there for me, and He did help me, and answer my cries for help! But afterwards ~ I went right back to my old ways ~ because I really didn't know Jesus, or His words, or what He wanted for me.

I didn't know what my purpose was in life."

I went on to explain, "Each time we sinned ~ our lives got worse and worse because we were going 'away' from God ~ not going 'to Him,' or toward Him." I told them, "My husband's motto used to be: 'If it wasn't for bad luck, I wouldn't have no luck at all!' But we learned that life isn't about good luck or bad luck. The Bible says, 'We reap what we sow.' If we sow good, we get good back. Just like when we plant a garden, if we plant corn, we get corn back. If we plant peas, we get peas back. So, when we plant 'good' in our lives ~ we get God's 'blessings' back. When we plant 'evil' ~ we give the devil ~ the right to bring 'evil' back to us.

We need to be very aware, and very careful about the choices we make. Because good choices bring us closer to God, and bad choices take us away from Him. We need to follow Jesus and stay on the right and good paths, and stay next to Him."

I told them the story of how Jesus saved me; how He answered my prayer, and proved to me that 'He loved me personally.'

At this point, you could hear a pin drop.

As I finished up my testimony, I told them all, that even though they went to church, "that doesn't mean you're a Christian, or that you'll get into Heaven. You have to 'know Jesus' yourself, as 'your' personal friend and Savior, and have Him in your heart." I told them, "You don't want to live a life of sin, and end up in jail ~ getting beat up, or raped, and feel so guilty that you might never forgive yourself, (and then, never ask Jesus to forgive you and save you,) and end up in hell!"

I told them, "That's why I'm here, to try to help you to never go that way!" I told them, "Jesus wants you to turn to Him, and give Him your heart, and all of your problems. He will help you through your entire life, and He promises to 'never leave you or forsake you'."

I saw them all looking up at me, and some looked so sad, and had tears in their eyes. I saw that same hurt in some of their eyes ~ that I had seen in my own eyes ~ when I looked in the mirror as a child.

The Holy Spirit led me to ask them, if any of them wanted to know Jesus as their Savior; I was going to pray and I'd lead those who wanted to know Him, in the 'Salvation Prayer.' I asked them to bow their heads, and I felt so humbled . . . to pray for them all.

When I finished the prayer, I asked them to raise their hands if they had prayed that prayer along with me, and had asked Jesus to be their Savior. I had tears in my eyes, when I saw about thirty-seven hands stretch up!

A 'Holy hush' was in that room like I'd never experienced before.

I then had a prayer of thanks, and asked Jesus to bless each and every child there, and to be with all those who had asked Him to be their Savior and Lord.

When I said, "In Jesus Name, Amen," they all looked up and there were many tears, some brushing them from their sweet little faces. I felt so sorry for some of them.

Many of them came up to me, shaking my hand and thanking me for talking to them, and telling them my story, . . . and some wanted hugs! They were all so sweet!

The church leaders seemed very happy with their decision to bring the kids in for a tour. I looked over at Jo and Sister Margaret, their faces were shining, and with tears of joy, they both thanked me. They were so pleased that I came to help them, and speak to these children.

They were so pleased in fact, . . that they asked me if I would consider coming to speak regularly to the women there, and counsel them, and eventually ~ they asked me to give Bible studies. I accepted their offer, and I was very honored to be a part of God's work, at Jo's women's mission.

God was leading me by His Holy Spirit, and was opening doors for me to tell others the Good News, that ~ "Jesus loves us!"

(I felt blessed each time I went there, and I thank God for those opportunities.)

I went in faith ~ and spoke the Word of God in faith ~ believing that God's Words would "not return void." And I just trusted the Holy Spirit, to bring them all closer to Jesus!

This is my ultimate goal and why I live my life for Him.

I often wonder how all those children's and women's lives turned out in the years ahead.

That too, is our Fathers business. His faithful, caring mission ~ is to bring us away from sin, to 'keep our souls,' and to finally, . . . grow us up, and 'fill us,' with His Holy Spirit.

All God asks us to do, is to be 'willing' to go tell people that Jesus loves them, and that He can forgive them of all their sins.

(Is there a mission you can get involved in? Or a hospital calling team, ~ or a Sunday school class?)

Maybe pass out Christian tracts, or place them in a doctor's office, supermarket, or a restaurant? "How beautiful are the feet of them that preach the gospel of peace, and bring glad tidings of good things!" (Romans 10:15)

He desires that everyone might "Repent," turn from their sins, and "be baptized in the name of Jesus Christ."

God's Word, the Bible, is the 'seed' of the Gospel.

When we speak His Words, He will water that seed, and His Holy Spirit will cause that seed to take root, and then to grow, and bring forth fruit for a bountiful harvest.

I always wonder, what kind of crop the Holy Spirit will harvest, through those times I went faithfully to that women's mission ~ and witnessed the love, and forgiveness, of Jesus to all of them.

The Bible says to come to Jesus as "little children," with innocent trust. That is the kind of faith He is looking for. Faith like all those little children had ~ on the 'Mission Tour,' who heard the voice of Jesus, and wanted to ask Him into their hearts, and keep Him with them ~ for all eternity!

May God bless them, . . . and may God bless all of us!

"Being confident of this very thing, that He which hath begun a good work in you will perform it until the day of Jesus Christ:" (Philippians 1:6)

"I write unto you, little children, because your sins are forgiven you for His name's sake." (I John 2:12)

"He shall feed His flock like a Shepherd: He shall gather the lambs with His arm, and carry them in His bosom, and shall gently lead those that are with young." (Isaiah 40:11)

"And whosoever shall give to drink unto one of these little ones a cup of cold water only in the name of a disciple, verily I say unto you, he shall in no wise lose his reward." (Matthew 10:42)

"Be ye therefore followers of God as dear children:" (Ephesians 5:1)

"The Spirit itself beareth witness with our spirit, that we are the children of God:" (Romans 8:16)

29. I KNOW HOW I'VE LIVED!

I have only met one person in all my years of hospital calling, that was 'not' willing that I should pray for him.

~ When I asked him, "Would you like me to pray for you?" He looked at me like the devil himself! His eyes looked furious, and he said in a mocking tone, . . "No, I know how I've lived!" Smirking, like 'he knew' that he was going to Hell; and he knew it was too late!

I told him, "God is willing to forgive you."

He adamantly said again, . . "No, . . . I know how I've lived!"

I said, "Well, I'll pray for you." . . He said gruffly, "You'll just be wasting your breath!"

As I walked out, the door to his room 'violently' slammed shut behind me! (It scared me!) He was lying in his hospital bed and was nowhere near the door! It felt like a 'demon' had slammed it!?

I opened the door and told him, "I'm so sorry the door slammed shut like that, I didn't do that!" He just glared at me with a smiling, evil smirk! He almost acted like 'he' did it, but it was only seconds before I re-opened the door! I knew that wasn't humanly possible!

This is the message ~ "If you know what you've done, God knows too.". . . Never think ~ God doesn't know!

"For if our heart condemn us, God is greater than our heart, and knoweth all things." (I John 3:20)

However, He says He can forgive anyone. ~ "For God so loved the world, that He gave His only begotten Son, that whosoever believeth in Him should not perish, but have everlasting life. For God sent not His Son into the world to condemn the world; but that the world through Him might be saved." (John 3:16,17)

Later, I found out the sad fact, . . (that still makes me feel sick to this day,) . . . that this man, was a child molester!

I had been asked by a lady I knew ~ to please call on him! I then had to come home, and tell her the 'sad truth.' He had rejected Jesus!

As for that man, "It were better for him that a millstone were hanged about his neck, and he cast into the sea, than that he should offend one of these little ones." As Jesus says in (Luke 17:2)

Come to Christ while you can! . . . Before your conscience is seared! Before you have no conscience left! We all have a conscience, as the Bible tells us in (Romans 2:15) "Which shew the work of the law written in their hearts, their conscience also bearing witness." But the Bible also says, that we can "sear our conscience!"

Because of 'sin,' we can become 'cold' to hearing the conviction of our Lord's dear voice!

Listen and hear, what our merciful and loving God is saying! ~ "Whosoever shall call upon the Name of the Lord shall be Saved." (Romans 10:13) ~ That means 'anyone' . . . Jesus is waiting!! ~

"Take heed that ye despise not one of these little ones; for I say unto you, That in Heaven their angels do always behold the face of My Father which is in Heaven." (Matthew 18:10)

"Speaking lies in hypocrisy; having their conscience seared with a hot iron." (I Timothy 4:2)

30. THOSE SIGNS DON'T MEAN ANYTHING

~ "The angel of the Lord encampeth round about them that fear Him, and delivereth them." (Psalm 34:7)

Doug and I have been privileged to witness some powerful miracles performed by our Lord Jesus. Some, I've said many times, that people would not believe. ~ This is one of them! This is the story of one of my strangest, and greatest miracles, and I pray you will be able to receive it in faith! We truly serve a great, and awesome God!

When we had to move out to Arizona for my health, I had to leave my dear Daddy who was suffering with cancer.

Doug had just started his new job at a boy's ranch, way out in the desert. He was working from 2:00 p.m. in the afternoon until 9:00 a.m. the next morning, four days a week, and then weekends. During his first week, our dear German Shepherd, who had been with us for fourteen years, became deathly sick.

Doug couldn't leave work, but our two new neighbor girls offered to drive our dog and I to their veterinarian. They were a real blessing!

It turned out, our sweet, loyal companion had developed 'cancer' throughout her body, and had to be 'put down!' Doug and I were both heartsick!

We always called her our "Angel Dog." She was part coyote and was very intelligent, obedient, and protective of us.

Once, she had even saved my life, by waking me up and leading me out of a fire! Losing her ~ was crippling to us emotionally; and was not what we needed!

Just shortly after this, I was invited by a dear older couple we had known for years ~ to go on a "sight-seeing trip" with them, out to see the desert. Another older couple (that I didn't know) were driving and they all picked me up in a passenger van.

Since Doug was working at the boy's ranch, I thought it sounded fun, . . . going along with these two older couples to view the desert landscape. So, I decided to go along. I thought it would take my mind off losing our poor doggie and cheer me up.

I was in shock however, when shortly into the trip, the man driving the van, turned out to be a terror! He was definitely not wise, and he was not a "nice" person ~ at all! It had been raining earlier and the sky looked as if it could start up again at any moment.

This man drove us way out into the desert mountains ~ to a very barren place, (a federal 'desert preserve' area.) All the roads were dirt roads.

He ignored all the signs not to go any further due to "flooding!"

At one point, he stopped the van, got out, opened the back doors, and took out some buckets and a two foot 'short handled' shovel. He gave no explanation! He then walked out into the desert; and started digging!

Suddenly, (to my horror,) I realized, "This guy is stealing cactus, from a federally protected 'National Desert Preserve!' We could all be arrested!" (In Arizona, you need government tags, attached by a federal employee, to transport certain cactus!)

He covered one large cactus with an old piece of carpet! He piled the cactus in the back, shut the doors, and then got back in the van and continued driving without a word! (I thought ~ "He's done 'this' before!")

We passed more 'Warning' signs about flooding! I finally spoke up, and asked, "Do you see those signs?"

He said, . . . "Oh, those signs don't mean anything!"

We passed several more signs. The next one struck fear into my heart, . . . it said ~ "Road Out!"

I questioned him on 'that sign' as well ~ he only 'giggled' at me like a teenager, (knowing I was scared!)

Well, you have to imagine, we were on small dirt roads, smaller than old rock roads out in the country. ~ They were mainly dirt mixed with very little rock, and we were miles off of any main road! The sun was starting to set, which also struck fear into my heart!

We came up to a very deep ravine, the water was rushing by, and you could see way down in, that it was very, very deep! (My stomach gets to feeling sick just writing about this.)

Then this mean, sadistic, and 'foolish' man, decided to scare all of us, and said, "Oh, it'll be okay, it's not as deep as it looks, let's just try and go across!" I jumped out of that van ~ before he could even finish his sentence!! (I thought, "What next?!")

I knew how deep it was, (and I knew he wasn't right in his head!) So, he inched up to this huge ravine, and now we could hear thunder in the near distance! We were all scared to death, (all but him!!)

He thought he'd 'inch up' ~ a little at a time, to scare us, (he was one of those types!) Suddenly, ~ the front tires dropped off the road and "Bang!" ~ they were down in the water! 'He' even looked scared!

The van was stuck, and now there was no way to get traction, and no way to get help! He kept running the engine and trying to 'pop' the van into a rocking motion, over and over, . . to try and get the front tires back up on the road.

Well, obviously, the van was now "high centered," and sitting on the frame! That van was not moving even a fraction of an inch! (By now he had also succeeded in flooding the engine, ~ and running the battery down!!) The sun was quickly setting, and soon we would be 'out in the middle of nowhere' in complete darkness! And no phone!

By now, I was so mad at this man, for messing with our very lives and safety, . . I can't begin to tell you!

We were already scared to death, and then, . . . we heard 'coyotes' howling nearby! Now, this genius started picking up some rocks (the size of cantaloupes,) and proudly proclaimed, "If we can find some more of these ~ we can build them up under the tires!"

I finally grabbed that rock out of his hands and threw it into the water in the ravine! It went down, . . down, . . down, and finally, slowly, landed way down at the bottom of the ravine.

I asked him, "How many years are you planning on being out here, to build this 'road of big rocks' under the tires?"

Oh! . . . I was livid!!

Silently, I was begging for God's mercy in my head, and finally God told me to ~ "Pray!" ~ I pulled the dear older lady aside (that we knew,) she was also a Christian.

I said, "You know we're never getting out of here, this way!". . .

With fear in her eyes, she whispered, "I know!"

I told her, "Okay, are you willing to pray with me, and are you ready to see a miracle?"

She said, "Yes Charlie!"

I said, "Come over here behind this bush and we'll pray!"

So, there we were, praying, out in the middle of the desert, with no way to get home, the sun setting, thunder in the distance, and the coyotes howling!! I prayed out to our Lord, "Please Lord Jesus, have mercy on us! We didn't know this man was crazy! Please forgive us of our sins, and have mercy on our souls, and 'Please' hear our prayer for a miracle, and give us a way out!! In Jesus Name, Amen!"

I promised Him, I would tell everybody about His Power, and Mercy, and Kindness, when He gave us our miracle!!

Well, if you have faith ~ believe me, this whole group of people 'instantly' witnessed the front of that van lift 'straight up in the air,' about a foot off the ground, and it was set back ~ about four feet!!

The lady I had just prayed with ~ immediately started to cry! Her eyes looked like she'd just seen a ghost!!

(I was also shocked, overjoyed, thankful, and relieved, but I was too mad at this man ~ to cry!)

'Everyone' was just standing there staring in shock and disbelief!

We could hardly believe our own eyes!!

The driver then got back into the van, and to everyone's surprise, the van started! It was no longer flooded! (Another miracle!)

Then, (to our shock and horror,) he 'headed right back toward the ravine,' and almost went off the road again!!!

This time I screamed at him, "What on earth are you doing? God has just given us all a 'total miracle,' and now you're going right back toward the ravine!!?"

He just 'grinned' and said, "Well, I had to put it in reverse, and when I do that ~ it goes forward first, because the linkage is messed up."

I yelled, "Not four feet it doesn't!! Now, get us out of here, before God strikes you dead for your ignorance!!" He just 'giggled' at me again! My patience was completely gone ~ and I was still in fear for our lives!

We all climbed back in the van. There was no 'turn-around' and the dirt road was so small, he had to drive in 'reverse' to get out of the place! . . Suddenly, it began to rain! We were in a "flood area" and we were 'all' scared then! (The roads which had been 'dirt,' were quickly becoming nothing but 'mud' from the rain!) The van began to slide!

When it finally seemed that we were making our way out of the preserve, this man stopped and got out of the van again!

I asked him, "What are you doing now?!"

He said, (still smirking,) "I have to shut a light off by the shed," (and the pole was metal!!)

Right as he touched it, ironically, lightning 'zapped' the pole and he got shocked! (I wasn't surprised at all!)

He snapped his hand back in pain! He kept rubbing his hand! I knew it hurt!! I told him, "You're acting like a complete 'fool!' Get in this van and get us all home!!" (Which he finally did!)

This was a 'big lesson' for me! I was always taught to respect my elders, but unfortunately, I don't trust a lot of them now, especially with my life! This was a horrible experience for all of us!

I missed my dear Daddy so much, and then to be disrespected and terrorized like this! I was totally numb in my spirit!!

When I finally got back to town, I went to the boy's ranch where Doug was working. I was a nervous wreck, and was shaking all over! That's when I began to cry!

Doug was really angry and upset that this had happened to us! And yet, we all knew, the Lord had saved us!

I told him all about the great Miracles that God had given us! He was very thankful to God, for getting me back home safe!

I will never forget, seeing that van 'supernaturally' lifted up and moved four feet backwards; and that 'dead battery' starting the van!!

When you see something that miraculous, that only God could do, (and right after you pray and cry out to Him,) you start praying a lot more, (and believing more!!)

You realize that our mighty Savior knows every little thing that's happening in our lives, and He can change it all in a moment! That's for sure!! Praise God He can!! (We have to pray, and believe!)

However, some people (like this rebellious and foolish man,) after being rescued and delivered by God ~ quickly head right back into their 'sin.' How many go 'right back to the ravine,' and the 'trouble,' after God gets them safely out of a jam?! (Are we thanking God when He helps us ~ or just going along, doing what we've always done?)

We Praise our Lord, and give all glory to our great and mighty God, for His miraculous deliverance!!

Jesus proved that He was with us, (and that He's always with us!!)

And we can tell you all for sure, that. . . "All things are possible with God!!" ~

"Call unto Me, and I will answer thee, and show thee great and mighty things, which thou knowest not." (Jeremiah 33:3)

"The righteous cry, and the Lord heareth and delivereth them out of all their troubles." (Psalm 34:17)

"When thou passeth through the waters, I will be with thee; and through the rivers, they shall not overflow thee: when thou walkest through the fire, thou shalt not be burned." (Isaiah 43:2)

"If ye have faith as a grain of mustard seed, ye shall say unto this mountain, Remove hence to yonder place; and it shall remove; and nothing shall be impossible unto you." (Matthew 17:20)

"God is our refuge and strength, a very present help in trouble" (Psalm 46:1)

31. THE 'OUR FATHER'

Doug and I were working with over a hundred kids at the boy's ranch here in Arizona. They had a senior staff member there, who supervised several "Wilderness Survival" trips every year with some of the boys and staff.

He had thirteen boys that had earned the trip, "for good behavior." He believed that these boys would benefit from this two-week trip, and ~ 'once in a lifetime experience.'

We were new to Arizona, and to the ranch, and the trip sounded exciting to both of us too! We were used to working with these types of boys back in Iowa, and we had no reservations about going along with them at all. We both came from rough backgrounds, and grew up in similar situations, so we got along with these kids real well.

The man who was heading up the trip ~ "Mr. Dan," was a good family man, and a tough old, World War II veteran. He had actually fought in the last three major battles of the war, culminating with "The Battle of The Bulge!" He was still in great physical shape, and all the boys looked up to him for his strength and bravery, and for his great 'story telling.'

He told us all, that this would be "an unforgettable experience," although we never fathomed, 'how' unforgettable it would be, and what would eventually take place!

Mr. Dan had told us all to 'pack light,' and he told us of the many things we could expect to see. We were all filled with excitement, and spilling over with anticipation! (We were all dreaming of the fun we'd have!)

He said we would be going to the "Four Corners" (where Arizona, New Mexico, Colorado, and Utah meet.)

He piqued our interest by saying we would have the opportunity to see wild horses, ancient Indian cliff dwellings, Monument Valley, Lake Powell, Utah State Park, and a very old, dormant volcano site in Flagstaff, Arizona. This was a chance of a lifetime for each of us!

On the morning we headed out, we packed up an older white van with a trailer, which carried the coolers and food to take along with us. Each boy had a few clothes rolled up in their bed roll.

As the morning sun came up, we were all more than excited ~ to get a break from the ranch with its vigorous routines of marching, early morning chores, and work crews. We all piled in the van smiling ~ like little children, free to dream, and enjoying the excitement of having no idea what might take place! We were all ready for an adventure!

We all prayed together in the van, that God would protect us, and 'keep watch' over us, and that we'd all enjoy our trip together.

With me being the only female in the group, I immediately took on the 'mother' role, and all the boys treated me with great respect the entire trip. They referred to Doug and I, as "Mr. and Mrs. D."

Mr. Dan gave us all informative and lengthy talks along the way, which made the travel time go faster. He told us about each state, and what we could expect to see as we visited each one! He was very knowledgeable about the history, agriculture, and highlights of every state; He was very interesting to listen to. We had never heard the boys so quiet!

One unforgettable memory was on a misty morning, when the fog was rolling in over Lake Powell. It was beautiful beyond words!

Mr. Dan always encouraged the boys, to "Make a good life for yourselves" so that they might be able to return and repeat this Four Corners state trip someday ~ with their wives and kids. So, they could experience with 'them,' the wonderful, awesome beauty we were all seeing together right then.

As Mr. Dan stared off over Lake Powell, Doug and I and the boys were all standing there ~ staring too; the mist falling sweetly against our faces. It was cooling, and made us feel as if we had all been transported to a different country! It was so beautiful! The views were breathtaking, and something none of us had ever had the privilege to experience before, (and maybe we would never get back to experience again.) It was like all of us being in a beautiful movie together! That enchanting, peaceful moment ~ seemed timeless!

Lake Powell was a glorious place, which stole my heart! There were beautiful twisted pieces of white driftwood, and sun-bleached branches that had been in the lake, and were now scattered and resting on shore. Being an artist, I could have camped there for months, and easily left the stress of the city life behind!

We had the awesome experience of walking through the many rock formations that were so magnificent ~ that there aren't enough words to describe their beauty! There were purple, pink, orange, and lavender mountains/rock formations that were very steep cliffs. The sand that we walked on throughout the narrow pathways ~ between the rock walls; was a fine, white, soft sand. The rock forms curled and twisted upward, . . and when we looked up to the tops, we saw the beautiful blue sky against the high purple and pink swirling rock walls. Sometimes, we had to crawl over the base of the rocks, because they were so tightly fit together.

I can only tell you ~ I fell in love with God's Holy Presence in that place! They were like Cathedral Coves!! His Voice was so close ~ in all His beauty! I never wanted to leave! It was an 'Eternal' feeling ~ the closest I'd ever felt to God in His beautiful nature and creation! The Bible says, "Be still and know that I am God." (I was living this verse!)

The questions were never answered in my mind, as to why the rock formations had tiny ridges all the way up, or how so many bright colors blended together to make soft pastels, or how it could all become so awesome, that it could make you want to stay, and leave the whole world behind! God showed me that memorable day, how His Heaven, His Kingdom, and His Holy Spirit, could someday (as He promises) wash away "all tears" from our eyes, and make us forget all sorrow from this worlds sin and grief! What a Mighty God we have!!

I was saddened that the day was almost over, and the darkness was falling fast. I wondered if the boys would be bored? ~ But no, we were all thrilled by the myriad of twinkling stars that night, and their magnificent parade ~ of all God's glory!!

We were given a perfect opportunity to talk to all the boys about our great God. There was a tranquil silence, and we would trade all the city lights for those beautiful stars, . . . any night, . . . any time!

The moon seemed to be shining extra brightly over all of us, as if watching over us~ while we slept out under God's angelic royalty!

When the glorious sun arose the next morning, we reluctantly loaded up the van, and pulled away from Lake Powell.

Our hearts were heavy, as I watched out the back window of the van ~ feeling I was leaving part of my heart back there, and somehow feeling I would never be whole without it! (I could tell the boys were feeling the same.) It was noticeably quiet. It felt much like a feeling of 'heartbreak' as a child. And it didn't let go!

We ventured on down the highway. We saw so much beauty each day, that we all had a hard time getting settled down to sleep at night.

Some of our favorite times, were sitting around the campfires at night, and listening to Mr. Dan's funny, and sometimes 'wild' stories.

He had an excellent sense of humor, and told great jokes, and with the campfire lighting up our faces, we were all laughing and having a great time! We each picked out a stick and skinned the bark from it, because Mr. Dan had brought a plentiful supply of marshmallows!

We all looked forward to that time of companionship each night. We were all growing closer ~ each day that we spent together.

We finally arrived in Utah. We all got out and stretched our legs and explored the land, looking for a place to camp and bed down later in the evening. Personally, I loved hunting for fire wood, and stacking a pile of branches, where we'd be starting a campfire ~ come dark.

Mr. Dan had always advised us, that no food was to ever be left in our backpacks, or bedrolls.

I had forgotten that I had a half of a granola bar in my backpack. We were from the Midwest, and when camping out ~ the only things we ever worried about were mosquitoes!

We started a fire, fixed dinner, and we were all waiting for more of Mr. Dan's stories and jokes! Of course, roasting marshmallows too, and trying to knock the other persons marshmallow out of our favorite spot over the coals! Occasionally, we lost a few marshmallows to the fire! ~ The woods seemed to fill up every night with a 'burnt sweet smell' ~ that added to the great fun of camping in the woods!

That night, the boys all went on to bed ~ all tired from the day's activities. Doug and I had set up our two-man tent, and it was there waiting for us when we were ready to turn in.

As the campfire was dying out, I decided to go out looking for more wood to take back and stoke the fire, so we could continue our talk, and all the fun we were having!

Mr. Dan and Doug were still talking over old times and laughing.

Finally, it was time to turn in, so we poured water on the fire and kicked dirt over the wood. We told Mr. Dan we had a lot of fun, and said, 'good night,' and we'd see him in the morning. Doug and I went into our tent, and it wasn't long at all before we both fell asleep.

A couple of hours later, I woke up to a 'strange feeling,' (my sixth sense) ~ one of danger! I listened closely, and the forest was now eerily silent. . . I knew in my heart something was wrong!

All of a sudden, I heard a noise outside, on my side of the tent, and it sounded like someone dragging their feet in the dirt! My heart seemed to jump up into my throat! ~ Total fear was overtaking me now! We had no weapons. I didn't want to scream, and I didn't want Doug to say anything, when I woke him! I knew it wasn't the boys. I was sure they wouldn't pull a prank on us, and chance getting their privileges taken away from them! My mind was racing as fast as my heart was! Fear came in like a flood!

Immediately, I knew we needed God's help! I heard in my mind, "Pray ~ the 'Our Father'." I decided to put my hand quickly over Doug's mouth, so he wouldn't say anything! I then put my mouth up to his ear, and as quietly as I could, I whispered, . . . "Pray the 'Our Father'!" It was pitch dark. His eyes must have been mirroring the fearful look ~ that I knew was on my face too!

Then he heard the noise too! I put my finger up to his mouth, to let him know not to say one thing! We laid there holding hands, each of us repeating silently, "Our Father which art in Heaven, Hallowed be Thy name . ." My heart seemed to be beating loud enough to hear it outside of the tent!

We knew for sure that it was something 'big' dragging its feet; on Doug's side of the tent now! All of a sudden, we heard something 'snort' really loud, and something 'heavy' . . . hit the bottom of the tent on Doug's side! We continued to hold hands, and then brought them up over our hearts. (We were in fear for our lives) waiting, . .

praying silently, . . we were laying so still; . . not moving one bit! The silence was so loud, . . and 'haunting!'

We were just listening, praying, . . and wondering! The next thing we heard, (we later considered a miracle,) were tiny raindrops falling on our tent. There was no thunder, just the loud pounding of our hearts, and . . 'little raindrops' falling. (This was the miracle!) For some reason, it was soothing and we eventually, miraculously, both fell back to sleep, being soothed by the softly falling raindrops!

When daylight came, we awakened to the birds singing in the woods. That sound, (of peace and hope,) was very welcoming! We were hoping that whatever was out there, had gone by daylight! We moved slowly, and sat up, and wondered if we should go outside the tent and see what we could see. (We were still quietly whispering in each other's ears!) Even though the fear remained, we decided we'd better go outside and look around.

We moved slowly, as we crawled out on our hands and knees and peeked around the side of the tent. The ground was completely wet. The rain had come down very softly, and had now stopped.

We got up and looked around the tent. On my side, there were big claw marks in the dirt! We slowly went around the back of the tent, and then to Doug's side of the tent. The ground had all been wet until we got to his side of the tent. We looked down, and the ground was dry in the perfect outline of a "large bear!!"

We knew then, that a bear had been outside of our tent, clawing, dragging his feet, snorting, and he'd decided to lay down by our tent to sleep!

We knew for sure then, that God had heard our prayers, and protected us from a bear attack!

We believe God let the light rain soothe the bear just as it did us! All we could do was thank God for His protection, and for sparing us both that night! Praise God!!

We told Mr. Dan about what happened and he looked shocked! He asked us if we had any food in our tent? I looked, and found the half of a granola bar I had forgotten about in my backpack! Again, we felt very blessed that God had heard and answered our prayers!

("And call upon me in the day of trouble: I will deliver thee, and thou shalt glorify me." Psalms 50:15)

We can call on God anytime, anywhere, and pray about anything! ~ "All things are possible with God."

That morning we happily packed up, and moved on to our next destination! We are still awed, and very thankful, for our Gods loving protection over us that night!

We will never forget the, "Four Corners," wilderness survival trip. We had grown very close to all the boys, and Mr. Dan, and especially to God! We were very thankful that we had the chance to tell them all ~ how Christ turned our lives around, and how we came to know Him as our Savior and Lord!

We have always called on Jesus in our times of need. We certainly called on Him that night, in that tent! He was real then, and He's been real every time we've called upon Him since!

Thank you "Our Father," for hearing and answering, even our 'silent' prayers! Amen!

"And He shall come unto us as the rain" (Hosea 6:3)

"For the invisible things of Him, from the creation of the world, are clearly seen, being understood by the things that are made, even His eternal power and Godhead;" (Romans 1:20)

"The Heavens declare the glory of God;" (Psalm 19:1)

"God is our refuge and strength, a very present help in trouble." (Psalm 46:1)

"My God hath sent His angel, and hath shut the lions' mouths, that they have not hurt me:" (Daniel 6:22)

32. I WANT TWO PRAYERS

We had only been in Arizona for about six months, and my dear Daddy was back in Iowa, his health worsening with cancer.

Doug was working at the boy's ranch with delinquent boys. I was accompanying him to work, helping the boys with school work, and counseling with them about their problems. I was also free to witness to them about the love of Jesus.

I felt so torn wanting to be home with my sweet Daddy ~ and yet, I wanted to be with Doug, who was working a treacherous 90 hours a week, (including the overnights.) He was also running 'work crews' by himself, with up to twenty-five boys in the desert heat every day.

It was one of the saddest times of my life ~ (both of the favorite loves of my heart, were suffering!) Looking back now ~ I know the only way we made it through; 'Jesus was carrying us!'

We had no savings to speak of ~ as we had spent so much money moving everything we owned out here, and then paying for a deposit on a rental home, utility deposits, and we now had a payment on a new car!

We were both very heartbroken about my dad, and didn't know what we should do. However, we knew that our Savior knew all about this heartbreak.

My health was not good in cold weather, which was the reason we had to move to Arizona. We never would have left our whole life back in Iowa, had it not been for my health, and the immense pain I was in. When we were living back there, it was so sad watching Doug struggling ~ trying to take care of me, (and all of our other responsibilities,) and maintain his job running his boy's home!

We knew we had to pray to our dear Jesus about going back and seeing my Daddy. God had always answered our prayers, and had carried us this far in life. (Doug and I prayed and put this burden all in our God's ~ Big Loving Hands.)

We asked Him for 'His will;' to 'provide a way' for us to go back, and to please, 'tell us' when my Daddy was going to leave us; to 'time it all out,' and to let Doug "get time off" from his new job!

163

(We were about to experience our God's loving care over us, and His very real presence in our lives; ~ as we watched our every prayer being answered, . . . step by step!)

My sweet aunt ~ (my Daddy's sister) lived here in Arizona, and we had re-united with her, and her only son, when we moved here.

(I hadn't seen her son for over 20 years.)

Shortly after we prayed, her son called me. He said his mother had told him that my dad's health was worsening; he asked if we were going back?

I was honest and told him, "We'd love to ~ but we don't have the money, and we don't know if Doug can get the time off from his new job. My health is also a big concern; going back into that freezing weather."

I knew that he had been unable to spend time with his own dad before he passed away. He retold the story about his dad and said, "If it's the money, and you can work everything else out ~ you've got the money! I'll give it to you, because I know how close you and your dad are."

I said, "I don't know how we'd pay you back ~ right now."

He said, "I told you I'd 'give' it to you, and you don't have to pay it back. Think about it, I'll be here, just call me back at this number."

Since we had only recently reunited ~ I felt very humbled that he made us such a loving offer. I was very emotional and taken back.

When I got off the phone, and told Doug my cousins generous offer ~ he had tears in his eyes, and we knew we needed to consider it. That was the 'first' miracle.

The 'second' miracle? ~ We had also prayed for God to show us when my Daddy was going to leave us, so it would all be timed out, and we could be there for him.

Soon after we prayed, . . my Mama called and said, "I don't know if this is a 'sign,' but things have changed." She told me some things that he was saying and doing differently, (she told me, "He just keeps looking up,") and she thought we would want to know. I knew she wanted us to pray for them, but I also knew, that 'God' was telling us ~ "This is the time." (Doug and I kept praying.)

The 'third' miracle? Doug asked his boss for the time off, and even though he'd only been working for the boy's ranch for a few months, he told him, "You can take a week off, with pay!"

~ We then decided, we should call about plane reservations. We knew God was moving in our lives, to work everything out for us to go back and be with my sweet Daddy.

These were all the signs we had prayed for, and our dear Savior was clearly speaking, 'His will,' to us.

We called my dear cousin and told him we would accept his generous offer, but only under one condition; we would pay him back.

He said again, "I don't care if you pay me back, I just want you to go back and be with your dad, because it still bothers me, that I couldn't be with mine." (I felt so bad for him.)

So, we accepted his offer, and later God blessed us to be able to pay him back in just a short time!

After we bought our plane tickets, and made all of our plans, we anxiously called to tell our folks we were coming back. We were all relieved, and felt that we were doing exactly what we should! We knew that we were completely in the Mighty Hands of our God, and His Will for our lives. It is so important to pray, and put everything in God's Hands, so that 'He' can help us, and work out 'His Will' in our lives.

We flew home, and when we saw my Daddy, we knew he was 'not long for this world.' Time was of the essence. We just wanted to stay near him, and not leave his side. (That's what he wanted too.)

He was in a hospital bed that Hospice had moved into their living room. We sat by his side and held his hands ~ I loved him more than words could say! We fed him little bites of food, as he was too weak to get a spoon to his mouth!

I remember sitting on his bed, and holding him like a child in my arms, and telling him we loved him more than he'd ever know; and that when it was time for him to go be with our Lord Jesus ~ we knew he would be well, and whole. ~ I told him it was 'okay,' for him ~ to leave us ~ and we knew he'd be with our dear Savior. He then seemed to be staring right into Heaven. ~ He seemed 'far away' in his eyes. I kept telling him sweetly ~ that we all loved him.

I was heartbroken he couldn't return my hugs now, or tell me he loved me; ~ but his love for me and for Doug was always evident, and in full color ~ when he was well. Every minute spent with him always seemed like the 'happiest' I could ever feel! I was content just to be with him ~ he was my 'Sunshine!'

Every minute that went by, the loving memories of what a sweet Daddy he was, opened up like a book in my mind. I re-read every chapter ~ as I sat beside him now, . . remembering. . .

He loved life; and he loved everyone! He hated arguing, and he believed in 'forgiveness.'

When we were growing up, he bought us baby chicks and ducks at Easter time ~ 'every' Easter! He would always taste a piece of candy out of each of our Easter Baskets.

Christmas was always so beautiful, and the presents were exactly what we wanted. He would have tears in his eyes, as our faces broke into joy and happiness as we opened our gifts!

~ Whether we ate soup, steak, or a bowl of ice cream with him, 'whatever we did,' we enjoyed every minute with him!

We all had wonderful family reunions, (and we would all have watermelon, or homemade ice cream, with fresh picked raspberries and strawberries.)

We all worked in his big gardens with him.

The pages of my memory book kept right on turning.

Each day, as we sat by his bed, each hour ~ was bitter sweet. We didn't feel the same. We felt too sad to eat. We felt sick! Many hours were spent, just remembering what a huge gift he was to our hearts, our lives, and to our family, and our friends. The days spent with him now ~ were going so fast, (too fast.) As my Mama said ~ 'things were different, and things about him, . . were changing.'

It was winter ~ and it brought back fun and exciting memories of him stringing up Christmas lights, and all of us shoveling the snow drifts out of our long driveways.

~ Now in this cold winter of our lives, the seasons of our best dreams together were freezing into memories ~ that we are hanging onto . . . even now.

As Daddy showed strong signs of leaving us, he wasn't getting up at all. I remember the air was so still! My Mama got frightened and said, "If he doesn't perk up, I may have to put him in a nursing home, I can't do all this by myself."

Nothing struck more fear into our hearts, than that statement! We couldn't even imagine getting on a plane and flying back to Arizona, knowing he was in a 'nursing home;' helpless ~ and maybe not being treated with love or respect! It was killing our hearts, (and our dear Lord knew it!)

We called the boys ranch and asked for more time. We told them that he was "bad," and close to death. They said "three more days" ~ but that was all ~ (ten days altogether.) ~ Our God, of course, . . knew this as well.

I asked Doug to come into the other room and pray with me! It was quiet, and more private. So, we went in and knelt down, and we cried out to our Great and Merciful God, knowing that He knew the heartache, and the crushed dreams of our hearts.

As much as we hated praying the words ~ we told our Precious Savior ~ "Dear Lord, You are Ruler over all the earth, and over our souls. We know that my Daddy is dying of cancer and we put him, right now into Your big loving hands, and we ask You, to please 'take him home' to Your Kingdom. We pray that he won't have to go to a nursing home; and we won't have to fly back ~ not knowing what's happening to him!! Lord, we ask You to time this all out, and take Daddy 'Home' before we have to go back to Arizona! Father, give us all, Your strength from Heaven, to make it through this, the worst sorrow of our hearts! Please dear God, take him home with You. We now commit him into Your loving care. In Your Holy Name we pray, Amen."

We knew that God heard us, and we believed He would answer our cries and our heart's desires! We walked into the living room and sat beside Daddy, and waited on our Great God. We believed that He had this all worked out ~ and in His perfect timing, we would see His power.

That prayer later gave Doug and I, and my dear Mama, (and all who heard the story,) the peace to 'know,' that Daddy was with Jesus, and the strength to carry us through the years ahead. It also gave us greater faith, to always believe in the 'miracles' of our Lord Jesus Christ!

Yes, our dear Savior heard, and answered our prayers! ~ the Bible says ~ "He is close to the broken hearted," and also, Jesus was "a Man of sorrows, and acquainted with grief," and yes, the shortest verse in the Bible; "Jesus wept." I believe Jesus was weeping with us too ~ as He began to answer our desperate prayer.

~ My Daddy was just 'skin and bones,' and he had a huge bedsore on his tail bone area. Daddy had not been able to talk, (he was too weak to even bring a spoon up to his mouth,) but all at once ~ he sat straight up so fast, with his arm raised up in the air, and he hollered so loud it startled all of us! My Mama was in the kitchen ~ and Daddy shouted, "Are you ready? I'm leavin' ya!!"

My Mama said in shock, "Where ya goin'?"

He said, "I'm goin' to Heaven, . . are you ready?! Are you goin' with me?" We were all shocked, but this was such a 'Holy' moment; the room was suddenly 'filled' with the Presence of God! . . Daddy's eyes were huge, and they shown with the complete 'Truth,' that 'what he was seeing' ~ was 'Real!' He wanted us all to go with him!

He then said, with an excited tone, "Call everyone and get 'em all here, and tell 'em to get here quick! I'm leavin' ya!"

Mama immediately got on the phone. She said she'd call his sisters ~ she called a few friends ~ and our brother-in-law, Rod, who said he was driving in from Texas!

Daddy then said, "I want two prayers. I want one now, and I want one later, and I want to hear the song "Amazing Grace!" I want Doug and Rod to sing it for me!"

Doug, and Mama, and I prayed with him, asking our dear Savior to give him, (and all of us,) His strength and peace, and let us know that He was with us all. We felt a very real Presence with us, that we knew was our Great God's Holy Spirit, and His perfect Peace.

While Daddy's sisters hurried over to see him ~ others started showing up.

Daddy had been so weak he couldn't even bring a spoon to his mouth, yet now, he sat in the middle of his bed, with no pillows behind his back or any support!

He still had that huge bed sore, but he sat up with his hands folded together around one of his knees!

(He sat like that for hours, and visited, and carried on a normal conversation with everyone, as if he'd never been sick!!)

That in itself, was something that still remains a beautiful (and awesome) memory in our hearts! Our Savior gave us so many signs that He was with Daddy, and all of us, (just like Doug and I prayed.)

More people started showing up, and they kept coming, and kept coming! Our brother-in-law was driving in from Texas in bad, snowy weather. We were all concerned that he would drive too fast to get there! He finally arrived safely.

I put in a call to our pastor from our inner-city church, and asked him to come when he could. He said, "I'll be there!" (That was just like our dear Pastor Alex) ~ he would go wherever God called him. If there was a need ~ he was there! Praise God for this dear pastor, and man of God! What would we all do without dedicated pastors and Christians?

The next day ~ after very little sleep, we sat in the living room chairs, wondering, waiting, for what Daddy would say, or what he saw! We knew he was leaving us, and we were praying, and believing God for His 'perfect timing.'

More friends and neighbors arrived, and came in to see Daddy. He spoke to each of them, but then started laying down, and talking less.

The room was filled with many friends from over the years, and the Hospice nurse was there also. ~ The room couldn't hold anyone else, (except for one very important man of God) ~ 'Pastor Alex!'

He came in and saw us all there ~ the room was full. There was a 'movie-like' atmosphere in the room that was felt by all who were present.

(Daddy was a humble man, who loved, and 'paid attention,' to everyone he knew, and here we were; he had 'all our attention now!')

There were tough construction workers and painters that Daddy had worked with for years in his painting business, there were loving neighbors, a 7' tall biker who was a family friend, and many others who would never enter a church!

Pastor Alex quietly said to me, "Sister Charlie, I see a real opportunity here for the Lord ~ do you mind if I take it?"

I said, "You go right ahead Pastor. I know God will speak through you, and many of these people have never been to a church!"

Let me tell you ~ when Pastor Alex spoke, you could hear a pin drop! We all needed a Word of Love, and Hope, and Encouragement from God! We can only tell you ~ that room filled with God's Perfect Peace. The Holy Spirit was so powerfully present ~ that when Pastor Alex finished his little sermon and beautiful prayer ~ we looked up, and (all) of us were crying, there wasn't one dry eye in that room!! I remember the Hospice nurse weeping at Daddy's bedside.

Pastor Alex went over to Daddy's side, and took his hand; he asked him, "How are you doing?" Daddy said, "I'm fine!" Those were the last words we ever heard from him!

~ Pastor Alex then had that 'last prayer' Daddy said he wanted. (He'd said, he wanted Doug to pray one now ~ and he wanted one later.)

Slowly, as Daddy was sleeping now, everyone began to file out.

One by one, they paid their respects. They all knew that God's Spirit had visited that day, and no one could deny it!!

We all had such a glorious little 'church service,' orchestrated by God Himself (and Daddy,) and we were just resting in "His Peace."

It was a matter of time now ~ everyone was gone ~ and we needed to hold on tightly to God's Peace in our hearts! The only ones left in the room were Daddy, Mama, Doug and I, and Dad's best friend that had worked with him for years. My Daddy began to lift his arms to Heaven. He was taking long, deep breaths, and we knew these were the last moments of my sweet Daddy's life here on earth!

What happened next ~ none of us were ready for ~ spiritually physically, or emotionally!

Suddenly, my dad's best friend started frantically yelling at my dear Daddy, telling him to "Breathe!" ~ that 'He could make it!' ~ "Breathe!!" He started shouting hysterically, "Come on, you can make it!" At this point my Mama tried to calm his friend down and said, "No, now, he told us he was leaving us." I went up to Daddy's friend and put my arm around his shoulder.

All of a sudden, he leaned forward, and began to physically 'beat' on my poor Daddy's chest! I looked at Mom and her eyes were huge! None of us could believe this was even happening!

I threw my arms around his friend's waist!! ~ I kept hanging on tight to his waist, struggling; I turned to look at Doug ~ like "Help me!" Doug was in shock too! These were my Daddy's last moments! ~ He was taking his last breaths!

So, Doug jumped up ~ but he only had room enough to grab ahold of my waist! He pulled and pulled, but we could 'not' pull this man away! He kept beating on my poor Daddy's chest, yelling ~ "Breathe! C'mon! You can make it ~ just take one more breath, . for me!"

At this point we were all so weak ~ and sad; we had no strength left, to get his friend to stop! As Daddy took his last breath, this man laid on his chest weeping, and talking to him, telling him, "I don't know what I'll do without you!"

The room had quickly changed from God's peace, to the complete hopelessness of a man who loved my dad with all his heart, but had no faith or hope to believe in Jesus, eternal life, or anything beyond this world! We just saw a poor man, who felt his life, his fun, and his joy had ended! We could identify with him on that ~ but we were still upset and angry for many years, that my sweet Daddy suffered that horrible treatment in his final moments of life! However, . . over the years, we have softened on that horrible experience. (Although we'll never forget it, we have forgiven this poor man!) We believe that God was showing us the hopelessness of all who are 'lost' and without Jesus Christ, our Savior.

Through that terrible experience, God has helped us to want to be more faithful in witnessing to the unsaved, and to help them to find His Peace. To faithfully tell them that Jesus loves them, and wants to give them His 'forgiveness, and eternal life!' (Jesus endured the pain of the cross ~ for all of us!)

After we had finally calmed Daddy's friend, we called the funeral home and while we were waiting ~ God sent my two sweet cousins over. (He knew we needed a hug.) We were so glad to see them. They said they were so sorry they were late ~ I told them, "No, you're right on time!" (We wouldn't have wanted them to go through what we had just endured; and we got through it only by the Grace and strength of God.)

Going through this, really brought my Mama, and Doug and I closer together. I don't think she could have handled that alone!

Two days later, we went to the funeral home and shared memories of Daddy with everyone at the "Visitation."

The next day, still numb after going through everything we had, we attended Daddy's funeral service. The church was packed!

Doug and Rod sang "Amazing Grace," as Daddy had requested on that last night and Pastor Alex sang his moving rendition of "Precious Lord." ~ The entire service was beautiful! Everyone remarked on the "beautiful songs!"

Our plane reservations could not be changed, and Doug had to be back for his job. Yet even then, we were talked down for not being able to take the time to stand around the grave and watch them lower Daddy's coffin into the cold ground.

People didn't realize ~ the physical pain I was going through in that freezing weather with my muscle disease! (And some didn't seem to care!)

They also didn't know the pain and suffering we had gone through watching my poor Daddy getting 'beat on' in the final moments of his life! Then we had to just leave my Mama and everyone behind, fly back home, and try to get through this traumatic loss ~ with no one around to comfort us. Why do people judge others so harshly? Word always gets back, and causes wounds that can hurt and sting for years. I often wonder how they sleep at night?

God help us all ~ to be more kind and loving toward others.

When we finally got back to the ranch; seeing the boy's smiles, and even seeing the little lambs they were raising ~ and sitting with them all in the big dining hall ~ still, it seemed like the fun of life had been stripped from our hearts. It was all a chore to cope; even smiling was a chore ~ after all we'd been through! We felt like we were working in quicksand ~ sinking, . . . as we went through the motions!

Doug and I were offered a promotion to "House Parents," and the administration offered us the best house on the ranch. However, I had no desire, and had to tell them, "No thank you." There were very dark days ahead for both Doug and I.

I remember being on my way to the grocery store one day and I had stopped at a red light. I happened to look over and saw a man on the corner with his hand on his hip, waiting for the crosswalk light to change. ~ He looked exactly like my sweet Daddy standing there! I broke out sobbing so hard, I turned and went back home, just hoping I'd get there, without getting into a wreck! No one knows what we went through. We know the family back home had their pain and changes too; but they still had each other. ~ They still had family reunions, they had lots of gatherings and lots of hugs, and the joy of all the little grandchildren. We had no 'family' here but Jesus, and our best friend, Kathy.

Jesus has been our 'everything, He has strengthened us, given us greater faith, and a ministry here that has proven His Faithfulness over and over. He had a special plan for our lives that we knew nothing about. We have 'grown up' in the Lord, and know and love Him so much more now!

Kathy was here, faithfully encouraging us, and supporting us with Christian love. She was our 'Angel' (that came to know the Lord back in Iowa.) God had moved her and her family out here at the same time we had moved, and she has been such a blessing to us!

~ My dear Mama eventually flew out to Arizona and visited us. Then later, Pastor Alex drove out with his dear wife and they stayed with us, which cheered us up as well. ~ God was strengthening us. Praise God for these dear Christians encouraging us, praying for us, and showing us the love of Christ, . . so we could heal spiritually, and emotionally.

Later, I was able to talk to my Daddy's best friend (the one who had been so distraught as my Daddy was dying,) and he told me, "I believe in Jesus now!" We were so very thankful for that!

Also, his oldest son surprised us, and called us in Arizona, and he wanted to know about Jesus! I was privileged to lead him to the Lord over the phone!

We have no idea what God is doing for His Kingdom! We have to realize that the Holy Spirit is always doing 'His work' of saving souls.

When we think back on how we prayed in faith, and asked God to 'provide a way,' and out of the blue, my cousin called offering to pay our way back. ~ We asked God to 'show us' when the time was right, and then my Mama called and told us "things were changing."

~ Then Doug's job gave him 'time off with pay,' and God in His mercy gave us quality time ~ to talk to my Daddy and Mama both. . . There were no doubts, . . we knew it was 'our God!'

We are 'still' in awe!

And finally ~ when we got down on our knees, and prayed, and asked the good Lord to come and take Daddy to Heaven ~ that very day, Daddy called out, and told us he was leaving us!

He then ended up orchestrating his own final little church service, asking for all his friends and family to come over; so God could use our dear Pastor Alex to comfort us all with God's Word, and witness God's love ~ to so many in that room!

We were there with Daddy, when he 'went home' with Jesus, and we were there when Mama needed us most!

Now ~ for all of that to be so perfectly planned out; . . all that happened could not be . . . a 'coincidence,' (for all who like to claim that kind of thing.)

Dear people, God is Real! ~ Our Lord and Savior answers prayers ~ and He is a loving, and very personal God!

He answered our every prayer! All praise to our dear Savior Jesus Christ! We Love Him so much!!

"Casting all your care upon Him; for He careth for you." (I Peter 5:7)

"Precious in the sight of the LORD is the death of His saints." (Psalm 116:15)

"God is our refuge and strength, a very present help in trouble." (Psalm 46:1)

33. HE UNDERSTANDS

Sometimes, when we are praying for someone and we want them healed so desperately, we just can't understand why God allows them to keep suffering. I've thought about this, many times over the years.

We do know this . . . God allowed His own Son, Jesus Christ, to suffer ~ and He tells us why. It was to offer eternal life to all the world, and to rescue us from our sins, and damnation!!

Yes, God has revealed to us the reasons for Christ's suffering, but we also know ~ (as God says through Moses,) "The 'secret things' belong to our God, but the things that are 'revealed' belong to us and to our children." (Deuteronomy 29:29). ~ When we are in the dark; when our mighty God cloaks His thoughts from us; we must have faith, (and trust in His great love for us.)

God is Almighty! ~ The terrible pain Jesus endured on the cross, was not just 'pain,' it was God's 'Divine Plan;' the 'Mission' of our dear Savior, to save us from our sins. Sins that were taking us to an eternal hell! Jesus knew the eternal consequences of those sins and He remedied that!

~ He took those consequences upon Himself ~ at the Cross.

When He died, He descended into hell, and rose victoriously on the third day! ~ And now, His "Salvation" is available to all who will accept the remedy ~ which is "Jesus Christ" Himself! He alone is 'our sacrifice;' and it is only "His blood," ~ that can cover and forgive our sins. Then, by accepting Christ, we can be "born again" ~ into God's eternal family!

Let me say this concerning suffering; this is something that our human minds cannot comprehend. These are the 'things of God!' God is constantly using these 'secret things' ~ to work out His plan of Salvation in our lives, in our family's lives, and in the lives of others.

We cannot see beyond their sufferings, and we cannot see beyond our own sufferings; but this is where we must talk to Jesus, and trust in Jesus! We can tell Him our true feelings! "He understands!!"

And He will comfort us through His Holy Spirit. "God is a Spirit: and they that worship Him, must worship Him in spirit and in truth." (John 4:24)

We have to realize that our sufferings will enable us to 'comfort others' who are suffering, as Paul wrote "that we may be able to comfort them which are in any trouble, by the comfort wherewith we ourselves are comforted of God." (II Corinthians 1:3,4)

We must lovingly pass on to others, the same comfort we receive from God. If we didn't, it wouldn't be right.

The Apostle James also tells us, "Knowing this, that the trying of your faith worketh patience. But let patience have her perfect work, that ye may be perfect and entire, wanting nothing." (James 1:3,4) Patience helps us to be satisfied and resolved, . . and resting in God's will.

We need to understand ~ that our God 'reveals' *some* things, but many times, . . in His wisdom ~ He also 'conceals' the reasons for our sufferings. We must remember that God has a plan; He has a mission; and some day He will reveal to all of us, what His plan was all about!

We all need to see, "that the sufferings of this present time are not worthy to be compared with the glory which shall be revealed in us." (Romans 8:18)

Let's look forward to that 'glory,' which Christ will reveal in 'us!'

For now, we must trust in our Mighty God ~ the Lord Who made Heaven and Earth, and everything in it!!

Pray for faith, and trust in our God ~ Who not only 'sees' into eternity, . . (Dear people ~ He's already there!) He knows everything from beginning to end!

Rest in His enduring Love, . . (the Love that Jesus proved to all of the world,) as He hung on the Cross for you and for me ~ Because, . . "He Understands."

"Draw nigh to God, and He will draw nigh to you." (James 4:8)

"I Am Alpha and Omega, the beginning and the end, the first and the last." (Revelation 22:13)

"These things I have spoken unto you, that in Me ye might have peace. In the world ye shall have tribulation: but be of good cheer; I have overcome the world." (John 16:33)

"Looking unto Jesus the author and finisher of our faith; who for the joy that was set before Him endured the cross, despising the shame, and is set down at the right hand of the throne of God." (Hebrews 12:2)

"Peace I leave with you, My Peace I give unto you: not as the world giveth, give I unto you. Let not your heart be troubled, neither let it be afraid." (John 14:27)

"Who is among you that feareth the LORD, that obeyeth the voice of his servant, that walketh in darkness, and hath no light? let him trust in the name of the LORD, and stay upon his God." (Isaiah 50:10)

34. HOME AWAY FROM HOME

When I think about the 'angels' that God sent to me in my early childhood years, I think of my little friend in kindergarten, her name was "Toni." She was everything to me!

She had long black hair, that she wore in a thick braid.

I loved brushing and braiding her hair. She cheered me up just by smiling at me; as she did all who knew her.

Her family was wonderful to me, and always considered me as "one of their girls." Toni's family was everything I needed. They had a stable lifestyle. To me, they were like a family show on television ~ like "Father Knows Best," or "Leave It to Beaver."

Every night, dinner was right on time, and we all helped wash and dry the dishes afterward. ~ Toni, and her dear mom and sister, all had wonderful voices, and sang together beautifully!

They would always harmonize together as we did the dishes. That was my favorite time every evening with them!

I stayed with their dear family so much ~ it was my 'home away from home.' Toni stayed with us, when I wasn't staying with her.

Later on, in her teen years, we all loved it ~ when she'd bring her guitar and sing for us. (She sings so beautifully!)

She also played piano, and wrote beautiful original music.

We loved music at our house ~ and we all loved Toni!

We appreciated her talent, and the love she brought to our family.

I truly believe ~ if she hadn't been my best friend, I wouldn't have lived very long. I can say ~ that Toni and her family were a beacon of hope to me. God knew exactly what I needed, and her family always accepted me unconditionally.

At Christmas time ~ Toni and I, (and her dad,) always had fun making the Norwegian cookies, (Kringle,) that we grew up enjoying. I was amazed at how perfectly they made them!

(Our Kringle's looked nothing like theirs!)

Toni and I enjoyed the times we spent together picking her dad's huge, beautiful red raspberries, that grew every year. Many time's ~ we ate more than we brought into the house!

We would often walk to the "Dairy Queen" for ice cream, and we enjoyed our lazy walk back home eating our cones. Sometimes, we would pitch a 'pup tent' in her back yard ~ and would stay up late telling stories, and sharing our feelings, (and secrets.)

I would do gymnastics in their yard as they all lovingly watched and encouraged me. The time we spent together was "gold" to me.

We played in her folk's basement ~ pretending we were grown up and had our own apartment, as the basement had a big old porcelain sink and counter, and also a full-size couch.

I got to travel to small towns in Iowa with them to visit Toni's dear grandparents ~ who were always so kind, and always welcomed us with open arms.

One summer, I was even included in their family vacation to the Ozarks, and we had so much fun with all the people there! We rode in boats, and met new friends, and yes, I even entertained them all doing gymnastics!

On Sundays ~ Toni would walk all by herself to a neighborhood church. Her parents didn't attend, but Toni always wore a beautiful dress, and I'd borrow an outfit, (and would wear her sister's shoes,) and we'd walk to church together. ~ We would enjoy the singing, and the sermon, and our peaceful walk back home.

Toni's home was always peaceful, always steady, with a simple routine each day. That was appealing to me, . . something I looked forward to.

We went to the movies, and went swimming together, and often walked to the Mall, to get a famous 'Younkers Frosty Malt,' 'Rarebit Burger,'~ and fries! Her mother worked for Sears and we always enjoyed going in to see her. Toni's dad worked for the post office and he was such a sweetie! He always had a big smile for us when he got home. We loved helping him in his garden and eating his homegrown tomatoes and veggies!

Toni's dear sister shared a bedroom with us, and we kept her up many nights ~ laughing and acting like "younger sisters" will! She was very patient with us, and I'm sure we helped develop her virtue of patience, for the beautiful children she eventually raised!

Toni and I grew up together, and went to school together, on through our high school years. She and her family saw me through so much. God knows, (and everyone knew) that she and I were truly "best friends."

We both married our 'first loves' and moved to different states, but we always stayed in touch. We both flew home to Iowa when both our sweet Daddy's had cancer. We took cabs from one hospital to the other to visit them. That was a very sad, but a very precious time we spent with our dads, (and with each other.)

We may never know how much God is doing through our lives, to influence someone's life for the better, to feel His love, and to make them feel 'accepted.'

I would challenge all who read this story to open your door to your children's friends, and let them be part of your family. ~ Make cookies together, . . and make time to include them in your family fun. You could be a light in their lives. Be steady ~ and show God's unconditional love to them. I know it helped me through some very rough times. God was showing me, that He was with me, (and I knew it!) Our God has a plan for each of our lives!

His "divine appointment" ~ was for this dear family to be a "home away from home," for a little girl named 'Charlie,' that needed His 'steady hand' upon her life.

And I know, that for now, our 'Christian family' here on earth ~ is our 'home away from home,' until we reach those golden shores of our eternal home in Heaven!

"Beloved, let us love one another: for love is of God; and every one that loveth is born of God; for God is love." (I John 4:7)

"Honor thy father and thy mother: and ~ Thou shalt love thy neighbor as thyself." (Matthew 19:19)

"My little children, let us not love in word, neither in tongue; but in deed and truth." (I John 3:18)

35. GOD KNOWS THE DESIRES OF OUR HEARTS

When we worked at the boy's ranch, there were nine homes on a huge acreage in the middle of the Arizona desert, with over a hundred boys housed there.

We had work crews, school, chapel and choir, group therapy, sports, and the kids were even able to raise and take care of the farm animals. We had older married couples as house parents that ran each home.

At Christmas time, we always made sure and decorated a tree, and made each home 'festive.' Every boy received a very nice gift, and a big Christmas stocking full of candy, salted peanuts in the shell, an apple, and an orange.

I had all of my shopping done for our home and each package was wrapped with nice Christmas wrap, ribbons, name tags, and (more importantly,) "Love." The gifts were all placed around the beautifully decorated tree, and the boys were anticipating what they were going to receive! Excitement and lots of love filled the air!

Surprisingly, on this Christmas Eve, we received a new resident, a young man who came in late in the evening. He seemed very nice, and he was a little more mature than some of the boys in our home. He was quiet, and had very good manners, and we thought he would fit in well.

We introduced him to all the boys, and after showing him his room, we told him to make himself at home. The boys seemed glad he was there, it added excitement to the 'Holiday Spirit.'

This young man came out into the big family room, where the Christmas lights were flickering, and the tinsel was shining amongst the lights and ornaments on our tree. As he was looking around the room in wonder, my heart skipped a beat; I suddenly realized that he had no present under the tree! We never, ever, liked slighting a child and making them feel left out (and especially at Christmas time!)

I brought Doug into the other room and we talked it over. I told him we needed a gift for this young man. He said, "It's too late to get a gift now."

"It's Christmas Eve and everything's closed this time of night!"

I was determined to find this boy a gift!

Doug and I prayed that God would help me find a gift for him . . one that he liked and wanted, and we asked God to watch over me as I traveled out.

I left the ranch, and drove down a very dark highway, until I came to some lights. We had only recently moved to Arizona and were new to the area ourselves. I was very happy to see a convenience store open, and I quickly pulled in.

The man on duty looked surprised to see anyone come through the doors on Christmas Eve. He politely asked me if he could help me. As I approached the counter, I smiled nervously and told him, "I'm on a mission."

I smiled, and told him our dilemma; about the late arrival of a young man at the boy's ranch. I told him I had no idea what I might find for him there ~ but, "I really need a gift tonight!"

The man was very nice and empathetic, and he helped me look through the few gifts they still had left on the shelves. I kept praying silently, "Lord, I need something this young man will like. Please help me with this. Thank You! In Jesus Name ~ Amen!"

This young man would not be happy with a toy, as some of our younger boys would. I didn't want to end up just giving him money in a Christmas card, when the other boys would be excitedly unwrapping their presents! So, I continued to search, and shop a little.

All of a sudden, I found a big glass case and looked inside. I saw a very nice wristwatch that was for an older teenager. It was really cool! It was very contemporary ~ (but it was also very expensive looking!) I knew I had to get this watch for the young man.

I looked at the nice man on duty and asked him, "How much is this watch?"

He looked at me and smiled. ~ He said, "How's ten dollars?"

(I couldn't believe it was only ten dollars!)

He smiled again and said, "It's the only one left. It's Christmas. If you like it, it's ten dollars even!" I knew he was giving me a deal, (and so was God!)

I told him, "Yes, I think he'll love it!"

He said, "It comes with a nice case as well."

He reached under the counter, brought out the case, and put the watch in it for me. I paid him and thanked him. He was smiling right along with me. He said, "I sure hope he has a Merry Christmas!"

I wished him a very "Merry Christmas," and we both parted with big smiles, and 'Christmas' in our hearts!

I left there so excited and happy ~ I tried not to speed home!

I kept thanking Jesus ~ for answering our prayers and letting me find such a nice gift!

When I arrived back to the ranch, I snuck in with the watch in my purse. I asked Doug to come into the office, and I was so excited to show him what God had let me find! His eyes looked so surprised, and happy, and he asked, "What did that cost?" I told him, "Only ten dollars!" He couldn't believe it! He thought it was a great watch!

On Christmas Eve, and so late at night, Doug and I both knew God had answered our prayers! I hurried and wrapped it up, curled the ribbon on top and placed the boy's name on a Christmas gift tag. I looked out and the family room was empty, the boys had all turned in and gone on to bed. I joyfully placed the gift under the tree, and filled another Christmas stocking with candy, salted peanuts, an apple and an orange, and excitedly hung it up on the fireplace with all the others.

I was remembering back . . . on all the many Christmas presents we were blessed with at home growing up. All the cookies, candy, popcorn; the Christmas songs, . . and the fun we had as a family.

We were 'their' family this year, and we're not sure they realized it, but 'they were our family, too!' We were responsible for showing all these boys God's love, and helping them ~ to get through a very rough time in their lives. . . Doug and I were missing our families, but we were all one big family there, and God had fatefully brought us all together in this 'season' of our lives; to all be encouraged and share in His Love. I'm sure, that some of the boys laid in their beds that night remembering, and missing the Christmas holidays they had spent with their families too.

Some were probably too excited to even sleep! ~ Some, I'm sure, were sad they'd be without their families this Christmas, (as we were also,) but we were trusting God to get us all through.

We went on to bed, looking forward to all of us being together on Christmas Day; opening gifts, sharing, and having a family prayer over a beautiful Christmas dinner together.

That morning, after the boys got their showers and dressed for the day, we all met out in the big family room next to the Christmas tree. Christmas carols were softly playing on the stereo. Each boy waited eagerly to open their gifts. We were all excited, and filled with God's love and joy; and we 'all' felt 'God's presence.'

The exciting moment came when we began to hand out the gifts; one by one, . . each boy waiting for the others to receive their gift. Finally, I waited, and the last gift I handed out, was for the new boy!

His eyes were so wide, and excited! He said, "I wasn't expecting a gift! I don't know who got me one?!" (I smiled, and my thoughts of how God worked it all out, were racing over my mind with great joy!)

After everyone had their gifts, we all opened them together, and so much excitement filled the room! ~ (We kept our eyes on the new boy.) As he opened his present . . . His face broke into a big smile, he looked so humbled, "How'd you know? How'd you know I wanted and needed a watch!?"

I looked at him, and pointed up, and said, "We didn't, but God knew!" He smiled at us and was so thankful, as he was looking his new watch over, and trying it on!

Each boy was happy with their gift and Christmas stocking, some were eating their candy and peeling their oranges.

God's joy was written all over their faces!!

This was a very special 'Merry Christmas' ~ for all of us, in our displaced situations. God was so good to all of us!! We felt the bond of God's Love in our spirits, and had a wonderful Christmas!

The time we spent together, I'm sure, still holds a special place in their hearts, as it 'still does' in ours! God brought us all together for a reason, and He was surely present there that Christmas Day!

~ God 'cares' about all of us, and he especially cared about ~ 'the boy that came in late.' He needed more than just a gift, he needed a 'family.' And he needed to know, that 'God knew' ~ and 'cared personally' ~ about him! We were so thankful to God, for allowing us to be a part of making him feel welcome, and more comfortable in his new home. Hopefully, he also felt more comfortable with our Savior ~ and realized that . . . "God Knows The Desires Of Our Hearts!"

(And may we all hold Christmas in our hearts ~ "all year round!")

"O Lord, Thou hast searched me, and known me. Thou knowest my downsitting and mine uprising ~ Thou understandeth my thought afar off." (Psalms 139:1,2)

"In all thy ways acknowledge Him, and He shall direct thy paths." (Proverbs 3:6)

"If ye then, being evil, know how to give good gifts unto your children, how much more shall your Father which is in heaven give good things to them that ask him?" (Matthew 7:11)

"Delight thyself also in the LORD; and he shall give thee the desires of thine heart." (Psalm 37:4)

36. THE 'WOULD BE' MUGGERS

We hadn't been out here in Arizona even a year and a half. My Daddy had recently passed away, and Doug contracted viral double pneumonia and had never been so sick in his life. (He lost 65lbs, and nearly died!) We had also lost our beloved German Shepherd shortly before that.

~ Right after Doug started feeling better, some really wonderful older Christian friends; "Tony and Sophie," from Iowa, came to visit us. They asked us to a well-known dinner buffet, which was in an old church, that had been converted into a restaurant in Mesa, Arizona.

The old building still had all of the decorative antique woodwork, and the huge beautiful stained-glass windows from the church. It was a very quaint place to meet and visit with friends.

Our older friends were dear Christians, both in their late 70's and they meant so much to us. We just loved them! We went to this dinner despite all the sadness we were going through, (and being physically and emotionally played out.) The part we really dreaded was having to say good bye to our friends when they left!

We had just enjoyed a great meal, and a wonderful time talking of sweet memories.

(Doug was still very, very, weak, and his clothes hung on him like a 'scarecrow!') On our way out to our cars, a young boy about nine years old stepped out from behind some bushes near the parking lot. It was dusk, and he looked me in the eyes and asked, "Do you know where KZZP is?" (It was a "hard rock" radio station.) This was an immediate "red flag" to me. I knew he was "up to no good!"

I said, "You don't want to know where a 'radio station' is, go on now, and leave us alone," but he just continued to stand there looking at us. Our friends, stood close in a circle waiting to pray, and say goodbye to us, but I kept my eyes on that boy!

Then suddenly there was a skinny, wild looking man (an obvious 'meth freak') that had quietly walked right up behind Doug! This man had his hands in his jacket right behind Doug's rib-cage! I had no idea if this guy was going to shoot Doug, or stab him, or kill us all!!

I was seeing the danger that none of the others saw, (and they all said that later.) I was in a dress, so I took my high-heeled shoes off, and held them in my hands, (figuring I was going to have to fight for all three of them, the shape they were in.) I've always been a survivor, and I'll never let anyone hurt my loved ones and friends!

But then ~ God did something, (that to this day,) we can only say was a miracle from God Himself!

All of a sudden, God's Spirit rose up in me! I raised my hands up over my head, and started praying out loud to God, pleading with Him to "have mercy." That prayer was coming out like I was ready to be caught up in the clouds! I felt a presence come over me, and the only way I could explain it was, . . . "God took over!"

I looked over at this meth freak and this young boy and their eyes looked as if they'd seen a ghost! ~ This meth freak just continued to stand right behind Doug, (normally Doug would have turned around to look,) but the man didn't move, and Doug didn't move. It was as if 'time stopped,' in that moment! Doug wasn't even aware of what was going on right behind him! Which was very unlike Doug!

My eyes were looking straight through this meth freak! He said to me, (with an evil look,) "What's a matter with you?"

As tough as I could, (and not even knowing what I was going to say or do,) I said, "Nothin' man, just go on ~ and leave us alone!!" This happened about three more times. He kept asking me, "What's a matter with you?" As I stood there with my shoes in my hands (to use as weapons,) I kept answering, "Nothin' man! Just go on and leave us alone!!" I kept crying out to God, (in my spirit,) tears were flowing down my face, and I kept thinking that I was going to fight these two guys, (and win!) I felt a great surge of power, and all of a sudden, the older guy says to the young boy, "C'mon, let's get outta here!"

And they quickly walked away, . . .'backwards!' Yes, backwards! The man started yelling now, "What's a matter with you?". . . and I yelled back, "Nothin' man, just go on, and leave us alone!"

As the two of them kept walking backwards ~ their eyes were 'wide,' staring back at us, . . as if they were seeing something that scared them!

The whole while, they continued walking backwards, and then ~ when a safe distance away from us, they both turned around and 'took off running!!'

I told Doug to get in our car, and start it up, and lock the doors! I hurried our older friends into their car, and told them to lock their doors! I quickly thanked them for dinner, and told them we would talk on the phone after we were all safely home.

When we called them later, they said, "Something came over you, Charlie!" They told me over and over, "Charlie, you saw something we didn't see!"

Well, we knew for sure, that God had given us all a 'miracle,' and had done something 'supernatural' to protect His children!

The next day, I called the restaurant manager and I told him what had happened to us; and that I wanted him to be aware of it. I found out he was already well aware of it! He admitted over the phone, that there had already been robberies, and 'muggings,' in the parking lot! He said, "You were (lucky) you didn't get robbed or worse!"

Then he told me, "There's a cheap, run-down, mobile home park right next door to the restaurant, that's full of drug addicts!!"

Well ~ we certainly don't believe in "luck!" We know that it was only Jesus Christ Who spared us that night!! I just want 'you' to know . . . Jesus is always watching over us!

He sees what these evil people do to His children, and He hates it! He says in Psalms: "He suffered no man to do them wrong: yea, He reproved kings for their sakes; Saying, Touch not mine anointed, and do my prophets no harm." (Psalms 105:14,15)

We need to believe in the Power of God, and thank Him for His all-powerful presence in our lives!

We have 'God's Spirit,' and He says, "I will go before thee, and make the crooked places straight!" (Isaiah 45:2). ~ This is a promise ~ that we've experienced many times!

And to this day, we don't know what those two guys saw, but if they are still in the land of the living, I'm sure they are still talking about it ~ just like we are!

All I know is, God knew all the sorrow we had been through, and He said to that devil, "Enough is enough!!" And we praise God we were spared; . . . all of us!

I am not Pentecostal, but the feeling I had inside of me in that parking lot, felt like something higher than I'd ever experienced in the flesh! It was God, and God all by Himself!

God is watching over us dear friends!! And for all we know, those guys were seeing a band of angels around us!! We won't know until we stand before our good Lord Jesus someday. We just thank Him for being there for us, . . and protecting us all!

God bless us all in these last days dear people! The End Times are upon us, and as Jesus tells us in Matthew Chapter 24 ~ (times will be getting worse and worse, . . right up until He returns!) Let's keep praying, and keep our eyes on Jesus Christ, our wonderful Savior!

"And he answered, Fear not: for they that be with us are more than they that be with them. And Elisha prayed, and said, LORD, I pray thee, open his eyes, that he may see. And the LORD opened the eyes of the young man; and he saw: and, behold, the mountain was full of horses and chariots of fire round about Elisha." (II Kings 6:16,17)

"For the eyes of the Lord are over the righteous, and His ears are open unto their prayers." (I Peter 3:12)

"The angel of the LORD encampeth round about them that fear Him, and delivereth them." (Psalm 34:7)

"Ye that love the LORD, hate evil; He preserveth the souls of His saints; He delivereth them out of the hand of the wicked." (Psalm 97:10)

37. THE WAY FORGIVENESS 'SHOULD GO'

For about two years, we managed a large mobile home park here in Arizona. When we accepted the job, we never imagined how many problems we'd have, or how many 'lost souls' there would be. It was a park for people 55 years and older. Many were in their 70's, 80's, and some in their 90's. It was an experience that God used to teach us a lot of lessons ~ about people. Some good; some bad.

I had just recently lost my Daddy to cancer, and I was very weak emotionally. God's Word says, "When I am weak, then am I strong." (II Corinthians 12:10.) Well, this story will show you that God can use us, even in our greatest weakness, and sorrow.

We were new to the job, and the owners of the park had just raised the rents on all the lots there. They had us mail out notices of the rent increase to each resident. Of course, many of the older people were furious at "the owners" of the park! We understood it was pretty hard for people on fixed incomes to accept.

One by one ~ they came through my door, wanting to 'let me have it!' ~ (I told them I had nothing to do with raising the rents, I was just an employee,) but most of the people didn't care! They just wanted to let somebody 'hear their anger!' Sadly ~ I felt like a tether-ball, or a soccer ball. Every night I went home crying my eyes out; over my Daddy dying ~ Doug almost dying from pneumonia ~ losing our German Shepherd, and now, everyone at my new job was angry with me! ~ I was taking a real emotional beating. I prayed for Gods comfort and help.

I felt like telling some of them off, but I knew I had to stay Christ-like and so I just tried to explain. But most of them didn't want any explanations! And nobody wanted to say "I'm sorry." This was one of the worst jobs I'd ever had! I was so sad and upset! We were now 1800 miles away from our families, and friends, and we were having to start over with our lives. However, we couldn't afford to leave this job! We were both heartsick! (So, we kept praying!)

One day an older man wearing a red baseball cap, (who was mad at the world) entered our office, (I will call him Mr. 'E.')

He yelled at me so hard, his eyes were bulging; the whites of his eyes were red, and he was shaking his hat around in my face, mad about the rent hike! I told him over and over, it wasn't 'us,' and that 'we' didn't raise the rent!

He didn't care!! I silently prayed, "Lord help me."

I heard later in the week, that Mr. E. went to the hospital with a stroke! I felt bad for him, but I also wasn't surprised; after the fit he was throwing in our office! He left my office in a rage!

However, I felt in my spirit we should go visit him in the hospital. When we got there, we found out that the stroke had left him unable to speak! I held his hand, and Doug and I told him we knew the good Lord Jesus as our Savior, and that we believed in miracles. I said, "If you believe that Jesus can heal you, and you want us to pray for you, will you please squeeze my hand?" With tears in his eyes, he nodded his head, and squeezed my hand! I smiled and patted his hand, and Doug stood with me ~ as we prayed for this poor man. His dear wife and daughter, who sat near the wall at the end of his bed, had also bowed their heads in prayer.

We traveled quite far to the hospital, and went twice to see him. While visiting with him the second time, a male nurse came into Mr. E.'s room, and (right in front of us,) started using a 'suction stick' to violently 'jab and stab' our Mr. E. in the mouth, and down inside his throat, as if we weren't even sitting there! Mr. E's wife was horrified, watching along with us, and crying her eyes out!

I yelled at this male nurse and said, "Hey, Hey~ there! That's way too hard!" Mr. E. came up out of his bed and spoke a single word . . . "Ouch!!" This male nurse was like a serial killer!! His eyes were evil, his face was red, and his actions were vicious!

We made sure he left the room, and I tried to comfort Mr. E. and his wife. We assured them we would go directly to the administration of the hospital and report him, and we did just that!

Upon hearing this horrific story, the administrator there was very apologetic; we told her, "We want this man fired!" ~ She assured us that she would let him go! Doug added ~ "This guy may have come up with a horrible new 'torture therapy' to make stroke patients talk! But even though it seems to be 'effective,' it's probably going to get your hospital sued!" She looked at Doug and I with a fearful look. She knew what Doug said was true! Mr. E's daughter and wife later told us, "that mean male nurse never came back!" They thanked us over and over, and hugged us, and were so thankful.

We need to remember that not everyone out there in this world ~ knows the Lord, or is going to treat you with Christian love and dignity (even in the hospital.) There are people filled with demons, and we had all just witnessed such a case!

To end this story (with all the glory to God,) Mr. E. received the miracle we had all prayed for, and he was released from the hospital in just a couple of days! He was completely restored, and was now able to walk and speak perfectly! All Praise to our great God!!

The next time I saw him, he entered my office without the anger, without throwing his red cap around, and he 'apologized' to me! He grabbed my hands, shaking, . . crying uncontrollably, asking, and begging me, to forgive him for the bad way he had treated me. I was never so humbled in my life. Of course, I said over and over ~ "I forgive you Mr. E." He kept asking me, because I believe he couldn't forgive himself. And too, he knew we came to pray with him, in spite of his meanness, and we took control of that mean ~ abusive nurse, (and had him fired from the hospital!)

Mr. E. had truly heard from God, through a total healing.

He admitted that day, God had heard our prayers, and healed him, and he was a different man from that point on! And we saw it!

All we can say is ~ "Praise the name of Jesus!!" What a plan He had, and He accomplished it totally!!

He saved His lost sheep ~ and we know we will see dear "Mr. E." again ~ in heaven someday! Hallelujah!!

Is there someone today you need to forgive? Forgive them from your heart. Jesus wants us to be kind and forgiving. God says ~ Love is the greatest gift. (I Corinthians 13:13)

Is there someone, you need to go to, and ask them to forgive your bad behavior? ~ Pray, and go to that person today ~ and ask them to forgive you.

It really meant everything to me, and made my day!! And it meant everything to Mr. E. too, that I forgave him! Amen!!

Praise to our Lord Jesus, who gave His life to forgive my sins, and the sins of the whole world! Hallelujah!! ~ Jesus wants us to love our enemies, and forgive one another, (so He can forgive us!) This story ~ 'shows us why!' ~ This is, . . .The way forgiveness ~ 'should go.'

"If we confess our sins, He is faithful and just to forgive us our sins, and to cleanse us of all unrighteousness." (I John 1:9)

"For if ye forgive men their trespasses, your Heavenly Father will also forgive you: But if ye forgive not men their trespasses, neither will your Father forgive your trespasses." (Matthew 6:14,15)

"Blessed are they whose iniquities are forgiven, and whose sins are covered." (Romans 4:7)

"And be ye kind one to another, tenderhearted, forgiving one another, even as God for Christ's sake hath forgiven you." (Ephesians 4:32)

38. IF YOU JUST GIVE ME A CHANCE

When we moved to Phoenix, we were both heartsick over having to leave my Daddy, (who had cancer,) back in Iowa. ~ We 'had' to move to Phoenix, because my fibromyalgia had become so severe that my doctors had recommended, "a move to a hot, dry climate." ~ I was in horrible pain, and Doug had to take care of me; helping me dress, and even had to carry me at times!

We walked away from our whole lives back in Iowa; Doug's job running his treatment center for boys, our relatives and friends, our church family, a new house we were buying, and so much more.

Shortly after we got settled in Tempe, Arizona, my Daddy passed away. Our beloved German Shepherd had died shortly before that, and then Doug almost died from viral double pneumonia! He lost 65 pounds in less than a month! He was so weak, he couldn't even hold my hand, or eat! He was so very sick, that I called on our best friend Kathy, and pleaded for her prayers! She was our angel! She prayed so hard for us, and continued to check on us. I frankly told her, "I don't know what we're going to do!"

Doug couldn't work ~ and I felt I needed to be with him 'every minute.' She told us she was praying for God to give us "a miracle!" ~ (He indeed gave us that miracle, and more!)

After we all prayed, Doug slowly began to feel stronger. We could only thank our Lord Jesus for healing Doug, and returning his health! ~ Our doctor, (who was also a friend,) had told us that, "most people with this virus have died!" He even told us, "You may want to get your affairs in order!" We were both worried! (I was in no shape to lose Doug too!)

Soon, our dear loyal friend called and told us about a job her folks were giving up; managing a large mobile home park ~ in Apache Junction, Arizona. The park had mobile homes, apartments, RV sites, and two clubhouses with swimming pools! At the peak season of the year (October through April) there were over a thousand people living there!

They thought Doug and I could do this job together, because they were coming into the "summer season." The business would be much slower as many of the residents would be going back east, or to the Midwest, for the summer. There were only a few residents who lived there year-round, so it wouldn't be that hard for us ~ just starting out.

The job included a new mobile home, free utilities and phone, a truck (with a gas card,) a golf cart, and a decent salary! We could be drawing a monthly check, and Doug would have time to get stronger, and physically 'well' by fall. Kathy's parents even set up an interview for us with the owners of the park!

The day of the interview, we were all praying. Doug still looked so thin, and sickly, I was afraid the owners wouldn't hire us. I asked Doug to wear a suit, so they wouldn't see how emaciated he was, and we prayed for favor. Well, we thank God He heard our prayers and we were hired on the spot!

The owners told us we could hire an assistant manager to help us. That job included a mobile home, utilities, and a weekly salary. There were several people who already lived in the park that wanted the position but Doug and I were praying and asking God for that 'special person.'

Then one day a little lady that weighed about 93lbs, came through our office door and asked if we had any work we could give her. She said she was a "hard worker!" She looked rough, and yet, she seemed like she had some common sense. I asked her name, and she said, "I'm Rose, and I go by 'Rosie'." She gave me a strong handshake, which I was always taught to do ~ when introducing myself. She was dressed in jeans, and she looked like she needed some food! She was very thin!

I asked her to tell me a little bit about herself. Half way through her testimony of what she'd been through, and about her struggle with alcoholism, she looked me straight in the eye, and said, "If you just give me a chance, I'll show you I can do the job!!" She was very, very honest with me, and told me she was living in her car, but she just needed a "break" in her life.

I spoke with her and told her our testimonies. She got tears in her eyes. She said she was going to AA, and she wanted to start working her program again. (Which she did.)

The Lord moved us to hire Rosie for our Assistant Manager. We bought her some groceries, and bought her a few dresses to wear when she was working in the office, and we bought her a Bible.

She helped Doug take the readings on the electric meters for the RV's, and she helped me clean the pools and clubhouses until Doug was strong enough to do that. She helped me with the bookwork and was such a blessing! She worked hard like a man!! And she was a loyal and kind person. You would have thought my dear Daddy had raised her!! We made a good team, and we all got along great! She started going back to her church, and to confession.

Then, about a year and a half later, Doug was offered another job running homes for kids and he decided he needed to take it. Sadly, we had to move back to Phoenix.

It was hard leaving Rosie, and others we had gotten close to.

Unfortunately, we lost touch with Rosie.

We were sorry that we did. We saw her just blossom, and grow to be a very responsible gal! (Praise God!)

About three years later, we were watching the news on television, when Rosie's picture flashed on the screen!

I yelled for Doug, "There's Rosie!"

We learned on the news, she had been working with an agency for disabled young adults in Mesa, Arizona. She had been driving a van with around five or six special needs residents, including twin sisters, . . . and there was a problem in the motor of the van. It caught fire; there was an explosion; and sadly, none of them had been able to get out! They were all killed instantly!!

It was such a tragedy! ~ The news crushed us! We just couldn't get over it!! I told Doug, "You know that if there had been a chance for Rosie to get out, she would have given her life trying to get those young people out of there!" He agreed!

But none of them had that chance!

It was devastating to everyone! There are no words to describe our sadness! We sat there in shock and disbelief!

However, as we thought about this later, we realized the many blessings God had given us all, in spite of this sad and tragic ending.

God was able to use us as the 'avenue' for Rosie to get right with Jesus again ~ who was definitely her Savior.

We gave her a Living Bible, which she read every day.

She returned to church and confession, and also to AA as she had wanted to do. She got her life together through Jesus, and knew she could go on to work a job with confidence.

Rosie knew others believed in her, and she believed in herself once again. (And especially, in Jesus!) She had obtained a great job that she loved! And the kids all loved her!

And although so many lives were tragically lost, we believe God will somehow use even this sorrow for good in His Eternal Plan!

I found out where her funeral was to be held, and I made it a point to attend! Doug had an obligation at work that day, but I went ahead and drove the 50 miles to be there.

The funeral home was packed, and standing room only!! Lots of rough people, some bikers, some cowboys, some common every day mom and pop people, a few women in dresses, and the special needs kids from her job were there too with their parents.

The priest gave a wonderful service. He spoke lovingly about how Rosie had gotten her life together. ~ How she was regularly attending AA, being faithful to her God, and coming back to confession. He said, "I knew Rosie, and even though she struggled at times, she knew that through Christ she could fight, and win." He offered anyone the opportunity to say something ~ if they wanted to 'remember' Rosie.

Suddenly, a tall, handsome young man about seventeen, (who was special needs ~ from her job), . . walked up to the priest, and said so seriously, "I wanna give this to Miss Rosie." (It was one, single long-stemmed red rose.) There was complete silence!!

There was an 8x10 picture of Rosie on the coffin. This young man knelt down, and on bended knee, he talked to Rosie out loud.

He said excitedly, "Rosie, you said I could do it, you said I could bowl over a hundred, . . and I did it! . . I bowled a hundred and 'one!!' I did it Rosie!" ~ Some older lady cried out, "God bless his little heart!!" And let me tell you, there wasn't one dry eye there! I will 'never' forget that day!

We know Rosie is in Heaven, and we know she is there because of the Grace and Forgiveness of Jesus Christ; and because He is a God of a second chance, and a third chance, and more ~ even when we mess up!

Friends, we'd better never underestimate our Saviors love for us, because "Jesus is alive!" He rose from the dead. He cares, and He transforms lives!!

Little Rosie was looking for mercy, and the steadfast love of our Savior, and she was looking for a break! (And she found it!) She was 'ready' to come back to Jesus, . . . and He was there waiting for her. I ask this question, . . . 'are you ready?'

I do know this; Rosie never imagined that she was going to burn up in a van with all those kids that day! So, . . we 'all' need to be "Ready" to meet our Lord and Savior, . . . just like Rosie was!

We were so blessed that God sent little Rosie our way ~ to help us in such a time of need. We really loved her and she was such a big help to us there ~ in Apache Junction, Arizona.

Thank you, dear Lord for being there for us, and also being there for Rosie! And Thank You Dear Savior, for Rosie and all the lives You touched through her ~ (especially ours!!) Amen!!

"Rejoice with me; for I have found my sheep which was lost." (Luke 15:6)

"If we confess our sins, He is faithful and just to forgive us our sins, and to cleanse us from all unrighteousness." (I John 1:9)

"And we know that all things work together for good to them that love God, to them who are the called according to His purpose." (Romans 8:28)

"Therefore be ye also ready: for in such an hour as ye think not the Son of man cometh." (Matthew 24:44)

39. OUR MARY ~ OUR 'BIG BABY DOLL'

If there was ever someone we were destined to meet in our lives ~ it was our "Dear Southern Bell," ~ "Our Mary."

We had just started our new job as mobile home park managers.

During the first week of the summer season, a man came into our office and introduced himself. He told us his name was 'Mack.'

He was a very funny and likeable character, and he immediately started joking with us. ~ He had us laughing the whole time we were together! (Which we really needed!)

He asked Doug if he could build a screened in porch (called an 'Arizona Room,') on his mobile home. He promised it would be very nice and "up to snuff," because he was a builder, and used to build houseboats at Lake Powell. Doug looked at Mack's plan on paper and agreed it looked real nice. Mack was so happy when we ok'd his room addition!

He worked very hard on the project, and had us down to see it when he was finished! We sat in a new 'glider' bench chair ~ and visited in their new Arizona Room, which was just beautiful! We complimented him on it, and he shook our hands and thanked us.

A couple of weeks later, "Our Mary" came into the office and introduced herself as, "Mack's wife." She told us that Mack had been hospitalized with lung cancer! We offered to go see him and she said she'd sure appreciate it. We drove her to see him, and he told us, "I feel sicker than I've ever felt before." He said he didn't know if he'd make it. The doctor's plans were to give him 'chemo.' We talked some, and Doug offered to pray with them both. We all held hands, and Doug had a prayer for Mack and Mary.

Mack had no Christian training, or knowledge of the Bible. He got home, and was taking the chemo, and he told us, "I don't know how long I can keep this up!" He said the chemo made him so depressed!

Mack's brother came to visit from out of state, and unfortunately, encouraged Mack to "take a cyanide capsule!" He said, "that's what I'd do!" His brother was way off base, he had no faith in God at all. He was definitely influencing Mack in the wrong way, and he kept calling him ~ after he returned home.

199

One day, not long after, . . . a helicopter landed in our mobile home park! One of the residents knocked on our door ~ telling us, "Mack shot himself in the head," (in their backyard,) while Mary was away at the laundromat!

The Life Flight took him to the hospital where he was pronounced dead on arrival. We found out Mary had been taken to the hospital by the EMT workers, to identify Mack's body. Doug and I felt we should go to the hospital to be with Mary. We arrived there just as she was walking down the hall alone, distraught, in 'shock,' with tears running down her face! Our hearts went out to her! We hugged her and told her we were both "so very sorry" that this had happened. She thanked us for coming, and she accepted our offer to drive her back home.

Once there, we listened, and sympathized, and tried to show her Christ's love. Before we left, we prayed with Mary.

Then she surprised me when she put both her hands on my face, looked me in the eyes, and said, "Honey, just promise me one thing."

"Anything," I said. ~

She said, "Never leave me alone on Holidays!"

We told her we never would.

(We were all, still in such shock.)

Well, God worked that 'promise' out to all our advantage over the years, and helped Doug and I to keep that promise to "Our Mary."

We found out in the days ahead, then months, and then years, how the promise I made that day to "Our Dear Mary" grew and blossomed, and shined, and multiplied, . . . into Eternity!

We learned that Mary had a son who lived in another state, who she loved very much. However, he had a demanding job, and also a wife who was very ill with a debilitating disease. He very rarely came to see Mary, even after his dad died. He never got along with his dad. This was a family that really needed to know the love of Jesus.

~ God used 'Our Mary' to graciously cook almost every evening meal for us when we got off work. What a blessing she was to us! She loved visits from us, and we loved visiting her, and we loved her cooking! She and Mack used to own a restaurant in Louisiana, and she'd always smile when talking about that; telling how everyone would "stand in line" for her fried chicken!

She was not just an excellent cook ~ she made the table settings, and all her recipes, 'festive.' We always looked forward to Christmas, Thanksgiving, Easter, and all of our birthdays at her little home. She made any time we spent with her, fun, festive, and filled with lots of smiles and laughs.

Mary was from "down south," very prim and proper, and always dressed up in a nice dress, (always with a white lace collar,) with nylons, and heels. She had lots of accessories ~ scarves, jewelry, (and especially her beautiful hats!) She was the perfect Southern Lady and we used to call her, "Our Big Baby Doll!"

We loved her so much, and knew she loved us. She told us all the time, "Honey, you're all I have! I love you like you were my own kids!"

We learned from her wonderful stories, that she had been born in 1907, and grew up in Mississippi, on a huge pecan plantation owned by her father and his family ~ for generations! She had also been an English, and History teacher, and told us stories of her childhood in the 'Old South' that would keep us entertained for hours!

She told us, "When the doctor had to come out with his horse and buggy, if it rained, he would have to stay the night, until the muddy roads were dry enough for his buggy to drive home on!" (Something we never think about today!)

Mary always told us that her mother was, "like Jesus walking on the earth!" Mary always seemed to think she could never live up to her mother's goodness!

She also told us that "way back," when her and her brother were little ~ her parents had a black nanny named, "Library!" Library had two children named "Ed" and "Becky." She said, "Library loved us like her own!" And they loved her! All the black families living and working on Mary's folk's plantation, were always treated with great love and respect.

When Mary's mother passed away, it was the custom for the coffin to be placed in the home for mourners to view the body. As these dear plantation workers were filing through, they all asked for some little thing of hers as a 'remembrance.' They all loved her (just as 'we' loved Mary!)

At her dear mother's funeral at the church, their plantation workers came to attend the service but the director didn't want to allow them in! (It was a segregated community and blacks were not allowed in white churches.) Mary was so angry ~ she told him off, and said, "Let them all in!!" And surprisingly, he did just that! He said, ~ "they'll have to sit in the balcony of the church."

She told us, "they all sang and hummed the song ~ "Swing Low, Sweet Chariot." She said it was a beautiful ceremony and she would "never forget that day!" (I'm sure Jesus Himself was up in the balcony that day with all those dear plantation workers ~ and He was singing right along with them!)

Oh, we could have listened to Mary's stories all day long! What an interesting lady! She taught high school, and spoke very fondly of her students, and they 'loved her, and her stories' as well!

We were all together for a purpose, and that purpose was to share God's love, and comfort one another, (we all knew that too.) With being new to Arizona, just uprooting our whole lives, and losing my dear Daddy, we needed her more than she knew.

And with her husband tragically dying, and hardly ever seeing her son, she needed us too, more than we knew.

Eventually, our Mary met my dear Mama, and step-dad, and other relatives, and Doug's grandpa and sister. They all loved her ~ and enjoyed her delicious meals, and festive table settings, and her entertaining stories. My Mama often said she was so glad we had 'Our Mary' to get together with on holidays, since we were so far away from home and family. (Mama knew we couldn't travel back home 1800 miles.)

One Christmas, Mary decorated the dinner table with a beautiful lace tablecloth, gold placemats, a candelabra with red candles, and had beautiful Christmas decorations ~ and little 'wreaths,' as napkin rings. We always looked forward to drinking out of her antique ruby glass goblets on thick stems; that she always placed on her table! It was exciting and fun to see the unique ways she'd plate her meals.

That Christmas, she spooned out the inside of oranges that she had cut in two, made fresh whipped sweet potatoes, and mixed in some of the juice from the oranges, along with cinnamon and butter, and then filled the orange halves. She then put marshmallows on top and browned them under the broiler. It was all so colorful, (and they were delicious!) It was a delight to sit at her table and enjoy her wonderful meals, made with her "Southern Love!"

As time went on, we had many opportunities to talk to Mary about God's love and His Word. She always asked "Douglas" to pray before our meals, and she loved that.

We bought her a Bible, and Doug bought her a set of dividers to put on the edge of the pages, which helped her to easily find all the books of the Bible. She often remarked how pleased she was, that "Douglas," took the time to fix those 'tabs' in her Bible for her!

At that time Doug and I were driving way into South Phoenix, to an 'inner-city' Baptist church, and stayed long hours. We knew it was not even a consideration, for 'Our Mary' to go to church with us, and sit for that long. We prayed about it, and asked God to help Mary to have fellowship, and get involved in a church in her area.

One day, we were talking to her dear neighbors across the street, Ray and Beulah, (some of the sweetest Christians there were!) They mentioned seeing Doug and I over at Mary's a lot, and asked us if we had a chance to ask her to our church? We explained our situation and our routine, (driving many miles each way.)

Ray and Beulah understood, although they were very concerned for Mary's soul ~ knowing she didn't know Jesus as her Savior. I asked them if they could ask her to their church? They both looked down and sadly said, they had already asked her and Mack both, but they said, they "weren't interested."

I said, "Well, let's all pray, and have faith, and since Mack's no longer here, maybe she'll say yes this time." ~ So, we all held hands and prayed in their living room that day, asking Christ to give them favor with Mary, and to soften her heart for our Savior. We asked the Lord to give Mary a desire to get out and go to church with Ray and Beulah. We finished praying, and we all believed that the Lord would answer our prayer.

In the next couple weeks, Ray and Beulah waited on the Holy Spirit to give them the 'right time' to ask Mary to their church again.

They received that opportunity, and when they asked, they offered that she could ride with them. We were all 'overjoyed,' when Mary accepted their invitation!

That next Sunday it just so happened that we were outside when they were all leaving for an early service. We watched them drive past our mobile home, with Our Mary, sitting in the middle of their van. (It reminded us of the movie ~ "Driving Miss Daisy!") We waived, and they all waived back ~ smiling!

Ray and Beulah (and Mary) all looked so happy! It was so sweet to see Jesus working through this dear couple who loved Him, and loved Mary too.

Mary really enjoyed the service, and liked the pastor a lot. Each week Ray and Beulah faithfully took Mary to church with them. She became a regular passenger.

One Sunday, Mary was moved by the Holy Spirit, and she walked forward in church, wanting to accept Jesus as her Savior, and be Baptized! We all praised God for her Salvation!

Mary was in her early eighties, and she really came to know Jesus in a close, personal way! She asked Doug and I, if we'd attend her baptism, and if I'd be willing to bring a hair-dryer, and dry her hair, and make her look "presentable" ~ to come back out after she'd been baptized. She chuckled and said in her southern accent, "I don't want to look 'spooky'!" We laughed and said we'd be glad to help her out! She had such a great sense of humor! She was such a blessing to us!

We sat in the pew with Ray and Beulah, and watched 'Our Mary' answer the pastor, that she believed ~ "Jesus died on the Cross, to forgive her of her sins. She confessed that He was the Son of God, He rose from the dead, and she wanted to follow Him in Believers Baptism, and live for Him!" What a wonderful experience to see God working in her life, and answering the prayers that we had prayed that day for her ~ in Ray and Beulah's living room! Praise God!

Mary developed many friendships over the years, with a lot of the people in her church. Mary began using her time to help others, and never told us what she was doing. We found out one day, when she was ninety-three years old. She told us she'd have to cut our lunch short because, "I have to go read to the 'old folks,' at the nursing home!" She had been going there every week to read to the sick and bedridden! (She was older than most of the people there!) Praise God ~ she really wanted to serve our Lord Jesus! She was an inspiration!

Eventually, Doug accepted another job working with delinquent kids, and we had to move back to Phoenix. However, we always kept our promise to Our Mary.

(Moving away from her was very hard on all of us. She was our 'second mother,' and we were 'her kids!')

We missed her, and her lovely meals, and our many great talks, and her words of wisdom; but most of all, 'her love.' We continued going to her home for holidays, we talked on the phone, celebrated our birthdays together, went shopping, and went out to lunch with her. She even sent me her delicious 'Southern recipes' on beautiful recipe cards through the mail.

I always looked after her when she was sick, or in the hospital. Once, she took a very bad fall! She broke her jaw in two places, and had broken her nose as well! I drove one hundred miles a day, and stayed with her. (I slept in a recliner next to her.) I bought her groceries, and blended her food in a processor, and also took her to follow up doctor's appointments.

I washed her dresses, and lace collars; ironed them, and kept her looking like the beautiful 'Southern Belle' she'd always been, (and everyone knew her to be!)

Mary was our 'Mother,' our 'Grandmother,' our 'Sister,' and our 'good Friend' ~ all rolled into one! We stayed close friends with 'Our Mary' for twenty-one years. We had so much fun together!

One thing we loved; on Christmas and birthdays, we'd no more than walk through her door (and get her big hug and kiss) ~ and she'd say, "Well, put your things down Honey, and let's open the presents!" She did it every time! She was like a little child excited about opening the gifts and getting to the fun ~ right away! We loved that about her!! She always made us smile!!

In the years ahead, our faith would be tested.

Unfortunately, as our Mary got older, we had to move her to ten different adult care homes. ~ We had so many problems with these homes! When we saw they weren't caring for her properly, or were even abusing her at times, we immediately moved her! (No one was going to disrespect "Our Mary"!!)

Trusting the staff in these homes was a true test of our faith!

We would have loved to have taken her into our own home and cared for her. However, we had a job that required a lot of our time, and we couldn't provide the level of care that she needed. We were also "on call" with our job.

The situation became very heartbreaking at times; 'care homes' promising such 'good care,' and then, 'not caring at all,' after they got her in!

We kept a good eye on things and cared for her the best we could. I often made dinners, and brought them in for the residents at the care home. They always loved my cooking, and baking.

One of our favorite sayings of Mary's was ~ "Honey, you can't help some people to help themselves!" She was reminding us that many people who wanted help, weren't willing to help themselves! That saying ~ has helped us so many times, to know what to expect from people. (And many time's what 'not' to expect from them!) We both loved her wise advice.

We loved 'Our Mary' ~ more than we could have ever imagined possible! God used her to help us through some hard times, and He used our lives to help her through many hard times too.

God brought Mary to His side through a terrible tragedy, (with her husband's death,) and she grew in her faith; and we did too. ~ We all enjoyed God's love and friendship together ~ and we created many beautiful memories.

The inevitable, sad day came, when we got the call that 'Our Mary' was dying. We turned our car right around and hurried over to see her, and be by her side. Unfortunately, she had just passed away, right before we got there!

When we walked into her room ~ the silence was so sad, because she always had a hearty, cheery greeting for us both, and her famous kiss and hug. Doug and I bent down and kissed Mary good-bye that day. That was one of the saddest days of our lives.

Earlier that morning, I had visited her and she told me, with a far-away look in her eyes, "I'm going to have to leave." (She knew.) She was a hundred and one years old!

(She had told us both a couple of months before that, "I think you and Douglas will do just fine without me," I had looked at her sadly, and disagreed. She said, "Honey, I just have to go!")

Mary had a 'pre-paid' funeral policy, and when we called them, they were very kind and respectful. They came to get her within the hour. We watched with tears in our eyes as the van drove away with Our Mary, and ~ 'a lifetime of beautiful memories' inside.

The next day, we drove out to the funeral home with Mary's legal papers. We talked with a young man who needed us to answer some questions about her policy.

We carried out her last wishes. She was to be cremated, and her ashes were to be sprinkled over the 'Superstition Mountains' where her husbands were.

The young man asked us if we were her children ~ we said, "no."

He said, "grandchildren?" We said, "no."

He smiled and said, "niece or nephew?"

We smiled back at him and again said, "no." Then, we told him the story about 'Our Mary,' (about her husband,) our long-time friendship with her, and how God led us to take care of one another.

We told him that we had a 'little deal' with Mary, that because we loved her so much, we were going to keep 'a little part of her ashes.' (She'd always smile, and chuckle endearingly when we said that.) We had no idea the funeral home had 'little tiny cremation urns' there. He smiled and said, "Let's go in the other room and look through them." We found the perfect one and bought it. It was bright red, with inlaid gold, about three inches tall.

As we were sitting across the desk from this young man, his eyes welled up with tears. We could see that God was touching his heart, and he was so amazed at our love for Mary. We told him that the Lord Jesus put us together to care for each other.

That testimony was shining out to him. He got so excited and said, "This is a story everyone should hear, it's beautiful! I'm going to go home and tell it to my wife!" He said, "Just think, if everyone took care of just one other person in this world, the world would be a better place!" His eyes were just shining, his smile was endearing, and he shook our hands, and thanked us for telling him our story, . . and Mary's story.

We give our dear Savior and Lord Jesus Christ, all the glory for helping us all through the tough times ~ And most of all, for Saving our dear Mary's soul, (and helping us to keep our promise to her.)

And we thank God for 'His promise,' that we will all be together again in His Kingdom!

Remembering our favorite saying of Mary's ~ "Honey, you can't help some people to help themselves!" ~ Well Mary, . . . We're going to use your saying, with a small twist, to sum up the end of our story; Mary, we couldn't help ourselves, ... 'to keep from loving you,' to your dying breath. We love you Mary, and because of Jesus, we can't wait to spend eternity with you!"

And we're sure ~ 'Our Mary,' will have another wonderful meal prepared, and she will be waiting for us, . . and Jesus will be seated at the head of that table!

"Pure religion and undefiled before God and the Father is this, To visit the fatherless and widows in their affliction," (James 1:27)

"And He said to the woman, Thy faith hath saved thee; go in peace." (Luke 7:50)

"Then saith He to the disciple, Behold thy mother! And from that hour that disciple took her unto his own home." (John 19:27)

40. THERE'S NO USE PRAYING FOR HER

I want to tell you about one of the greatest miracles we were ever allowed to witness! It was very scary, . . . (but also very awesome!)

When we were members of our black inner-city church in South Phoenix, Arizona; some church members told us about a single lady who had young children, who was very sick, unto death. I decided to go down to the 'County Hospital' to call on her. (The County Hospital can be a scary place in itself; with many crimes in the parking lot, Police bringing injured suspects in and out, and the gatherings of indigent, drug addicted, and homeless individuals!) However, I felt the Lord telling me, I needed to go see "Sandra."

I didn't know her; I had only seen her a few times when she dropped her children off at the church. She was not a regular member ~ but her children were in my Sunday school class, 'every Sunday.' Others from church who had been to see her, believed she "Wasn't going to make it."

As I was waiting in the lobby to go in and visit with her, I noticed her small boy, maybe seven years old, and he had lost all hope. He had shut down emotionally, and wasn't speaking to 'anyone.' He was just staring out the window of the lobby.

I was talking to him, but sadly getting no response.

The nurse came to tell me that I could go on in to see her. When she brought me to the room . . . I was shocked!

She was lying on a gurney, and my first thought was that the nurse had taken me into the wrong area. I pointed to the very obese woman lying there, and I said, "Are you sure, . . . she is Sandra?"

The nurse said, "Yes!"

I asked, "What's wrong with her?!" (She looked horrible!)

She was so swollen and puffy ~ she didn't look like the same person! Sandra normally weighed about 98lbs. ~ But now, she looked like she weighed over 300!! (I was horrified to see that 'this' could happen to someone; almost overnight!) The nurse never answered me.

Sandra was so very ill, that she was unable to even talk!

A tall doctor who was standing there spoke up. He stared directly at the Bible in my hands, and with one of the most evil faces I have ever seen in my entire life, looked me right in the eyes and said, . . "There's no use praying for her! . . . She's at deaths door!!"

He then walked out ~ and 'slammed' the door hard behind him!! I immediately thought, "What an 'evil' thing to say in front of Sandra!"

Those words were so 'final,' and said with such 'meanness!!'

(That cruel, heartless scene still plays over in my mind!!)

~ I kept wondering what poor Sandra was thinking!!

Well, I had instant 'righteous anger,' which made me want to pray with greater faith and show him; . . . God is Real!!

I took Sandra's hand and said, "Sandra, this is Sister Deitrick, and I'm going to pray for Jesus to give you a miracle! Would you like that?" All of a sudden, she gripped my hand so hard, and pulled me down ~ with such force ~ I lost my balance and almost landed on top of her chest! She was trying to tell me ~ "Yes!" with no words, just physical power!

I said, "Okay Sweetie, I'll pray with you." ~ I was shocked! That was the first time I'd ever had anyone do that!!

I knew from that moment on, that she had 'faith,' and desperately wanted God to heal her! I said a prayer, "Dear God, please stay right here with Sandra, please heal her, and cast all evil and sickness away from her, in Jesus Name! Amen!" I told her, "Don't lose hope honey, and don't listen to that devil! You just keep praying the name of Jesus in your mind. Jesus will stay right here with you." I told her that I was going to talk to her family and her children, and I would be back; . . and that the whole church was praying for Jesus to heal her!

Now, I can't write the whole story here, it would be too long! But our Lord and Savior, Jesus Christ, did heal Sandra!

Jesus is 'Real' dear friends!

He's worthy of our praise, and our faith in Him! (I only wish I could have seen that evil doctor's face, when he heard that Sandra was 'healed,' and went home to her family!)

One Sunday, some weeks later, someone entered the door of the church, and they wheeled this lady through the door to the altar for prayer! It was Sandra!! Everyone looked as if it wasn't real! She was now so tiny and thin! She was so weak ~ she couldn't stand up, but we all gathered around Sister Sandra in her wheelchair and stretched out our hands to touch her shoulders. We all prayed at the altar in the "Mighty Name of Jesus," thanking Him ~ for bringing her back to health, and to life itself! We prayed that Jesus would continue to heal her ~ and give her complete strength back to her body, and restore her to good health! (That was a very powerful prayer!)

Praise God, He did just that!

She was in church every Sunday after that! Her children were so happy that they had their dear mother back!

After Sandra had been 'healed,' and was strong enough to walk, . . I asked if she could go to a department store with me. She smiled and accepted my invitation. I still didn't know her that well, but God led me to buy her a whole new outfit. I told her I wanted to give her a blessing, because she had suffered and been through so much.

She was just overtaken with emotion ~ smiling and just beaming! She asked my opinion as she tried on several dresses, and decided on a beautiful white dress, shoes, nylons, and jewelry! (I had encouraged her to go on and "pick out a whole new outfit!") We had fun!

When we got in the car to go home, with all those sacks of gifts, she said she really wanted to thank me . . . for all the love I had shown her, and all the prayers. And then she said, with a humble look, "You didn't know this, but you just bought me ~ my wedding dress."

I was so surprised! She said her boyfriend had told God, that if He healed Sandra ~ he would marry her, and take care of her and her children forever. I had no idea! All Praise to God!

You see how God can answer prayer, if we are willing to step out in faith, and pray, and follow Him, and just do as Jesus did? Let's begin to "believe" Christ's words, and His power to heal and to Save, and let's be those people who are bold in our faith, to pray for others! Let's give God our lives, and ask Him to do miracles through 'us,' for the glory of His mighty Name and Kingdom!!

"All things are possible with God!" ~ Amen!!

Sandra's story is a perfect picture of the love of Christ.

We are all ~ sadly, "Dead" in our sins. . .

When Jesus comes to us, He gives us life, and heals us; He clothes us in the beautiful "robe of righteousness," that He 'purchased' for us,

. . . and He promises to take us, and make us His Holy, loving Bride, and take care of us, . . forever!

We are all waiting for that glorious day!

All Praise to His wonderful Name!

"And He said unto her, Daughter, be of good comfort: thy faith hath made thee whole; go in peace." (Luke 8:48)

"And all things whatsoever ye shall ask in prayer, believing, ye shall receive." (Matthew 21:22)

"for I am the LORD that healeth thee." (Exodus 15:26)

"Bless the Lord, O my soul, and forget not all his benefits: Who forgiveth all thine iniquities; who healeth all thy diseases;" (Psalm 103:2,3)

41. GOD'S RELENTLESS LOVE ~ AND THE CHOCOLATE CHIP COOKIES

When Doug and I were working as managers of the "fifty-five and older" mobile home park here in Arizona, each new resident would check in at our office and tell us how long they planned to stay. We would rent RV spaces and apartments on a six-month basis. We heard a lot of stories from people; some very interesting, and some very sad. This particular story began as the latter ~ very sad!

Many times, we are completely unaware of the paths, and the situations, that God is leading us into. As Christians, we need to pray each day that Christ Jesus will lead us, and use our lives to help others to know Him. By faith, we follow Jesus, . . His Words, . . and His miraculous leading!

Jesus leads us and guides us when we are praying, and 'willing' to 'follow His leading.' Where many Christians go wrong; 'they' have an agenda, 'they' have 'their own plans' and desires, and 'they' have no desire to go into the 'trenches of life,' to get involved, or to be the stabilizer (if need be,) in someone else's 'storm!'

One day, a very nice couple came into our office telling us they wanted to rent an RV space.

They had given up their home in California, and had come to Arizona to care for his father, who was elderly ~ and very ill with cancer. His father, (who I will call 'Mr. H.',) was one of our residents that had a mobile home, and lived there 'year-round.'

His son and daughter-in-law, "John and Mary," were very sincere Christians, and very quiet, humble people. We found out they were committed to helping their dad through his last years, and were willing to give up 'their lives,' to take care of him, and look after him.

This is a quality that is almost extinct today, even among many Christians! Knowing them was a breath of fresh air. Their lives were a beautiful picture of what it means to be surrendered to Christ. We had never met anyone else who had ever 'given up' their own home, to take care of their ailing parent! (John and Mary were now living in a very small travel trailer.)

They were asking Doug and I to pray for God's strength for all of them ~ but especially, to pray for John's dad's 'Salvation.'

He was ninety-one years old, belonged to an older 'main-line' church, and still did not know Jesus as his Savior.

As Christians, we know the Word of God teaches ~ that without Christ as our Savior, we will never enter the Kingdom of God.

~ There is a glorious Heaven awaiting all who believe in Jesus Christ. There is sadly, also a 'hell,' for all who reject the blessed Son of God, and His plan of Salvation and forgiveness for the world. This plan includes each, and every one of us ~ (including Mr. H.) ~ who had sadly rejected Jesus all of his ninety-one years of life.

We had been at this job a few months, and the residents who were "regulars" year-round, just used our office mail-drop to pay their rent. We had never met many of them ~ and we had yet to meet John and Mary's dear dad.

I felt I should bake him some chocolate chip cookies, and go over to visit 'Mr. H.'

When he answered his door, I introduced myself and told him that I was very glad to meet him. I also told him I was very happy that his son and daughter-in-law had come to help him out. He didn't seem too talkative, which made my initial visit a little short.

His eyes lit up like a child's though, when I said I had baked him some chocolate chip cookies! That seemed to really cheer him up! I wondered how long it had been since he had home baked cookies, as he was a widower and his family had all lived in California until now.

I talked to him about his health and found that his cancer wasn't new. He had been suffering with spinal cancer for "nineteen years!" I asked if he had a pastor that came to see him?

He looked down and with a sad stare in his eyes, he said, "Well I do, but he's busy building a church." I smiled and said, "Well, that's why God sent me!"

(Let's never get so busy that we forget the poor and the sick!) The Bible says that when you visit the sick, you are really visiting Christ Himself! Jesus says, "I was sick, and ye visited me." (Matthew 25:36)

And, "Verily I say unto you, Inasmuch as ye have done it unto one of the least of these My brethren, ye have done it unto Me." (Matthew 25:40)

I immediately felt God's Spirit moving in my heart ~ to stay right with him, to encourage him, and just be a friend.

I began to visit Mr. H. regularly. We had some very nice talks, and a few laughs together as well.

He told me one story that we'll never forget; ~ He had a very nice, new big white Cadillac he'd named 'Betsy.' He said, in his soft, calm voice, "Oh, she was fast!"

He told me, "One day I was on 'a long stretch of highway,' and a police officer pulled me over! He asked me if I knew how fast I was going?"

Mr. H. had replied, "No, . . do you know?"

The police officer said, "I've been following you for two miles! Why didn't you pull over when you saw my lights flashing?"

Mr. H. told him, "Well, I was trying to officer, but Betsy here has a mind of her own, and it took me this long just to slow her down!"

The cop said, "Do you know I could give you a ticket for ninety dollars for speeding like this?!" To which Mr. H. responded, "Oh my! That sounds like an 'awfully' lot of money to me!!"

~ The officer just chuckled, and gave Mr. H. a 'verbal warning,' instead of a ticket. (Mr. H. was so sweet, and he had a very 'serious' demeanor.)

We enjoyed many chats together and became good friends.

Doug and I prayed each day for Mr. H. We prayed for his health, and for a chance to talk to him about our Savior, and the condition of his soul.

We had many years of calling on the sick with 'Hospital Calling Teams,' through the churches we attended, so I felt I was right in 'my niche' ~ visiting Mr. H. It felt very familiar, and I felt good about God using us in this dear man's life.

So, we kept right on praying and visiting him.

Mr. H. was suffering great pain ~ and we were able to talk about this. I told him, "When Jesus walked the Earth ~ He healed many people; all who believed in His healing power." I told him I had been healed many times, and was also healed of "stage four cancer!" Our eyes connected and suddenly I saw 'hope' in his sad, blue eyes.

God's Word says, 'Hope,' and 'Faith,' are necessary for receiving Christ's miracles! ~ "But without Faith it is impossible to please Him: for he that cometh to God must believe that He *is*, and that He is a rewarder of them that diligently seek Him." (Hebrews 11:6)

I explained to Mr. H. that "Jesus rose from the dead, . . He's alive, . . He still heals, . . and His Holy Spirit is here with us." We asked him, if he would like to pray and ask Jesus as his personal Savior, and to have Him in his heart forever?

He said, "Yes I would!"

He was very open to praying with us! Doug was right there with me, and we stood around him in his recliner.

We held his hands, and Doug prayed for Mr. H. and asked that he would "feel the presence of Christ's Spirit, and know that Jesus is real." He asked Jesus to ~ "come into his heart as his Savior."

When Doug finished that prayer ~ we looked up and smiled at Mr. H., and he had 'Joy' in his face!

His face was just shining ~ his eyes had filled with tears, and he had so much excitement in his voice saying, . . . "I feel His Peace! I feel His Peace all around me! I have no pain!" (He was so happy!!)

We knew he had truly accepted Jesus as his Savior, and had been touched by Christ Himself! What a glorious time in God's Holy Spirit that was!! We thank the Lord for that sweet moment!

We had such wonderful talks, after his decision to accept Jesus as his Savior. He was a lot more comfortable in talking to me now about his personal feelings. I quoted many Scriptures to him in the days ahead. He listened very intently.

One day he confided in me, that he wished he had gotten to know Jesus sooner in his life. He told me that he wished he knew the Bible Scriptures like I did. He said, "I think what kept me from ever really getting to know God, is that I was always too 'scientific minded'." He admitted that he had tried to "figure everything out too much." We continued having wonderful talks, and times of encouragement.

We thanked God for this opportunity, and for the time He gave us with Mr. H.

Later, we had a taste of what the Lord must have felt like, when the religious leaders of His day, (the Pharisees and Sadducees,) were condemning Jesus for healing on the "Sabbath," and associating with 'sinners.' Jesus could just never please that type of people!

We too, had dealings like this, among some of the residents there. We heard that some of the women were wondering why I was visiting Mr. H. so often ~ especially since he was a 'widower,' and I was a married woman? (The man was ninety-one years old!!) Those women had little minds ~ and such shallow hearts!

How sad that made us both feel, when all we were doing ~ was showing the love of our Savior, and caring about this dear man's soul!

"Blessed are ye when men shall revile you, and persecute you, and say all manner of evil against you falsely, for my sake. Rejoice, and be exceeding glad: for great is your reward in Heaven: for so persecuted they the prophets which were before you." (Matthew 5:11,12) We truly experienced this verse in our lives!

We have seen a lot of this judgmental thinking out of people, even in those who attend church. ~ We must all stay away from judging people's 'motives.' Only God knows our hearts and motives.

If we were watching a man building a house, and just staring at the foundation, and we began putting him down, and saying, "What a silly looking house!"

We would be very 'simple,' foolish, (and small minded,) to think some cement blocks ~ were the end result of this mans finished work!

Be very careful not to fall into judging another man's work. "But why dost thou judge thy brother? or why dost thou set at nought thy brother? for we shall all stand before the judgment seat of Christ." (Romans 14:10) Remember ~ we will all eventually see the finished work.

A lot of women might have been hurt, and turned away from the Holy work that God wanted to do in this man's life, because of this malicious gossip. But, because we had worked with delinquent kids half of our lives, this discouraging gossip didn't stop me at all, (I just baked more cookies!)

One day we got an urgent call from John and Mary ~ they were so upset and asking my help ~ Mr. H. had taken a turn for the worse!

His home health care nurse had "disappeared," and Mr. H. was in excruciating pain! I told his daughter-in-law, "I'll be right over!"

I made a heated call to the home health agency, (some people you have to hunt down, call them up, and give them a 'sermon' to get them to do their job!) I asked to talk to the director, and when I told her their nurse was ~ "Missing in Action," she tried to make every excuse for her!

I told her emphatically, "If this was 'your' dad, that nurse would be here! This man is hitting the walls with his poor hands!

Get your best nurse out here as soon as you can, and they better have something to soothe his pain, and make him comfortable!" Let me tell you, God worked out a real blessing for our friend, Mr. H. The director immediately sent out a very sweet, southern, tall black nurse to his home, and we couldn't have been happier! This lady gave him a shot and he was totally at peace, almost instantly!

We all saw this as a real Victory! This nurse was so faithful, and came to see Mr. H. regularly. Doug and I continued our visits as well.

One day Mr. H. smiled and said, "She is so good to me ~ when she picks me up, she is so gentle, she's just like a 'big black angel'!" (And to this day, we're not so sure she wasn't!)

~ Mr. H. was totally comfortable after that, and always so happy to see us, as we were to see him as well.

Eventually, we got a call from John and Mary, . . . that their dear daddy had gone to Heaven in the night. He slipped away, and thanks be to God ~ he knew Jesus Christ as his dear Savior, and we know we will all see him again ~ in God's Glorious Kingdom!! We will always believe our friendship was a 'divine appointment!'

God watched over him for ninety-one years with 'His Relentless Love,' and Mr. H. was supposed to meet Charlie and Doug!

(And we were blessed to know him!)

But most importantly, he had an appointment to meet 'Jesus,' our dear Savior and Lord! Thank you Father!

Growing up I always heard, "The way to a man's heart is through his stomach." Jesus opened the door of this dear man's heart with chocolate chip cookies! . .

And the sweetest ending of this story is that Mr. H. is walking the hills of our God right now, . . . with Jesus! He is with his dear wife, and he is going to be with his son John and his wife Mary, and with Doug and I ~ Forever!

(And I'm sure ~ we'll all be having a batch of chocolate chip cookies together,) only this time, . . . Jesus will be joining us!!

Dear people, Jesus is Real!

And His Great Love is . . . Relentless!

"For I reckon that the sufferings of this present time are not worthy to be compared with the glory which shall be revealed in us." (Romans 8:18)

"He healeth the broken in heart, and bindeth up their wounds." (Psalm 147:3)

"And if thou draw out thy soul to the hungry, and satisfy the afflicted soul; then shall thy light rise in obscurity, and thy darkness be as the noon day." (Isaiah 58:10)

"Blessed are they that mourn: for they shall be comforted." (Matthew 5:4)

"He that heareth My Word, and believeth on Him that sent Me, hath everlasting life, and shall not come into condemnation; but is passed from death unto life." (John 5:24)

42. I CAN'T TELL HIM!
(Do unto others)

One day I was talking with a young lady we knew very well here in Arizona, . . she had been going with a very nice Christian man we also knew. Neither had ever been married, and he was so in love with this young lady, he was willing to wait for her. (He had already waited seven years!)

She attended church and claimed to be a Christian and believe in the Lord Jesus Christ.

As she and I were out having lunch, she told me he had given her a nice ring, and had asked her to marry him. I was so happy for them! I saw the ring on her finger and I congratulated her!

Then she said, (very seriously,) with an embarrassed look on her face, "Oh I'd 'never' marry him!!"

I was so shocked, and hurt for him! . . . I knew how badly he wanted to marry her! Imagine, seven years of your life wasted!!

I immediately felt led to scold her in a loving manner, and I asked her, "Why would you keep going out with him then, and leading him on?"

She boldly told me, "Because I love to have him take me out to lunches and dinners, and I like his attention!" I strongly disagreed!! (Right is right, and wrong is wrong . . . dear friends!)

I stood up for him right there and took his side!

I said, "Well, you're going to give the ring back, aren't you?"

She said, "No! . . He gave it to me!" Then she said, "I can't tell him I don't want to marry him, that would hurt him!"

I nearly fell over in my chair!! I asked her, "What do you think he feels like ~ when you're stringing him along?" (My Goodness!!)

She had no intention of telling him!

So, right then, the Lord burdened my heart to tell him, in the kindest way I could! Some people might have just left it all alone, (but not me!!)

Here was a lady, (almost middle aged,) leading this man on ~ for how many more years?

Doug and I prayed about this, and I went and told this dear man the truth! He had tears in his eyes, and was visibly hurt, angry, and embarrassed! I'm telling you ~ this was one of the hardest things I've ever had to do!! However, I am here to report: God wanted me to follow through with (His Truth!)

Doug and I continued to pray for him, and he later met a beautiful young Christian lady at his church, who had just lost her husband due to a massive heart attack! She had four children. He dated her, and fell in love again, and she fell in love with him. They were married, and he became a wonderful husband and father to her children.

They have been married now for many, many years, and have several grandchildren! His family is an inspiration to us!

We thank God ~ He worked this all out for His Glory!!

Dear people, sometimes it's a 'hard thing,' to do the 'right thing!' But when God leads us and guides us, we must always obey the voice of our loving Savior, . . and always stand on the side of 'right' and 'good!' Amen!

Men, and women, please . . . do not lead others on, 'in the name of love.' The Bible says we will surely "reap what we sow," when we do those mean (and selfish) things!

Let's always be 'honest' with one another!

(The young lady we knew, never found love ~ and never married.)

Dear God, please help us all to respect, and love each other ~ and "Do unto others, as we would have others do unto us!"

"Therefore all things whatsoever ye would that men should do to you, do ye even so to them: for this is the law and the prophets." (Matthew 7:12)

"And they will deceive every one his neighbor, and will not speak the truth: they have taught their tongue to speak lies, and weary themselves to commit iniquity." (Jeremiah 9:5)

"Be not deceived; God is not mocked: for whatsoever a man soweth, that shall he also reap." (Galatians 6:7)

43. SUDDENLY BLIND

A good friend of ours ~ who was in his seventies, had a sudden, strange attack upon his eyes! He could not open them!

We received a frantic call from his wife saying ~ "Please come over, . . something's happened to my husband!"

I got in my car to go over, and she had already called the rescue unit. She asked me if I would go to the hospital to sit with her, and be willing to bring them home later on.

I was glad to help. I asked her husband, "What are you feeling?" His eyes were watering excessively and he told me, "I can't open my eyes!" (I was afraid it might have been a stroke!)

The rescue unit came and took him and his wife, and I followed them to the hospital. I helped her fill out the lengthy paperwork while he was sent back through the double doors on a gurney.

As soon as we were done with the intake, she asked if I would go check on him. She anxiously told me to, "Pray for him!"

As I started to go through the double doors, I turned and gave her a look, like ~ "Pray for Me!" She and I were both Christians ~ but he didn't know the Lord Jesus as his Savior. When she said, "Pray for him" ~ you need to know 'why' that struck a nervous chord in my heart. He was a tough ex-lifetime trucker, a 'Teamster,' and he was very rough ~ a stubborn man, and many times rude ~ just not the kind of man that would be open to me praying with him! ~ I thought, "Please God, hear my prayers!"

I asked a nurse where he was, and she pointed to an area behind a curtain. I went in, and as I saw him lying there ~ my heart went out to him! I told him I was there, and that I would sit with him a while.

He laid still, not moving one bit. I knew how frightened he must have been. (I was frightened for him!) I sat and prayed a silent prayer to Jesus ~ asking Him to work through me, and to give me the words to say when I prayed with him.

When I felt God's leading, I first asked his permission. I said, "Do you mind me having a prayer with you?"

Eerily, his hands were folded across his stomach, as if he were lying in a coffin! God used this 'visual' ~ to cause me to forget my fears about praying for his Salvation.

I waited for him to answer me ~ and he barely spoke under his breath, and he finally said, "okay." He didn't look happy about me praying for him. Sadness seemed to fill the whole room around us.

Boldly, I put my hand on his hands (and again said a silent prayer) ~ "Oh Lord ~ please give me the words, and the power, to pray in Your Spirit for a healing for this dear man." Then I prayed out loud to God and I asked, "Lord please hear my prayer, and heal his eyes, in the name of Jesus Christ." Amen.

(We were always taught early on by our pastors, that, according to God's Word, there is "Power" ~ in the mighty name of Jesus!)

I knew what Jesus had done to turn Doug and I around ~ from a life of sin, and a wild background, so I never doubted God's Power.

(I was expecting God's blessing as I prayed!)

~ All of a sudden, I looked at this dear man, and I thought of all the people in the Bible that Jesus healed. I began to feel strength and even greater boldness to pray for his healing. Right then, I was led to say something that shocked ~ even me! . . . I called his name, and told him I felt that God wanted him to ask Jesus as his Savior!

His face didn't flinch. I then said, "If you pray, and ask Christ into your heart, you will be healed, and you will be able to see!"

Immediately, I thought to myself, "Charlie! What did you just say??" (Sometimes, God causes us to say something in His Spirit, that we would 'never' say otherwise!) ~ This was definitely one of those times! I thought, "Please God, answer me!"

He turned his head about a fourth of an inch, and he looked upset. There was no answer! (In a case this intense, I had to keep strong faith in Christ to even continue on.) ~ I asked him again, (his eyes 'Still Closed!') . . . "Would you like to open your eyes and be able to see? I'll pray with you to receive Jesus as your Savior. You can just say the prayer after me in your head, and say "Amen," when I'm done."

He was still reluctant, but then he said, "oh, okay," like a mad, pouting child. I thought, "Thank You Lord!"

So, in faith, I prayed the Sinner's Prayer for him and said, "Dear Lord Jesus, please come into my heart and life as my Savior. Lord, please change my life, and heal me, and let me be able to open my eyes and see. We ask this in the mighty name of Jesus Christ, Amen!" I waited only seconds, and I heard him quietly say, "Amen." I asked him if he would try and open his eyes and he said softly, "okay."

This was a very tender moment in God's Spirit.

In a few seconds, I saw him struggling to open his eyes ~ as if he was looking into the bright sunlight. His eyes were watering, and tears ran down the sides of his temples as he laid there on his back.

I took his hands and asked him to sit up for me, and it seemed as if his attitude changed, and he had opened his eyes a little more.

I sat beside him on the gurney. I smiled at him, and I told him I was so glad he had prayed with me. (His eyes were open now.)

He took out his handkerchief and wiped the tears from his eyes. I asked him if he could see me, and he said, "yeah!"

I asked him if he thought he could walk with me to the lobby, to see his wife.

He looked at me, and connected with my eyes; . . . he had a look of hope, and he said, "Where is she?" I said ~ "I'll take you to her." I grabbed his hand and we walked back through the double doors. His wife looked hopeful too!

They grabbed each other's hands and then hugged each other!

I told her ~ that he and I had prayed, and that he had asked Jesus into his heart! "We prayed for a healing miracle, and Jesus healed his eyes!" She smiled, and he humbly smiled at her.

Then he smiled at me, and told me, "thank you."

We were all so thankful that he could see! Praise God!

We talked a little with the nurse and doctor, and they seemed to think he'd do alright going on home. Surprisingly, they didn't do any blood work, tests, or x-rays! It seemed that God had allowed all this (without tests and people running in and out) to give me a quiet time to pray with him! They just told him not to drive.

I told them, "that'll be 'my job' for a few days."

We all smiled, and we were so happy he would be going home! (And Jesus would be accompanying him home today!) Praise God!

We can only thank the dear Lord for our friends healing and Salvation that day.

We are so glad to be able to report that this man who was so gruff, and rude, began to change completely!

He smiled more, asked us to dinner, went on trips with us, and we grew to really enjoy being with him. We grew close to him as a good friend. He would eventually pray with us over meals, and would also pray with us in times of need.

Jesus 'really' came into his heart, and changed him to be a nicer, kinder man! He even told Doug and I, that he loved us more than his own kids! That was a sign to us that he was experiencing a 'spiritual,' and 'eternal' love from Jesus, which sadly, he never had with his own children.

Some years later, he went home to be with our Lord. However, we know without a doubt, we will see him again, . . He will be waiting for us in Heaven! We know he will always be happy and thankful, (along with us,) that he reluctantly, prayed the Sinners Prayer that day in the hospital in Phoenix, Arizona! He received his sight back, and also received Jesus into his heart and life, and he will be in the family of God for all Eternity! What a glorious reunion that will be!!

~ Thank You, dear Lord Jesus, for loving tough and stubborn sinners, . . . (such as us.)

"One thing I know, that, whereas I was blind, now I see." (John 9:25)

"Whosoever shall call on the Name of the Lord shall be Saved." (Acts 2:21)

"As the Father hath loved Me, so have I loved you: continue ye in My love." (John 15:9)

44. THE OLD BOX OF LEADS

I was working in sales, as Marketing Director, for a very reputable company that sold air-cleaning vacuums called, "The Rainbow." They are so helpful for people with allergies, asthma, or other breathing problems. We believed in it, and sold many of them all over Arizona. Doug came on board, and we both worked for Rainbow for around two years.

One evening, I was there all by myself, making calls to set up new appointments. Something told me, to leave the list of current 'leads,' (people that wanted 'call backs,') and try some of the older ones.

My boss had told me months before ~ "If you ever need leads, there are plenty in this box in the bottom drawer of your desk."

(I didn't know it then, but I was being led of God's Spirit to get into that box, and pick out a card.)

Since it was an old lead, I called the woman and talked for a few minutes about the Rainbow. She said, "Oh, honey, I know it's a great machine, but I wouldn't be interested in one, because I don't even want to live! I'm sitting here thinking of suicide!"

I was completely shocked! I said, "Oh no! Please don't do that! Will you please talk to me?"

She said, "I don't think it'll help, honey, but I'll listen to what you have to say."

I wrote a note to my boss, and put it on my office door. It said, "I had to sign out for a while, 'on personal time,' and I'll explain later." (He was gone, but if he came back ~ I didn't want him to think I was on the clock.)

I got down on my knees behind my desk and said a quick prayer, that God would "help me ~ to help her!!"

I told her our testimonies, and then, how I came to find her phone number! I told her, "Jesus loves you; He 'led me' to your number, and He has a plan for your life!"

She was so thankful, (and joyful,) that I took the time to talk to her about her situation, and to talk her out of "suicide!" She then told me her story and why she was so depressed.

I asked her if she had a church, and she said ~ "Yes, but I haven't been there in the longest time." I told her that we would be willing to go with her sometime. (She asked me if we could join her that coming Sunday!) I told her, "We sure will!" We ended the call on a hopeful, and positive note. I thanked God. I felt so relieved!

When I got off of the phone, my boss returned, and I told him I had taken a little time off, and told him what had happened. He said he was "okay" with that, and seemed to take it to heart. (He knew we were Christians.)

So that next Sunday, Doug and I, and our foster daughter, went to her church to meet her. I told her we would meet in the lobby of the church, and we would have our foster daughter with us. I told her, "I have very long, brown hair, down to my knees! You can't miss me!"

She and I both giggled.

When we arrived at her church, she had been watching for us, and came right up to me and hugged me!

This dear lady was about sixty-five years old ~very, very, sweet, and she seemed like someone we had known all our lives.

We all felt 'instant happiness' to be sitting there together with her in church! It was a very nice service.

She told me later over the phone, "It did me good to go back and reunite with friends, and I'm going to start attending church regularly again!" We stayed in touch for quite some time! (And we had a new friend!) We thank God for her life, and we were very thankful for the opportunity to help her! That was definitely a "divine appointment!"

What were the chances, that I picked her phone number, from the middle of an old file box, . . right at the time she was thinking of committing suicide? (That was God, and God all by Himself!)

We learned from our church in Des Moines, Iowa, (when we were new Christians,) . . . that God has 'divine appointments,' and perfect timing, for us to reach, and help others! ~ And we Praise God for all He did here! We give Him "All the Glory!" (And it all started with a 'little feeling' from God's Spirit) ~ to drop what I was doing, and pick the first name out of the middle of ~ "The Old Box of Leads!!" May God help us all to follow up on "His leads!!" Amen?

"And we know that all things work together for good to them that love God, to them who are the called according to his purpose." (Romans 8:28)

"Fear thou not; for I am with thee: be not dismayed; for I am thy God: I will strengthen thee; yea, I will help thee;" (Isaiah 41:10)

"For the Lamb which is in the midst of the throne shall feed them, and shall lead them unto living fountains of waters: and God shall wipe away all tears from their eyes." (Revelation 7:17)

45. LET US DO GOOD UNTO ALL MEN

I've worked managing wealthy homes here in Phoenix for many years. . .

Taking care of children as a nanny, hiring contractors for services, and construction projects; and when the owners were out of the state (or the country,) taking care of all the 'day to day' household needs. I also did interior decorating for many of the home owners.

We had one monthly contractor that I often witnessed to about the love of Jesus. He was part-owner of the pest control service we did business with, and he was also trying his hand as a palm tree trimmer. His name was 'Ted.'

One day, around 15 years ago, he was up about 30 feet, trimming a palm tree on another property. A powerful gust of wind hit; they are called "dust devils" here in the desert, and are like a mini-tornado! He had chosen that day not to use his safety belt, (never a good idea.) He always felt very 'invincible,' (can't be beaten.)

That dust devil came out of nowhere, (as they usually do,) took him, and threw him down to the ground, sadly crushing both his legs and ankles!

We heard about his accident, and my foster daughter and I went to visit him in the hospital. It took prayer to even go in there, because I knew he would be very upset and depressed.

She and I prayed that God would give us the words to say to him, and the 'power' to pray, and see God's blessings over his situation! We also asked God to somehow use our 'smiles' ~ to cheer him up.

We went in and talked a little while, and when the nurse came in, I questioned why he kept 'hiccupping,' (so loudly that it frightened us,) and we wondered why he kept hiccupping so often?

She said, "When someone takes a fall from that high up in the air, it jolts their whole system in an extreme way, and he may always have hiccups like that!" She added, "Some people never get rid of them!" He looked scared! (It was frightening!)

My heart broke for him!! I looked at him, and he looked at me like a little kid, not knowing what was going to happen to him! We were told ~ his legs, "might never be normal again."

I had witnessed to Ted many times and he knew what we believed ~ I asked if he wanted us to pray with him; that he would get over those hiccups, and that God would help him to be able to walk again?

He seemed very eager to have my foster daughter and I pray with him.

We reached out and he held our hands, and I prayed and asked God "in the name of Jesus" ~ to deliver him from those horrible hiccups, (that shook his whole body,) ~ and we prayed that Christ would ~ "take them away!"

I also prayed for his legs to be "healed" so he could walk again!

He didn't have much hope about that ~ but we prayed in faith, believing!

My foster daughter had lovingly taken him some of those 'gold foiled chocolate coins.' He smiled when she handed them to him. He was smiling by the time we left. God had lifted his spirit through our prayer and our visit with him, as God so often does when you visit the sick. (And we had specifically asked God to cheer him up!) Praise God for answered prayers!

The next time we went to visit him, we saw the numerous pins, screws, (and orthopedic braces,) that had been attached by the doctors to try and repair his extremely crushed legs and ankles! We noticed right away his hiccups were gone! Praise God! ~ We mentioned that his hiccups were all gone, and Ted told our foster daughter that it was the "gold coin chocolates," that healed him!

She smiled, and I told them both, "We know. . . 'Who' took them away!" Amen! We thanked our Savior and gave him the Praise!!

Later, (much later,) we saw God's plan work out for all of our lives together.

The braces on his legs would have to remain for many months, and then he would need physical therapy. We knew that we had to help him.

Doug and I and our foster daughter ended up moving him, from his 2nd story apartment to a ground floor apartment in the same complex. He could not do stairs. He could only sit on the step and scoot down, step by step, on his bottom, in a little kid's fashion. . . He was very humbled. He was a body builder, very ego-centric, and was not the type of man that would ever ask for help at all.

To make a long story shorter, he became very depressed when he began therapy, and realized his physical limitations. We kept praying for him. I had a long talk with him about his business. I told him he could "switch it up," and "do things a little different." He didn't think so.

Well, I won't stand by and let someone give up and sink into depression! So, I told him to hire a couple of young men who were eager to work, train them, and he could be the boss, and they could build a small business together. He was still very negative. He asked how would he get the work started? He had no faith at all, and began staying in his apartment, only becoming more depressed.

We finally got him convinced to find a couple young men to help him with his tree service, and eventually he added landscaping. Praise God!! I would load up his wheel-chair every day ~ in the back of my truck. He bought a magnetic sign to advertise his business, and stuck that on the side of my truck.

My foster daughter and I rolled him up to the houses to bid jobs, and she and I canvassed neighborhoods, passing out flyers for him. Later, God worked it out where he was able to walk with a cane; and with all of his new customers, his business really took off! He even learned Spanish! Praise God!! ~ He really blessed Ted, and He heard and answered our many prayers for him!

One day, he told me that a wealthy man he had met, told him that he had been out of work, and he had seen us helping Ted. He got the idea to start his own business, re-inventing peoples job descriptions (from watching us!)

When someone was out of work, he would find new opportunities for them to use the talents they had already developed. He would help them figure out which way to go in their future occupation, like I had done for Ted. We should never forget that people are always watching us ~ whether we know it or not! There is an old saying, "You are the only Bible, some people will ever read!"

Well, I wish I could tell you that Ted got saved. I really hope he will someday. But let me tell you, he can never say that God didn't help him! Because one family stepped up to the plate, and wheeled him around in a wheel chair for many months, in the boiling desert heat; from house to house, to get his new business started!

We give God all the glory for this; for all the answered prayers; whether Ted will ever humble himself to give God the glory or not. We'll praise God, and tell all of you ~ how good God was!

We worked very hard to help Ted, and I know God was pleased with our service for our Lord Jesus. God will get the glory for all that He did through our lives, for the glory of His Kingdom! All praises to Him!

When we pray and ask God to use our lives, we never know what job He will send us to do. But our God is faithful, to Christians and also to the unsaved. (God is good to both the "just" and the "unjust!")

No one will ever be able to stand on Judgment Day and say, "God you never gave me a chance to know you," because He gives us all many chances to know Him, . . and then some!

Have you decided to tell Jesus, "Lord, I need you, I repent of my sins, and I ask You to Save me, and be my Lord and Savior?" I know He will be waiting, . . 'just for you!' . . ~ Amen and Amen!!

"That ye may be the children of your Father which is in Heaven: for He maketh His sun to rise on the evil and on the good, and sendeth rain on the just and on the unjust." (Matthew 5:45)

"As we have therefore opportunity, let us do good unto all men, especially unto them who are of the household of faith." (Galatians 6:10)

"A man that hath friends must shew himself friendly: and there is a friend that sticketh closer than a brother." (Proverbs 18:24)

"When I sit in darkness, the Lord shall be a light unto me." (Micah 7:8)

"Therefore to him that knoweth to do good, and doeth it not, to him it is sin." (James 4:17)

46. THE RAY GUN

Just a while back, I was driving home on a neighborhood street. Suddenly, I saw a young boy, about seven years old, quickly duck and crouch down behind the back end of a car parked on the street! I was not sure he wasn't going to dart out in front of me!

So, I slowly approached him, and quickly 'beeped' my horn. He looked up, stood straight up, and gave me a look to kill! He had a 'ray gun' in his hand!

Just then, I saw two older boys about nine and ten, coming to see where this boy was hiding.

The boy with the ray gun, had a very visible look of disgust, as he glared at me! He had been "found out" by his friends, when I honked!

He gave me a disgruntled look, as if to say, ("Thanks a lot!")

His plans were foiled! I had ruined his plan of cover! The game was up!!

Later ~ as I sat at home and thought this over, (and thanked the Lord, I didn't hit him) ~ I was thinking of our own lives over the years. We were young, and full of excitement and plans, and never looked ahead much ~ to see what might cause harm or danger.

We were so focused on 'our plans,' that we never gave our future much thought; where we were going, or what plans God might have for us.

We prayed, yes, but were we committed to 'God's plan' for our lives? Or were we just running and playing it all out ~ hiding, and not wanting to be found out in our own plans?

Sometimes, even knowing we were hiding from God's plan, but we were too into 'the fun' of our own games of life, to seek 'His will.'

God has a plan for each of us. He is a God who even had a plan for His own Son, to save us from all our sins.

Sometimes, He may have to "honk the horn" at 'us' ~ to get our attention! I know He has sure done this to me! However, it is God's loving duty to warn us, so we won't get hurt!

He knows our 'games,' and our 'plans,' to "hide from Him," and others. And He knows the future for each of us ~ and he loves us more than we will ever know.

The question remains, are we thankful for His warnings? Or do we stand straight up, and give Him a look of disgust, as he turns 'His' ray-gun on our plans, and finds us out!! Let's think about that, the next time our Savior corrects us, and warns us through His Word, (and through others.)

Let's be willing to say, (when He honks at us,) "Okay Lord! I'll stop, and do things Your way. Just give me Your direction, wisdom, power, and strength!"

Let's allow His light to shine the truth in our lives, and lead us on His paths. Let's trust God to be our Father!

He surely wants to be! Amen?

Dear Lord Jesus, please help us to be real with you, and never ignore You, or try to lie to You, or lie to ourselves! Help us to never play games with You. Please, give us a desire to know 'Your Words' ~ and follow 'Your paths.'. . Help us to live for You, and to love You, and to serve You more faithfully. Amen!

"I will instruct thee and teach thee in the way which thou shalt go: I will guide thee with mine eye." (Psalm 32:8)

"Thy Word is a lamp unto my feet, and a light unto my path." (Psalm 119:105)

"But He knoweth the way that I take: when He hath tried me, I shall come forth as gold." (Job 23:10)

47. DO YOU SPEAK SPANISH?

~ If God told you to do something, would you do it?

It just feels so good to follow through on something you can do, . . "in Jesus name."

One evening, Doug, our foster daughter, and I, were having dinner at 'Chili's' Restaurant. Many times, I know when God is asking me to do something in the Lord's service. This was one of those times.

Doug was ready to pay the check when I told him, "I'll be a few minutes." I told them both, "I'll meet you out in the car in a little bit." (Doug knew, I was telling him I had a 'little mission' from God.)

The young man that was bussing tables was clearly angry ~ (for whatever reason,) and I felt that he was unsaved. He looked 'mean,' and the Holy Spirit spoke to my heart and asked me to tell him the Gospel message. This young man's name tag said, "Juan."

I started to speak to him, but he said, "No habla englais," (he didn't speak English.) In my heart I said, "Lord, I thought you wanted me to witness to him about the Love of Jesus?" As I looked around, I saw a beautiful girl at the front hostess desk. I looked at her and had a feeling of hope, (she was Spanish.) . . . She was very sweet. I asked her, "Do you speak Spanish?" She said, "Yes I do."

I asked her if she could get permission from the manager for me to give 'Juan' a message? She politely agreed, and asked Juan first.

She came back smiling, with Juan following behind her, but Juan looked the same ~ very unhappy, and sad.

I asked her to please interpret, as I spoke. I prayed in my head, "Lord, please give me the words. I have no idea what You want me to tell Juan, so Lord, 'You' speak to his heart, please!"

As I spoke to him, through the Hostess ~ God's Holy Spirit began working, and it was so visible in Juan's expressions. First ~ there was sadness; then conviction, then happiness, then tears!

The Hostess looked as inspired as Juan did, and I had God's Spirit upon me, full to overflowing! ~ And I felt it!

I told Juan, (through her,) that ~ "the Lord Jesus Christ wants me to tell you something. Would you like to know what it is?"

He looked to the Hostess, and he looked scared, but shook his head 'yes.'

I told him ~ "God has been wanting you to surrender your heart to Him for quite some time, but you are running with the wrong men. And your mother has been worried, and asking you to attend church with her."

God told me to tell Juan, "Jesus died for your sins, He loves you, and Jesus wants you to serve Him with your life, and someday be in Heaven with Him, and your family."

I asked the nice young lady to ask him, if he had ever asked Jesus into his heart?

She asked him, and he looked to her and said, "No."

I asked if he wanted to know Jesus as his Savior?

Humbly, he said "Yes!"

That's when the Hostess knew that God had really told me to give him that message! Her eyes were very serious and intense!

I told the Hostess, we would say a prayer, and Juan could repeat it in his heart after me, and ask Jesus into his heart and life. But first, I told him, "God wants you to turn around and quit hanging with (that gang.)"

The 'second' I said that, Juan's eyes changed into a scared look! And then, . . he agreed he would "get away from them."

After we prayed together ~ his face looked 'radiant,' and almost glowing! He shook my hand and kept saying "Gracias, Gracias," over and over, and he was extremely thankful!!

He happily shook the hand of that sweet Hostess, and thanked her for interpreting. I thanked her for everything too!

(Juan may have never come to Christ, without her willingness to help us both!)

We all had tears in our eyes! The Lord was so obviously present, and that thankfulness, and (the 'Presence' of the Holy Spirit,) stayed with me, long after that!

One amazing miracle was; for the entire time we were talking and praying ~ not one person came into Chili's, (and this was a busy night!) God allowed this Holy moment, and His perfect timing ~ all for 'Juan's Salvation!' All praise to Jesus, our compassionate Savior!

I went out to the car, and told Doug and our foster daughter how the Lord Jesus had blessed us, and that Juan had accepted Jesus! They were so encouraged, and really happy to hear the story!

I had told Juan, through the Hostess, we would be back in to see him, and told him we'd all be praying for him.

He gave me a big smile!

Well, we did go back in to see him several times. He was always so nice to us, and had such a beautiful smile for us!!

I asked him if he was going to church, and he nodded 'yes,' and pointed to his heart. He knew what I meant.

Then later, he was riding his bicycle and he sped up real fast to get beside us in our car, to wave at us, and was waving so excitedly! We all waved back at him, and he was smiling and so happy! We were all thrilled to see him again! We only wished we spoke Spanish!

We saw him several other times on his bicycle, and each time he sped up, . . to wave to all of us! We knew, God had changed his life through Jesus, our beautiful Savior. May God be glorified through this testimony of His Great Love!!

Well, I still pray for Juan, and hope that he is doing very well with our Lord. I often wonder ~ what God's plan is for his life!

We will definitely meet up with Juan again, in Heaven one day. And we will be able to praise the Good Lord together!!

And the wonderful thing is, . . . there will be no 'language barrier' there!

"Whosoever shall call on the name of the Lord shall be saved." (Acts 2:21)

"And He saith unto them, follow Me, and I will make you fishers of men." (Matthew 4:19)

"For Thou Lord art good, and ready to forgive; and plenteous in mercy unto all them that call upon Thee." (Psalm 86:5)

48. THE TINY BROWN LEATHER DIARY

We had an elderly neighbor just down the street; a widower, who was in a wheelchair and lived alone.

He was very likeable and had a great sense of humor. He had very funny stories of his experiences in life, and he could entertain us for hours. We prayed for him, as we knew he wasn't a Christian.

He was a 'tough' man, and had been a downtown Phoenix bar owner in the fifties, a member of the Teamsters, (he once met Jimmy Hoffa in Oakland, California,) a Black Jack Champion in Las Vegas, and finally, a Real Estate Broker in California, Mexico, the Bahamas, and Arizona. Sadly, he was also a dabbler in 'Tarot Cards,' and the occult. He had made a fortune in real estate, but ended up spending it 'all,' on medical costs for his dear wife, who he loved so much. She had needed a series of 'new,' 'experimental,' (and very expensive,) operations for her heart, her lungs, and eventually for cancer, (which sadly ~ ended up taking her life.)

One time he asked me if I wanted him to ~ "read me," (with Tarot cards.)

I told him, "No, I don't do that, the Lord Jesus took us away from all that years ago." He looked at me "with respect," and thankfully, he never asked me about it again.

We became very close friends. I went to the store and shopped for him, cooked for him occasionally, and did what we could to help him.

In all the years we knew him ~ his daughter and his grandkids had never been to see him.

He would speak of them often, and he had such love for them. He talked about them fondly, as if they were all very close. He kept a picture in a frame, that one of his little granddaughters had colored for him, of 'the family.' They were all just cute 'stick people,' but he still loved looking at that sweet little picture. He kept it close, where he could see it every day.

He was a very friendly man who loved people and really enjoyed company, and he always looked forward to our visits with him. He had a big tomato patch, that we all tended to ~ and he bought a small, light-weight, "Mantis" rototiller, so we could till up the ground every year, and plant the tomatoes. We'd go visit, and water the tomatoes with him. When the tomatoes were ripe ~ there were always so many ~ that we gave most of them to friends. It was a fun "family project," that we all enjoyed together! Our time together was so important to all of us, . . we were family!

One year, I asked him what his plans were for the Fourth of July? He just looked down, and sadly said, "Awh, just the same as any other day." (We knew his family wouldn't be coming.)

I asked him, "If we grill hamburgers, would you like one?" His face lit up with a child-like smile, and he said ~ "Oh, that sounds good!"

He didn't know what I had planned ~ but I went to the store and bought hamburger ~ and Bratwurst; I also bought buns, and squeeze bottles of mayonnaise, mustard, ketchup, relish; some potato salad, and chips. When I got home, we wheeled our barbeque down to his house, and a couple other friends were there. We had an instant picnic! He couldn't have been happier! His smiles said it all! He was so surprised we had planned this for him. We had a great time and a lot of fun! (He ate two cheeseburgers, and two Bratwursts!)

We had never seen him eat so good!! God's Spirit was really with us, and blessed us that whole day! (Whenever you help the poor, crippled, and elderly ~ Jesus says you have done it unto Him.) Amen!

Then one day, a friend of his knocked on our door ~ to tell us that he had fallen, and had broken his hip!

He was taken to the hospital, and eventually to a 'rehab center.'

(Back then, for an elderly person, a 'broken hip' was pretty much viewed ~ as a "death sentence!")

I noticed every day I visited him, that he was slurring his words.

When I asked him why he kept slurring his words, he said, "the nurse is always bringing me that pain medicine." (We knew 'from our own experience,' that rehabs often 'over medicate' elderly patients; the patient would begin to lose ground, and then they would try to get them into their nursing homes.)

A couple of times, over the phone ~ he could barely talk!

I told him, "You need to wean yourself off of that medication." He had completely lost his appetite.

Then he spoke up and sadly told me, "The nurse is talking about sending me to a nursing home!" ~

(Because he wasn't eating and gaining strength.)

I asked him ~ "How bad do you want to get outta there and come home?"

He said, that was what he wanted, "more than anything!"

I told him, "Alright then, I have a plan. Are you willing to do what I say?" He said, "I sure am."

I told him ~ "Okay, the next time that nurse comes in, and hands you those pain pills, put them under your tongue and just swallow the water. When they leave ~ put the pills in your drawer in the side table.

Cover them with a napkin, and when I come up ~ I'll dispose of them." I told him, "You'll have to take at least one bite of each thing on the plate to build up your strength."

He followed all that I told him, and we prayed for him each day. Thank God he came out of his 'stupor,' from those strong pain pills ~ and he was clear headed again! He got his appetite back, and could carry on a great conversation! The rehab workers were very surprised, (and I think a little disappointed,) at his comeback!

We kept talking with him about all the fun we'd have ~ when he got home! I told him, we'd start having glazed doughnuts, and coffee, together again in the mornings. That put a big smile on his face!

Then, on one of my visits I brought our foster daughter with me. We prayed before going up to his room, and I asked God to give me a chance to tell him the Gospel, and tell him that Jesus loved him, and died for him. (I was a little nervous, because as I told you, he was a 'tough' man, and I really didn't know how he might react!)

I took my Bible in with me. I remember looking over at my foster daughter, knowing she was praying for me.

(I had even made a 'promise' to God in my prayer in the car, that if He let our friend accept Him as Savior ~ I would get down on my knees beside his bed, and thank the Lord Jesus ~ right there in his room!)

Well, I asked him if he would mind me sharing a few Scriptures from the Bible, and he was very open to it.

He said ~ "Sure, go ahead." So, I felt more comfortable ~ and yet I could feel a strong, 'spiritual battle' in the air! I went ahead and read several Scriptures ~ depending totally on the Holy Spirit ~ to lead the conversation, and bless 'His Words,' to this dear man.

As I read the Bible verses to him, he began to cry, and suddenly he blurted out ~ "My grandmother used to read those verses to me when I was young!" I kept right on reading, . . and he kept weeping.

I then asked him (boldly,) if he would like to know Jesus as his Savior, and 'know' in his heart, that he would have Eternal Life when he died and left this world. He looked me straight in the eyes and he said, "Yes I would."

I told him, "Now ~ I know that the Word of God says we must 'repent' of all our sins, and be willing to go God's way." I looked him in the eye and said, ~ "You know, that means you must 'turn away,' from those 'Tarot cards' ~ because that's connected up to the devil."

He nodded his head ~ "yes."

I asked him if he was willing to let go of all that, and ask Jesus as his Savior and Lord. He said, "Yes I am!"

It was truly a miracle to see this strong man, who had spent his whole lifetime, (doing so many wrong things in his life, . . going his own way, . . being rebellious against Jesus) ~ and here we were ~ just about ready to pray to Him!

I asked him to pray with me ~ I told him, I would say a prayer, and he could say it in his heart. He looked so thankful to do just that! I prayed the Sinners Prayer and we said, "Amen."

When we both looked up, he was weeping. His eyes looked up at me with relief, and 'Joy,'. . from Gods Spirit. Here he was accepting our dear Savior, who he had sadly been ignoring his whole life!

I then remembered my prayer, (and promise,) to Jesus. So again, I boldly asked, if we could have a prayer of thanks for his Salvation. He eagerly agreed.

I took his hand and knelt down by the side of his bed, and thanked God for answering my prayers for our dear friend, and saving his soul! (His grandmother's prayers, had just been answered!!)

We thanked God for all He was going to do, to let him go back home, and to answer all our prayers for his healing. We continued to see him through his recovery.

Then, one day we got a call from him, and he was so happy! He told us the social worker came in and had a talk with him, and said if he had someone to help him at home ~ they would release him to go back to his house!

(Otherwise, he would have to go to their nursing home.)

Well, along with us, and another good friend who was willing to help ~ he was able to return home! We all pitched in and helped him every day, and Doug covered him up at night ~ and we thanked the Lord for answering all of our prayers! We continued to pray with him on a regular basis.

Every time we visited him, we would pray before we left. He looked forward to it, and so did we! We'd always have a prayer for God to "bless him," and continue to heal him.

We can tell you, . . . God did just that!

Miraculously, our dear friend had five more years at his home, and we had plenty of good times together!

We were all so thankful ~ that he was able to avoid the nursing home, and stay in his own home! Praise God!

When he was younger, he had personally known some old country music stars, and he would get out his collection of 'classic' country music records, which we would listen to for hours as we visited.

One evening Doug took his guitar and sang some songs for him ~ and he had no idea Doug used to sing professionally. He was so proud of him, and happy Doug shared his music with him! ~

He then brought out a guitar that had belonged to his late son.

He wanted to give it to Doug! We were honored ~ but we insisted on giving him the money for it. He was happy with that.

Eventually, he had to go to the hospital due to breathing problems, and sadly he died there after an emergency biopsy on his lungs, which showed emphysema. He didn't even last a week in the hospital.

We hung out in his room and we told him ~ "We'll just move in here with you," and he said, "I'd like that!" with a sweet smile on his face.

I remember being at work the next day and I told Doug, "I don't feel like being here today!" I felt God wanted me to go to the hospital and be with our friend ~ which I did. He was dying and I knew that. ~ I sat with him a long time, and then went on home.

Later that day, I felt I should call the hospital. The nurse said he had, "just passed away." We knew that the Lord had come to receive him into the glories of His Kingdom. We thank our dear Lord, he was Saved!

Now, I can't tell you the emptiness we felt in the loss of our good friend. We had all been through so much together! We went through a wonderful growing process, in seeing him come closer to Jesus. We all loved each other in the Lord, and truly cared about each other!

What a miracle, that 'all' of our prayers had been answered, and God graciously allowed him to stay in his own home for another five years! Praise God, . . . now he is in his 'Eternal Home!'

He isn't crippled now, and no longer needs his wheelchair.

We are looking forward to that wonderful day that he'll be waiting at the gates of Heaven, to welcome us home!

Now, before I close this story ~ I want to say ~ his daughter and granddaughters finally came, (to prepare his home to sell!)

They took only a few things, and then called a company to bring a big dumpster to the yard. They filled that up, and put all of his personal belongings on the patio. We saw antiques, and collectables, and books. After a few days, we called the family and asked if they were coming back? They said, "No, we're done and out of there."

We asked about all the things on the patio, and they said, "you can have anything you want. In a day or so, it will all be at the dump!!"

To say the least, we were shocked!! We couldn't believe their lack of appreciation for his antiques, and his old books, and all the other interesting things that he'd collected over the years. Many were very nice and valuable keepsakes.

Doug and I ended up being the ones blessed with so many of his antiques and collectables.

(His collection of 1940's "Zane Gray" books alone was valued at $1200 dollars!) We knew we were being blessed by God to receive them, and we thanked Him for all of His blessings.

In looking through his books, we found an old, tiny, brown leather diary. We saw that our friend had penned his thoughts there when he was very young.

On one page, it read, "I'm nine years old, and my dad just died." That was all it said on that page. It was so sad. We never knew that. . .

I put it all together then; when I was reading the Bible to him that day in the rehab hospital; he had told me, those were the verses his "grandmother," used to read to him.

That little diary told the sad story of a young boy, whose heart was aching. Now, in his last years, he 'sat for years' waiting to see his family.

His son had been murdered, and his wife had died of cancer years before him. God, in His mercy, moved us into his life, . . to show him that God was with him, and had never abandoned him. God says, "I will never leave you nor forsake you." For years, 'Jesus stood waiting'. . . . sadly, it was our dear friend that had shut Jesus out.

Just remember it's never too late to turn to Jesus, and ask Him to be your Lord and Savior. Our dear friend was proof of that! This story still encourages our hearts; that Christ is 'always' with us.

We can't wait ~ to be reunited with our dear friend.

We will all live in God's wonderful Kingdom, . . and be neighbors once again, . . forever. We will all walk the hills of our God, together. . . with our wonderful Savior and Friend, . . Jesus!

"Cast me not off in the time of old age; forsake me not when my strength faileth." (Psalm 71:9)

"And even to your old age I am He; and even to 'white hairs' will I carry you: I have made, and I will bear; even I will carry, and I will deliver you." (Isaiah 46:4)

"For Thou, Lord, art good, and ready to forgive; and plenteous in mercy unto all them that call upon Thee." (Psalm 86:5)

49. HE'S SOMEBODY'S SON

Years ago, I was a run-a-way. Since God turned my life around, "Now, I look for the run-a-ways!" The good Lord has given me many "divine appointments," and used me to help these kids.

I want to lift high the name of Jesus through the personal stories He has given us. These stories are God's handwriting in our lives; He alone brings them ~ 'truly alive,' and gives them a purposeful ending! ~ Why? We believe it's because we have prayed for "greater faith," and that faith ~ is in our Savior ~ Jesus Christ Of Nazareth! ~

These hopeful endings are possible, and given, because Jesus is "Alive!" He walks with us, and we ask Him ~ to lead us and guide us, to those who need to know Him! We give all thanks to our Savior and Lord!

One day I was coming out of a Walgreens store (here in Phoenix, Arizona.) I noticed a very thin young man sitting there on a bench, staring down, . . with that 'lost look' I can 'detect,' even many feet away. I went and stood in front of him until he looked up. I asked if he was homeless, and he said, "yeah." I said, "Wanna talk?" He looked at me kinda surprised, but he answered, "sure." I sat down next to him! To my surprise, I felt I was talking to a college educated counselor!

After talking a little while, I told him, "You're a very intelligent young man, you could be a counselor for kids. My husband and I have worked for years with delinquent kids, and you would make a great advisor for wayward youth."

He smiled, but his head was still hanging down. I asked him if he was hungry, and he said, "yes." I immediately got in my pocket and handed him some money. He thanked me for that.

I asked him to tell me what had happened in his life. He said, he was "really angry with his family. They didn't understand him, and they didn't want to listen to him, . . or help him."

Once we got to talking, he told me his family name ~ which told me volumes of what his background was like, and who his relatives were.

This family has a very prominent standing in society, and there's even a street named after the family ~ in Scottsdale, Arizona.

We had dealt with them, and I knew exactly who they were.

I thought when he was talking to me, "you poor kid!"

If I didn't know how God had used me in the past, and how He answers the prayers of His people, I wouldn't have had much hope for this young man! Isn't that how God keeps many of us alive ~ through 'Hope,' in rough and difficult times?

I listened, and kept letting him know that I cared ~ and told him, "Jesus cares," and that my husband and I would be praying for him. I felt led to give him our phone number, and told him if he ever needed food, to call us, and we would be there for him.

Now, this was certainly not the last time God had me meet up with 'Matthew.' There were many times!

We lived, and worked in a wealthy neighborhood, and I saw him whenever God allowed us the privilege. One time, he called me and told me he was hungry.

He said, "if I just had a peanut butter sandwich, or an apple, that's all I'd need." That was the fastest lunch I ever got together! I took off to meet him.

Some weeks later, I saw him going into the Seven Eleven store.

I pulled over, and got out of my truck, and hollered his name. He turned around, and I saw his army jacket was very dirty and dusty. He didn't look good at all!

He said, "I'd hoped you'd never see me like this." I said, "Come here and give me a hug. I love you, and God loves you, and neither one of us cares about the way you look."

He hugged me back, and I felt that was a real break-through. I told him we were still praying for him.

We saw him later ~ a couple of times, and then we didn't see him for the longest time.

One afternoon ~ months later, I was picking up a couple things in a place called "Honey Baked Ham." They sell fresh cooked hams, and also sides of casseroles, and vegetable dishes. I grabbed a couple of side dishes for a lady I knew, went to the cash register, . . and there stood ~ our "Matthew," working next to the manager! I went over and shook his hand, we were both smiling!

I said, "How are you doing?" He answered quietly, . . ("things aren't as rough for me now.")

I tell you, my heart was crying and smiling, both at the same time!

I stepped over to the manager, and told her I wanted to give him a holiday gift, (it was Christmas time.) . . . She smiled, and said, "sure." (I didn't want her to think any of the money was being mishandled!) She was happy about it!

I told him I was proud of him, and proud of God too! I also told him, it was the best Christmas ever, to know that he was on his feet! I handed him twenty dollars, and wished him a very merry Christmas, and then told him I loved him. He was still looking at the twenty and he looked up with a big smile, and said, "I love you too!"

We both waved 'good-bye,' smiling, and wished each other a very "Merry Christmas!"

All praise to our mighty Father and Savior, Who loves and helps the poor and down-trodden! My motto about the homeless has always been, "What if that was my brother? ~ He's somebody's son!" (There are girls out there too, and she is somebody's daughter!)

Encourage them!! Show them somebody cares!! Be the answer to a mother's prayers. Talk to their son or daughter, help them if you can, and tell them, . . . 'Jesus loves them!'

We ended up moving away from the area and we've never seen Matthew since ~ but we know that wherever Matthew is, Jesus is walking with him, . . . we really believe that! Jesus loves the lost and forgotten. All praise to our loving God in Heaven.

Remember; let's seek out the helpless, and the needy, . . . and let's be 'good listeners.'

After all, he's somebody's son, . . and she's somebody's daughter!

Be the answer to a dear mother's prayers!

"The Lord is nigh (close) unto them that are of a broken heart; and saveth such as be of a contrite (humble) spirit." (Psalms 34:18)

"Blessed is he that considereth the poor: the LORD will deliver him in time of trouble." (Psalm 41:1)

"And if thou draw out thy soul to the hungry, and satisfy the afflicted soul; then shall thy light rise in obscurity, and thy darkness be as the noon day." (Isaiah 58:10)

"Follow Me, and I will make you fishers of men." (Matthew 4:19)

50. THE ANGEL

We have no idea why ~ but I have a 'gift' to retrieve stuffed toys out of those coin-operated, 'crane machines.'

I just have that ability!

One day I walked away with ten of them, with only one try each! I have given many of them to children.

Well, one day we were just coming out of a restaurant ~ and in the lobby, stood a little three-year-old girl who was crying, 'so hard!' ~

We stopped and asked her sister and her parents what was wrong? Her sister, (about six years old) said, "Oh, she wanted a toy out of the machine, and she didn't get one."

Doug smiled at me, and said, "Here" and handed me a dollar. He said, "get her one." (And I got her one, . . first try!)

I smiled, and handed her the toy, and said ~ "Looky there! See? You got one!"

Her face stared at that stuffed animal for about three seconds, and she threw that thing down on the floor just as hard as she could! She threw her head back, and cried even harder!! She began to stomp and get 'dramatic' ~ on all of us!

Her parents said, "What's wrong, . . the nice lady got you one!?" Between gasps, she pointed at the machine, cried out and said, "I . . . wanted, . . that one!!" We all looked into the machine, and she was pointing to . . . an "Angel!"

Well, I had to explain to her the cold hard facts of "crane fishin!" I tried to explain that a lot of the good toys are buried under other toys, packing them down, and they have too much weight on them to be drawn out and retrieved. (That didn't help a bit!) In her little mind, she only knew, . . she didn't get the one she wanted!

That left a vivid picture in our minds that very day. . .

As Doug and I walked to our car, I asked him if that looked like us as Christians sometimes? . . . . We're praying, and praying, for a certain prayer to be answered, and God 'gives' us an answer. But it wasn't the answer we "wanted," or "expected," and so we get mad, and throw a fit, and cry! We don't care 'why,' ~ we just want what we want!!

He agreed, and we watched as the parents took the girls to their car, scolding the little one for ~ "not being nice, . . . to the nice lady!"

Let's try not to get mad at our dear Savior, when we don't get just what we want! His answers are best for us, He knows the future, and He knows what He's doing.

Let's trust Jesus, and just say "Thank You," and believe it's the best answer for us. Let's be thankful!

He gives us all so many blessings ~ let's not be 'brats,' and throw fits, and get mad, and cry, when we don't get . . . "The Angel!!"

"Not that I speak in respect to want: for I have learned, in whatsoever state I am, therewith to be content." (Philippians 4:11)

"Humble yourselves in the sight of the Lord, and He shall lift you up." (James 4:10)

"But my God shall supply all your need according to His riches in Glory by Christ Jesus." (Philippians 4:19)

"My help cometh from the Lord, which made Heaven and earth." (Psalm 121:2)

51. HE'S IN THERE!

We worked for eleven years ~ with a special needs man. He was in his forties, and we just loved him to pieces! He loved us too! He was just so sweet and innocent, like a little boy, and he loved stuffed animals and little toys. They made him so happy!

One year, his sister, (our boss) took him to the mall ~ to buy Doug and I Christmas presents. They had the store wrap the gifts while they waited. His sister 'swore him to secrecy' and told him, "Now don't tell Doug and Charlie what their presents are!"

Then, one evening, . . way before Christmas, . . we were all sitting in the living room, and there were our Christmas presents underneath the tree. He looked over at (my) gift, pointed, and raised his voice in loud excitement; and so 'serious,' he shouted, "He's in there, . . it's a dog, . . he likes me!" His excitement got the best of him!

He had picked out a very soft stuffed dog for me, and he was saying it liked him! He wasn't supposed to tell us what it was, but his mind was so excited to let that dog out of that box! (He wanted him for himself, and we knew it.)

I motioned to his sister to come into the other room and asked her what the gift was and where they bought it? The next day, Doug and I went to the mall and bought him a 'lion,' at the same store.

Then on Christmas ~ I got the dog, and he got the lion. We were both very happy with our gifts!

Sometimes, . . we get so excited that we just can't keep it to ourselves. Our excitement gets the best of us!

I thought, . ."We should be that way about our Lord and Savior, Jesus Christ!" Let's be 'so excited' to tell people, "He's in here, (our hearts) . . He's God, . . and He loves me!". . . Let's not hide our love for Jesus!

What a beautiful lesson!!

"Then I said, I will not make mention of Him, nor speak any more in His name. But His word was in mine heart as a burning fire shut up in my bones," (Jeremiah 20:9)

"No man, when he hath lighted a candle, putteth it in a 'secret' place, neither under a bushel, but on a candlestick, that they which come in may see the light." (Luke 11:33)

"What I tell you in darkness, that speak ye in light: and what ye hear in the ear, that preach ye upon the housetops." (Matthew 10:27)

52. THE BIG WHITE DOGS

A few years ago, Doug and I worked for a lady, who supplied a beautiful home for us in a very nice neighborhood, as part of our job.

I had started my day with a prayer to Jesus, as I always do.

I asked Jesus to help me, and to "go with me to help others around me, and allow me to 'be a blessing' to them." I went into our garage, and as the garage door opened, I walked around the back of our truck.

I looked outside and noticed two 'big' white dogs on the corner of our lot, standing there looking at me. Their eyes were cold, and they didn't look 'nice.' They were staring at me like I was, 'dead meat!' I had never seen these dogs before, and it was very unusual to see dogs running loose in our neighborhood.

Immediate fear struck my heart! I went back around to a counter in our garage and I saw a big hammer lying there. I grabbed that for 'personal protection,' in case they were still around when I got back home! I went back and got into my truck, and now the dogs were nowhere to be seen!

This neighborhood was near a big mountain preserve, and many people walked the area for exercise, and for hiking the mountain trails. This particular day, fortunately, there was no one out and about.

As I backed out of our garage, I looked over, and I was horrified to see those two big white dogs surrounding, charging, and jumping at the nice young man that lived adjacent to our home! (He was a doctor who made prosthetics.) I didn't know him well, but he always smiled and waved, and he was always busy! Once in a while, I'd see him jogging with his dog along beside him.

As I got closer to his house, I could see that he was desperately struggling to hold his dog up above his head, to protect it; and his dog was bleeding! (His dog had to weigh 60 - 65lbs!) This man was very red in his face, and I knew if these big dogs got a hold of him, both he and his dog could be torn apart and killed!

Instantly, a plan entered my mind. I stepped on the gas pedal and sped toward our neighbor and those dogs, and laid on the horn! I kept going toward them, and I never let up on the horn! Thank God, He let me scare those two big white dogs away from them!

Those dogs kept running down the street looking back at me, and I followed right after them; still laying on the horn and not letting up! I saw them run up to a backyard gate half way down the street. So, I sat outside the house ~ continuing to just lay on the horn ~ the dogs just standing there staring at me!

Eventually, a couple in their late sixties came out of their front door. I rolled down my window and yelled at them ~ and told them ~ "You'd better get those dogs locked up 'now!' They just attacked our neighbor and his dog." They went over to their gate, opened it, and both dogs ran right in. She closed the gate, (and never said one word to me!) Immediately, our neighbor who'd just been attacked, ran up to my truck and yelled ~ "Are those your dogs?"

I said, "No, they live right here, and I'm calling Animal Control right now!" We were both traumatized just knowing those big dogs got loose, and could have killed him and his dog! It was very hard for me to get on with my day after that!

Our neighbor rushed his poor dog to the vet for surgery! I decided to go and get some doggie treats, I bought a nice card, and wrote our neighbor a note; that I hoped when his dog felt better, he "could give him some treats to enjoy!" I wrote our phone number in the card and left it in his mail box. I was hoping that he would let us know how his dog was doing, and I told him we would be praying for them.

Surprisingly, I 'never' heard back from him. Each day that passed, I wondered how his doggie was, but I never got a call.

Several months later, I answered the phone and I was shocked to hear our neighbor on the other end, apologizing for not calling me. He said his mother had 'shamed him' ~ asking him, "Haven't you called that nice lady yet, to thank her for saving your life?" He admitted, "I should have called you before now."

He continued to tell me exactly what had happened that day, after I had seen those two big white dogs in my yard, staring me down with that cold, mean look! Within seconds they had left my yard, and gone to my neighbor's home. When he had opened his door, and came out with his dog to go jogging, those two big dogs had viciously attacked his dog! When our neighbor tried getting his dog back inside his home, those big dogs came charging inside, and started 'tearing his dog apart!'

He swept his dog up above his head and went back outside, and was stuck there just holding his dog up in the air to keep it from being killed! He had no way to get them away from him! He also told me that when the dogs had chased his dog inside, they trashed his home!

His dog had to be hospitalized, needed surgery, a draining tube, and also IV's!

Thankfully, the owners of the dogs paid for all the costs. (Which they should have!) He ended up by saying, "I was sure glad you came along when you did, because you saved our lives!"

We give our God all the thanks and praise for his perfect timing! The Lord blessed my neighbor, and his dog, that day. However, He also blessed me, by answering my prayer to use my life to help those around me. I was so happy this man finally called me and thanked me, and told me the whole story.

God answered our prayers ~ and healed his doggie too!

Knowing how it all ended up ~ made us feel good, and confident that we can call on God in a time of need!

This experience reminded both Doug and I of the Bible story in Luke, when Jesus healed the ten lepers, and only one came back to thank Him. ~ Many time's, people get too busy, and forget to thank God, (and others) for His deliverance out of their troubles. Let's remember to always be 'Thankful' to God ~ for His answers to our cries. (And let's not take God's answers to our prayers for granted!) ~ Thank you, dear Father, for saving our nice neighbor and his sweet doggie that day!

"And Jesus answering said, Were there not ten cleansed? But where are the nine?" (Luke 17:17,18)

"In the day of trouble I will call upon Thee; for Thou wilt answer me." (Psalm 86:7)

"At the voice of thy cry; when He shall hear it, He will answer thee." (Isaiah 30:19)

53. JESUS

One of our sweetest miracles from God happened some years ago. We desperately prayed for Him to help us. We were in a major move, (we had only two weeks to move out) ~ and needed laborers to finish our home before we could move in!

We had a lot of work that we needed done, and we had no idea where to look. Having worked with contractors for years, we knew that many times, they don't even show up to put in a bid!

It can take weeks to find good people, and even longer to get the job started! We prayed, and asked our God to "Please, send someone to help us!"

We know very well that you can't trust just anybody, so we asked the good Lord to give us wisdom, and to "let us know" ~ when it was from Him!

Well, As God has always done for us ~ He told us 'loud and clear' ~ that He was with us! The very next day, a Spanish man wandered onto our property ~ He asked if he could work for me? I asked him what he did? "Cement," he said. I asked his name ~ and he said, "Hesus!" (Spanish for, "Jesus!") I hired him that day!

He was an excellent cement worker! He had a whole crew, and they did a wonderful patio for us, along with some other cement work, for only $500.00! Praise God!! We gave him a very good tip! He was thrilled, and so were we!

That same week, a painter came by, (out of nowhere?) He asked if we needed a painter? I told him, "We sure do." We needed to have "the whole inside of our house painted." I asked him his name, . . he said "Hesus." He seemed very nice and I hired him on the spot. He also did an excellent job, and his price was only $700.00! We also tipped him very well!

That same week ~ another Spanish man came by and asked if we needed a worker? We had a 'texture guy' here, to get ready for the painter. I was gone at the time, so our texture man said, "here's a pen, write your name on the drywall over there, and your cell number, and I'll have her call you when she returns." When I came back, the texture guy told me, "a worker stopped by and I told him to leave his name and phone number on the drywall there."

There in big, bold letters, was the name . . . "Jesus." (Hesus!)

He also did an excellent job for us!

I kept thinking, "What a wonderful Savior we serve!!"

God is just such a personal God! ~ When we try our best to serve Him, obey Him, and (pray) ~ we will find out just how much He loves, and cares about us!

We could have never found such good, (and honest,) workers if we'd tried! (And what are the chances that all three of them would be named "Jesus?") ~ But our great God knew where to find them, and He sent them, . . . right to us!

However, there were actually 'four men named Jesus,' working for us! Miraculously, our dear Lord Jesus was our 'foreman,' and we didn't have to go looking for any of them!

They completed everything within our two-week deadline; and we still praise God every time we think back on this miraculous answered prayer!

(And we've 'never' had any workers wander onto our property, before, . . . or since!)

When you need help ~ call on our great God and Savior! 'He is God ~ and God all by Himself!' ~ Praise His Holy Name!

Thank you, dear Lord Jesus, for all you have done for us!!

Dear people ~ Jesus Christ is Real!

Pray, and Believe, and 'expect' Him to answer ~ and you will find out ~ "All things are possible with God." Amen! ~ and Amen!

"And call upon Me in the day of trouble: I will deliver thee, and thou shalt glorify Me." (Psalms 50:15)

"Then shalt thou call, and the Lord shall answer; thou shalt cry, and He shall say, here I am." (Isaiah 58:9)

"The Lord thy God, He is God, the faithful God, which keepeth covenant and mercy with them that love Him." (Deuteronomy 7:9)

54. THE LITTLE VISITOR

Yesterday, (Good Friday,) was a very different day for us, as we had a "little visitor,". . a small doggie, . . that stayed in our front yard, . . and would not leave!

She was a beautiful little (red) Miniature Doberman Pinscher, and had obviously been well cared for.

She would not let us come close enough to pick her up, or even touch her. She was hungry, and thirsty, so we fed her some chicken from the refrigerator, and we gave her a bowl of water. She would lay down, but several times, when we slowly tried to get close to her, she would 'bark,' and 'snarl,' at us! She was scared to let us get too close!

We kept talking to her, and feeding her, trying to win her trust . . . but to no avail! She was definitely a "one-man dog!"

Three different people walking by asked if she was our dog, and when we said, "No, she's lost," they tried to catch her! She would not allow them to get close to her either. (She was very fast!)

We prayed to know what to do about her, knowing that someone was surely looking for her, worried, and probably praying to get her back home. For some reason, she would *not* leave our yard! (And we are right across the street from a small park!)

We finally gave her a big box, turned on its side, with a bath towel inside, to sleep in that night.

She was so lonesome, she kept howling and crying all through the night. We were not able to sleep much either, . . hearing her cries, and hearing how sad and lonely she was. Doug kept going out, talking to her, and feeding her. We both tried coaxing her into our gate, but she wasn't going for any of it! She would not allow us to comfort her.

Finally, the next day we were forced to call the, "Animal Control Department." We didn't want her to 'run off,' and get hit on a nearby busy street. We prayed they would "send out a good person, who was nice, . . (and could catch her!)"

While waiting for the person to come out, I went to McDonald's, and bought a cheeseburger for this little dog. I gave her a couple small bites, and she loved it! I saved the rest, until right before the Animal Control person would come to try and catch her. I sat for several hours waiting, knowing I had to keep her attention, (and keep her around.) Doug kept talking to her too. (We would want someone to do this for ~ 'our doggie.')

The man finally showed up, and used a big net. She ran from him, and he scrambled to catch her, and he finally did! Then, while he went back to the truck, he had 'me' ~ hold the long pole with her in the bottom of the net, scurrying around inside, trying desperately to get away! . . (He came back with a 'noose' on a pole!)

He stuck the noose down into the net, looped it around her neck and tightened it ~ and was then able to pull her out, and put her in a compartment on the side of his truck. He used a 'scanner,' to see if she had an 'identification chip;' sadly, she didn't.

We told the man, we hoped that this would be a happy reunion with her rightful owner, to make some little child, or a widow happy ~ having their prayers answered for Easter, to have their doggie back.

Now, we mentioned to him, that if no one came for her ~ we were "interested in adopting her."

He smiled, and took our names. He shook my hand and thanked us. He told us we would have to wait for three days (until Tuesday) to apply to adopt her.

That Tuesday, we were ready to go pick her up.

We had bought a 'pet carrier' ~ to bring her home in, and we bought food, and shampoo. We decided we'd better call ~ before we drove all the way over to the shelter.

The nice lady I spoke with, asked me, "May I have the little dog's number?" I gave her the number that the rescue man had left with us, and with an excited voice, she said, "Oh! The owner came and picked her up!" We thanked God that He answered all of our prayers!!

Doug and I had both agreed the night before, that even if we had her for a month or more, if the rightful owner was found, we would give her back to them.

Then Doug said, "Just think, even though our God is all powerful, and created the entire universe, He still cares about a little lost dog and her owner." (And He surely does!)

The way this all happened; and this little dog absolutely refusing to leave our yard, . . we were sure ~ that the owner must have been 'praying' to get their little doggie back.

Many of our on-line friends were praying too!

We give God the glory for answering all our prayers!

(His eye is on the sparrow, and I know He watches over me!)

Thank you, dear Jesus!!

~ Let me tell you what God brought to my spirit about this entire experience. He brought this verse to my memory: ~ "O, Jerusalem, Jerusalem, thou that killest the prophets, and stonest them which are sent unto thee, how often would I have gathered thy children together, even as a hen gathereth her chickens under her wings, and 'ye would not'!" (Matthew 23:37)

I told Doug that I had thought of this verse out of Matthew, and he smiled, and told me that he had the same thought, and the same verse had come to him that day!

God loves us all, and He wants to 'adopt us' into His Heavenly Family. Jesus said, "I go to prepare a place for you." (John 14:2)

Are we resisting our loving God, as this little dog was resisting us and our love?

Are we running from 'adoption,' and the many blessings He wants to give us in the family of God? ~ Or are we just 'staying outside,' the gate, 'crying,' and 'lonely,' but refusing to go into His Kingdom?

Let's 'give in' to Jesus! Let's run to Him and just say "Yes Lord!"

God please give us all, the confidence to come to you in trust, and love, . . and faith, ~ knowing that You loved us enough to give Your very life for us. Lord, please help us all, . . . to 'want' your blessings!

Thank You for being our dear Blessed Savior, and always having Your loving arms open to us. Amen!

"Come unto Me, all ye that labour and are heavy laden, and I will give you rest." (Matthew 11:28)

"I will seek that which was lost, and bring again that which was driven away, and will bind up that which was broken, and will strengthen that which was sick:" (Ezekiel 34:16)

55. "KIMO"

Today, I dropped Doug off at the Safeway store to pick up a few groceries, and parked the car to wait for him.

I noticed a homeless man with a grocery cart, very unlike anyone I'd ever seen on the street. He was at least 6'5" tall, and looked like a biker, with a lot of tattoos.

I was prompted by the Holy Spirit to go over and talk to him.

I got out of the car and walked up to him as he sat at an outside table, where people drink coffee and sit to enjoy our wonderful winter weather here in Phoenix.

I saw a lady on a motorized wheel chair go up and look through some DVD's that he had in a plastic bag. She asked me if I wanted any? I said, "No, you go ahead." She gave a quick look, smiled, and said none of them were anything that interested her. She thanked him, and she went on. A young man with a writing board sat at the table next to him. I started to look through the bag of DVD's ~ and asked him a few questions.

I asked if he was homeless and he said, "For quite some time." He said he was going to look for a job.

I asked him how he became homeless? He said, "Many reasons." He told me he had "been in the service and almost died a number of times." He had also been in prison, "on and off for the last sixteen years." He was very soft spoken, and a good-looking man. He did not look like the average homeless person I was used to seeing.

I asked him if he knew the Lord Jesus? He looked down and told me he had heard of Jesus, and he thought "people who believe in Him are cool." But he said he had always gone along with the "Aryan belief." (Not such a good thing to believe.)

We talked a little, and he said he thought he would probably stick to what he believed. I said, "Well, you can stick with it, that's your choice. But if I came to you, and stopped your car, and told you the road was out up ahead, would you listen to me, or keep driving and go off the cliff and die?"

He looked a little taken back. I told him, "You need to know, . . the road you're on, is out ~ up ahead, . . and you will die, no matter how much you want to believe your way! Jesus says, 'I am the Way, the Truth, and the Life, no man cometh unto the Father but by Me'."

I felt led to tell him that Doug and I ran with bikers, and were heavy into drugs and crime, but when we asked Jesus into our lives, He turned us around, and Saved us.

"But," I told him, "we had to 'repent.' We had to get off the road we were on ~ that road was taking us to Hell."

I told him according to the Bible, what a terrible place Hell will be, and that there was "no hope," of ever getting out!!

Suddenly, right when I said, "no hope of ever getting out," there was a loud "Bang!" right next to us, that startled us both!

~ It felt like 'God Himself' was right there with us, stressing my warning about hell!

We both looked over, and the young man at the table right next to us ~ had dropped his writing board, right at that moment!

I went on and told him, "Years ago, we began 'backsliding.' We had a job working construction and started going back to the things we used to do before we became Christians." I told him how I got stage four cancer, and had to go in for surgery.

I told him, "After the surgery, God gave me a vision while I was wide awake in my hospital room!"

"He showed me a bright white screen with our lives playing back everything we had been doing, 'since' we started backsliding!"

I told him, "It was awful, . . seeing all those sins shining through that Holy light! I thought about putting the pillow over my face to block it out, but then God said to me, 'Go ahead, but it will shine right through!'

It seemed like God was communicating with me 'telepathically' somehow ~ because God knows our thoughts!"

I told him, "God said to me, 'If you keep going on like this ~ I'm going to have to take you! I can't let you go on like this.' I told God (in my mind,) 'I'm too weak Lord, I can't live the Christian life,' and God said to me, 'I'll be your strength.'

I told Him again, 'I'm too weak!' He just repeated, 'I will be your strength.' This happened one more time.

After the third time, (and after thinking it over a while . .) I said, 'Okay Lord, . . You be my strength.' He said to me one last time, 'I'll be your strength!' And I thanked Him!

And since that day, He has truly been my strength! He helps me one day at a time . . . to live for Him."

At that moment, Doug came out of the store. He looked at our car and saw that I was gone. I yelled to him, and waved my hand. He saw me and waved back. He went on to the car and waited for me. (He's used to seeing me talking with homeless people along the street.)

I could see that this man was very 'convicted,' and believed that what I was telling him was all true!

I said, "That man over there, Doug, is my husband and he can tell you my life has been very different since I saw that vision, and his life has too!" I told him, "Jesus healed me of that stage four cancer, and I didn't even need any chemo or radiation!!"

I asked him if he would like to pray to know Jesus as his Savior? He looked at me with a very welcome look and he moved up closer to the table. I said, "Do you want to pray?" He said, "Yeah." He reached out and locked hands with me in a "brotherhood" handshake. I asked him his name? He said, "Kimo." (like, kēmō.)

I prayed the Sinners Prayer with Kimo, and after we prayed, he looked very uplifted, and encouraged. I knew he was glad he gave his life to Jesus! (And so were we!)

I gave him a Christian tract along with a few bucks, and told him, "Now expect your life to change!" I told him, "Jesus promises, He will never leave you or forsake you." I said, "The disciples were told to throw down their nets and follow Jesus."

I then told him that whether he was homeless, or whether he got a job, Jesus was with him now. He smiled. I asked him if he would be around, and he said, "Yes."

I said, "Maybe we'll see you again." I smiled, and he smiled back.

I walked to the car . . . and as we backed out and were leaving, he walked over to our car, and gave us the plastic bag of DVD's he had been selling! He smiled and said, "Maybe you'd like some of these." We thanked him.

We were all smiling, and we could feel the love of God! ~ This man was truly thankful someone cared enough to share the love of Jesus with him, and we were thrilled that he had opened his heart to Jesus!

The Bible says, when one sinner repents, all the angels in Heaven rejoice! They were all singing today ~ dear friends!! Please pray for Kimo. Let's ask our Savior to stay very close to him, and show him what He wants for his life.

God bless this man who is homeless, and has even been in prison, but now he has been given the power ~ to 'become a son of God,' and is on his way to Heaven!! "But as many as received Him, to them gave He power to become the sons of God, even to them that believe on His name:" (John 1:12)

I Praise the name of Jesus Christ ~ for the opportunity to witness to Kimo, and for his desire to know the Lord! ~ God bless us all ~ to tell others what Jesus has done for us, and that He loves them too!

God wanted Kimo to know that 'the road was out up ahead.' ~ He decided to get off of that "broad road that leadeth to destruction," and try God's "narrow road" that "leadeth unto Life!"

~ The road Kimo is traveling now, will lead him safely to the beautiful gates of Christ's Kingdom, and we are looking forward to seeing him there! I ask you, . . . "Which road are you traveling dear friend?"

God Bless you all.

Love, Charlie.

"Likewise, I say unto you, there is joy in the presence of the angels of God over one sinner that repenteth." (Luke 15:10)

"For God so loved the world, that he gave His only begotten Son, that whosoever believeth in Him should not perish, but have everlasting life. For God sent not His Son into the world to condemn the world; but that the world through Him might be saved." (John 3:16,17)

If you have enjoyed this book and have any comments or questions please feel free to contact us at:

divine.appointments@aol.com

or

Find us on Facebook at:

Divine Appointments
(Book Series)

(Also, watch for our next installment of
"DIVINE APPOINTMENTS")

Postscript

I hope and pray that you have been blessed and encouraged by our book. However, . . this is not really 'our book,' it is 'God's book.' He wrote these stories in our lives. Doug and I only lived through them!

These personal stories are about all types of people; little children, delinquents, bikers, the elderly, pastors, witches, the homeless; people from all walks of life. Jesus walked among all types of people when He walked the earth, and He helped them all! He still walks with those who believe in Him, and have His Holy Spirit living in them.

When we prayed years ago, and asked Jesus to be our Savior, we had no idea that we would both be privileged to witness His Great Power and miracles, working in and through our own lives!

My message to everyone is ~ "Jesus is Real!" Anyone can reach Him through prayer; and there is 'Forgiveness' and 'Hope' in Jesus, our Savior!

Whether you're a Christian ~ or you are still searching to know more about Jesus; or you have possibly drifted away from the Lord; these stories are proof of a great Holy Power ~ far beyond anything we ourselves can do! This Power is, 'in Jesus Christ,' and is given to us to accomplish "God's Will," (not 'our own.')

"And this is the confidence that we have in him, that, if we ask any thing 'according to his will,' he heareth us:" (I John 5:14)

I hope, that as you have read these true "Divine Appointments," you have felt Jesus closer to you!

Hopefully, you have heard the voice of His Spirit speaking to your heart, and calling you ~ to a closer relationship with the only true and Living God! Maybe you know someone that would be helped and encouraged in their faith ~ by reading this book.

Jesus will show His Great Love and Forgiveness ~ to all who call on His Name in faith, and ask Him to be their Savior. Our only desire is for God to use our lives to help "anyone" find and know Jesus. He loves us all, and wants us to live with Him in His Kingdom, forever. (John 3:17) ~ Because of Jesus, and His Great Love, . . .

We truly love you all,
Charlie and Doug

CPSIA information can be obtained
at www.ICGtesting.com
Printed in the USA
FSHW021122150421
80439FS